Twins

AND TWIN RELATIONS

66

Twins

AND TWIN RELATIONS

By HELEN L. KOCH

THE UNIVERSITY OF CHICAGO PRESS

CHICAGO AND LONDON

Library of Congress Catalog Card Number: 66–20591

THE UNIVERSITY OF CHICAGO PRESS, CHICAGO & LONDON
The University of Toronto Press, Toronto 5, Canada

© 1966 by The University of Chicago

Published 1966

Printed in the United States of America

To my mother,
whose membership in a twin pair sparked my interest
in the subject of twins.

Acknowledgments

This study was supported in part by Grants No. USPHS 07098 01 and USPHS HD 00888 01 and in part by a subvention from the Elizabeth McCormick Memorial Fund of Chicago. The support is very gratefully acknowledged.

My obligations for assistance are too extensive to recount in detail, but a few sources should receive special mention. To the child subjects who bore with us those prying "queries," and to their cooperative families, we feel deeply indebted. A hundred or more school systems extended themselves to scout for subjects for us. The teachers of the twins studied gave generously of their time to make the thoughtful assessments of the children that are so important a part of the data. Edith Cope assisted with some of the face-to-face work with the twins. Dr. Helen Heath read the manuscript and made valuable suggestions. Ismael Maung, Richard Blough, Elliot Simon, and Dr. John D. Jackson were helpful in programming as well as in other statistical aspects of the investigation. Toni DeKoven did most of the scoring and analyses of the CAT protocols. To all of these persons the author wishes to make clear the depth of her appreciation for the competent and willing assistance that did so much to facilitate the explorations attempted.

Preface

It has been assumed in the preparation of this monograph that some readers might want to become acquainted with its contents without wading through the detail of its statistical and technical analyses. The last chapter has been prepared with especially these readers in mind. It summarizes without much technical cluttering the major issues with which the investigation deals and its essential findings. A scanning of chapter 1, which describes procedures, methods, and major tools, is also encouraged for all readers. The statistical tables, which are in essence the evidence the author is trying to interpret, have been placed in the Appendix. These tables will be most meaningful to the reader prepared to struggle through the whole text, but ever occasional reference to them may prove clarifying.

Since our study is chiefly an exploratory one and covers only one small area, it opens up many more questions than it settles. The problems of twins interactions with and influence on each other, as well as the effects of other unique biological and social forces that typically play upon twins are exceedingly complex ones. One problem that is in great need of exploring is the influence of family size and structure upon twins that are included in the sibship. Indeed, even the siblings of twins deserve some study. It is important to probe systematically, too, the outcomes of various educational programs—e.g., separation of twins at school—the attitudes the culture holds toward twins and twin rearing, and the developmental picture in twin relationships from the very early months to the adult character that emerges from various backgrounds. It should be emphasized that twins, and their parents, siblings, and friends have much to contribute toward filling the gaps now occupied by our ignorance.

HELEN L. KOCH

Contents

Tables

CHAPTER I

Problems, Subjects, and General Research Design

PROBLEM AREAS

Most of the psychological studies involving twin subjects use the latter chiefly as tools, e.g., as a means of controlling variables such as the genes. A large mass of studies dealing with the so-called heredity-environment problem has to do with the question of the role of genetic and non-genetic forces in the determination of individual differences. (See Newman, Freeman, and Holzinger 1937; Eysenck 1951, 1956; Thurstone, Thurstone, and Strandskov 1953; Cattell, Blewet, and Beloff 1955; Kallman 1959; and Shields 1962). A recent parallel, but quite different type of study, took advantage of a condition of natural crossed circulation in a pair of conjoined twins to explore the question of the relative merits of the hypnotoxic as opposed to the neurological theories of sleep (Ohira 1958).

The present investigation, in contrast to the types sketched above, is concerned with twins as such—their characteristics, the nature of their relations in pre- and post-natal life, the effects of these relations, and the social forces that play upon twins because they are twins. To spell out some of these problems that challenged the investigator, a substantial number of questions will be posed. Are twins particularly close in their relations to each other? If they are, what influence does this have on their relations with others, both children and adults? Does the close relationship isolate them from others, or perhaps, instead, facilitate friendly intercourse? Does the close relationship and

1

similarity between twins increase their confidence, make them rivalrous, or reduce their ambition? It is alleged that twins tend to have a difficult time learning to speak. If this is a fact, is it because the children are poor speech models to each other, or possibly, because internal relevant complications before, during, or after birth have occurred (prenatal interference, prematurity, or even obstetrical difficulties)? Parents often worry about the extent to which one twin dominates the other, or leads, while the other follows. If such relationships do exist, are they usually initiated early and do they tend to be inclusive or areal? Does one member of the twin pair tend to be markedly dependent and lacking in originality? Twins, as a rule, are compared much. What is the effect of this on their competitiveness and confidence? Twins also tend to receive highly similar treatment. Does this lessen rivalry, diminish ambition, and constrict the range of experience, or does the treatment do the reverse? Some contend twins do not contribute as many of the very ablest persons to the population as their numbers would dictate. Is this correct? If it is, is this because of prenatal complications that often leave permanent handicaps, or because of unfavorable effects of prematurity, or because of lesser drive or competitiveness? Twins are not infrequently separated at school. Why is this done? Is it always helpful? What are the consequences, biological and social, of having a twin of the opposite sex? Does this, for example, make for sissiness in the boy and boyishness in the girl of the pair? Are the boys in opposite-sex pairs in the prenatal period physiologically the more "aggressive," with the result that the girl gets a poor start? Since boys and girls tend to develop at different rates, what is the influence of this on the self attitudes of the pair members?

Although the present investigation has contributed virtually nothing toward the solution of biological problems, yet, since in interpreting the psychological findings reference must often be made to biological considerations, it seems well to acquaint the interested reader with the specific nature of some of these ramifications. What, for example, produces twinning in the first place (see Newman 1917, 1923; Arey 1934; Corner 1955; Lilienfeld and Pasamanick 1955, 1956; Shettles 1960; Hartman and Leathem 1963)? Does a tendency toward twinning run in families and, if so, is there such a trend for both types of twins (Dahlberg 1926; Greulich 1934; Wilson and

Jones 1931; Waterhouse 1950; Oettle 1953; Kallman 1959)? To what extent do unfavorable biological and psychological effects stem from the prematurity so common among twins (Douglas and Mogford 1953; Knobloch *et al.* 1956; Wiener 1962; Potter 1963; Drillien 1964)? What is involved in the prematurity complex, either as causes or effects? Could mild prematurity be an advantage to twins? What are some of the sequelae of mutual circulation in identical twins (Schatz 1888–1910)? Does this condition ever occur in fraternal twins (Osborne and DeGeorge 1957; Walker 1957), and what sorts of complications do some believe develop as a result? What mechanisms lie back of blood chimerism, i.e., the possession of two kinds of blood? How common is the condition and what are its consequences (Dunsford *et al.* 1953; Booth *et al.* 1957; Nicholas, Jenkins, and Marsh 1957; Chown, Lewis, and Bowman 1963)? What, if any, developmental defects occur more frequently in one type of twin than in the other? Are congenital defects more common among twins than singletons (Guttmacher 1939; Price 1950; Stevenson, Worcester, and Rice 1950; Bender 1952; Russel 1952; Karn 1953; Ross and Philpott 1953; Guttmacher and Koll 1958)? It is alleged that gemini tend to remain somewhat small. Why is the deficiency not routinely compensated by later growth (Alm 1953)? Why is the death rate, prenatal and postnatal, higher among twins than singletons (Russel 1952; Potter 1963; Drillien 1964)? Why does the postnatal death rate tend to continue relatively high (Osborne and DeGeorge 1957)? What are the influences of monoamniotic and monochorionic conditions, as well as those of placental fusion, upon twin well-being and development (Schatz 1888–1910; Stevenson *et al.* 1950; Potter 1963)? Is sinistrality more frequent among twins than among singletons or among one twin type than the other (Wilson and Jones 1932; Rife 1940)? Since the two varieties of twinning are different—double ovulation being responsible for producing fraternals and fission or division of a blastocyst for identicals—does the physiology of the mothers of the two tend to be different in basic ways (Karn and Penrose 1952; Karn 1953; Lilienfeld and Pasamanick 1956; Folsome *et al.* 1956; Anon. 1965)?

Such, briefly, are some of the questions with which our data may be meshed. Let it be stressed again, however, that the present study has contributed little to their clarification.

SUBJECT SELECTION AND ITS IMPLICATIONS

To show the bearing upon our investigation of some of the studies of forces influencing the composition of twin populations, it seems well first to describe our subjects and to make clear some of the implications of the selective forces that will need to be taken into account in interpreting the findings of the present study.

The subjects investigated were 59 to 86 months in age (see Table 1),[1] were the only children in their families, were white, urban or suburban dwellers in the north central area of the U.S.—chiefly within a hundred-mile radius of Chicago. The children were all native born; came, so far as could be discovered, from intact families; were, with the exceptions of two pairs, the biological offspring of the parents with whom they lived. They were normal enough to be enrolled in a regular class in the public schools. There were ninety pairs about equally divided by plan among identical male pairs (MZm), identical female (MZf), fraternal same-sex male (DZSSm), fraternal same-sex female (DZSSf), and fraternal pairs whose members were opposite in sex (DZOSm and DZOSf). These subgroups did not vary significantly in age but did differ some according to social class (see footnote, Table 1). Hence, in the analyses concerning those attributes that social class influences considerably, this factor was usually discounted by an individual matching or an appropriate analysis of variance technique (Scheffé, 1959, p. 98 ff.). The variables, social class and twin type, interact somewhat, however. Thus by controlling class when dealing with matching groups, we may be partially masking twin type differences. But more on this anon.

Since for the purposes of this study prematurity was considered virtually inherent in twinning, we did not, except in a few exploratory sallies, try to control this factor in our analyses. The reader may want to keep in mind, as group differences are interpreted, that factors correlated with birth weight may be involved in the picture.

Our interest was chiefly in zygosity and sex differences as well as in twin-singleton disparities. The content focus was intertwin attitudes, generalized social behavior and attitudes, some language character-istics and a few physical particularities that might have profound effects upon the social behavior. Since the focal concern of this study

[1] All tables are placed in the Appendix.

was the effects that twin pair members have upon each other, an effort was made to avoid having the picture complicated by group differences in family composition or complexity. Hence the study was limited to twins who were the only children in their families. The procedure followed has thus placed definite limits on our findings and generalization range. The singleton group with whom the twins were compared had been the subjects in an earlier investigation of siblings and the bases for their inclusion in that study were essentially the same as those employed for our twins (see Table 1). All came from two-child, native-born, intact, urban families from the area of Chicago and its suburbs. The singletons fell within the same age range as the twins. Since there were a considerable number of singleton subjects from which we could draw, when we compared twins and singletons, the two groups were matched rather carefully and individually in sex, age, sex of sib, and social class in addition to the other variables mentioned above (Table 1). The number of these individual singleton matches varied from one to four per twin, depending on the measure. The matching yielded a better and more extensive comparative group of singletons than is usual. The singleton groups contained in about equal numbers children whose sib was older by under two, two to four, and four to six years, as well as subjects younger by the same spacings.

Ours, then, was a highly selected group of twins and singletons. That the reader may realize how selected they were and some of the implications ensuing from this fact, a number of these implications will be spelled out.

Because interaction with twinning or twin type is common among a portion of the variables with which we dealt, there is always the danger that in our zeal to rid the investigation of possible consequential obscuring effects and to maximize the influence of zygosity and sex, some variation of interest might have been eliminated. It should be stressed, therefore, that our twins are not broadly representative of twins.

As explained earlier, among the questions of interest to us were those of likenesses and differences on various physical and behavioral dimensions between our twin zygosity and sex groups and the differences in patterns of behavior between twins and singletons. Hence, our objective brings us immediately face to face with the problem of what types of twins there are. The dominant view for the past 50 years has been that there are two types only. One type, the identical, is alleged to be the result of a very early split (probably during the blastomere, gastrula, or early embryonic axis stage, less than two weeks after conception) in a cell mass that would normally have developed into one individual. Fission occurring later than about 14 days is believed to result in conjoined twins. The twins occasioned by early fission have presumably identical genes and, hence, are called identical, monozygotic, or one-egg type. The other kind of twin is alleged normally to be the result of the near-simultaneous fertilization of two ova by two sperm; the resulting individuals, genetically not different from singletons, have been called fraternal, dizygotic, or two-egg twins. The view taken here is that the deviation consists in two ova being available for fertilization or being able to develop simultaneously. This takes us back to the basic question of whether in humans only one ovum is usually extruded each month, or if not, whether only one can usually survive and why. Ohno, Klinger, and Atkin (1962, and in later, unpublished studies) and Hartman and Heatham (1963) have called our attention to the role of inductor cells in ovum fertilization in some mammalian forms. Only very slowly are we coming to understand the role of the inductor, granulata, and zona pellucida cells.

Through the years there have been the stubborn scientists who have insisted, usually without entirely convincing data, that there was at least a third type of twin possible—identical in maternal contribution and diverse in paternal. The statistician Fisher (1925) for a brief time felt that the twin similarity data available could be best explained in terms of three types. Recent studies of oögenesis and fertilization *in vitro* have provided more directly relevant data. For example, Shettles (1960) has suggested a possibility that would perhaps account for substantial difference in twin maturity or size at birth, as well as for a third type of twin. In his study of human gametes, he observed directly *in vitro* the meiotic division of oöcytes and the fertilization process. He noted not only one oöcyte with two nuclei but, among many fertilizations conforming to the usual pattern, there were a few instances in which a sperm entered the second polar body and initiated development. Of course, what the history of such an incident might have been had it occurred *in vivo* is a question. No relevant evidence is available.

There have been those workers who did not necessarily favor the theory of three genetic twin types but who have called attention to the facts that twins from a given pair may arrive at times separated by at least several months or that twins, being born at the same time, may differ greatly in size and physiological maturity. The first phenomenon has been called superfetation, if there is evidence a second fertilization occurred at least a month after the first. Although superfetation seems to take place in some animal stocks, there has been much debate about whether it occurs at all in human beings and, if so, whether it is necessarily the cause of marked differences in maturity in twins at birth (Meyer 1919). Studdiford (1936), quoting DeLee, mentions that American and French biologists have, in the main, been skeptical of the concept, whereas the German and English are more inclined to accept it.

The present investigator, faced with no convincing evidence as yet that she might be meeting with three types of twins, has acted on faith as have most other investigators and has used the binary classification of twins, monozygotic (MZ) and dizygotic (DZ). But this decision concerning classification, even if it is correct, still leaves the problem of diagnosis of zygosity, which investigators to date have attempted to solve chiefly by a study of co-twin similarity. It is true that different experimenters have made their diagnoses on the basis of twin similarity in different traits, but the general procedure, although it has had many variations and supplementations, is always basically the same. Some investigators have assumed that the greater the number of the more strongly gene-influenced or penetrant traits on which the twin pair members are similar, the greater is the probability the pair is an identical one (e.g., Siemens 1927; Mueller 1930). Substantial differences, however, in any one of the more critical traits, such as eye pigmentation or in a blood fraction or sex, most present investigators take to negate such a classification, but similarity in many traits does not necessarily establish monozygosity. Smith and Penrose (1955), who have developed one of the more rational procedures, have elaborated a probability formula that takes into account the frequency in the population of the traits considered diagnostic, as well as their likely association. Of course, the frequency of the observation of the trait, on the basis of which its probability of occurrence is estimated, may vary with the population. This can be troublesome.

We shall describe later in detail the diagnostic procedure used. Suffice it to say here that one's classifications may suffer from selective errors—ones that are more common in classifying one type of twin than the other (see Gottesman 1963). Although serological tests involving as many as six to ten qualities are the most satisfactory means to date of arriving at a diagnosis, there are difficulties even with this method, especially when the blood fractions studied are few and when parent blood composition is not known (Wiener and Luff 1940). It has been estimated by the investigators in several carefully conducted studies that as many as five to ten per cent of the subjects may have been misclassified (Wilson and Jones 1931; McArthur 1938; Shields 1962). Gottesman (1963) believes even more incorrect diagnoses may be the rule. The work on zygosity determination has been based on essentially circular procedures because there are no entirely dependable independent criteria of zygosity.

There is the further question of how good a sample the present study has of the population to be represented (Price 1950; Allen 1955). The subjects, for instance, were all alive at five to six years of age. This fact alone means the study clearly has no adequate sample of the twin population available among newborns. Potter (1963), as a result of a sixteen-year study involving 51,909 births at the Chicago Lying-in Hospital, reported that the neonatal mortality of twins was seven times as great, and fetal mortality three times as great as that of singletons. Mortality and morbidity rates vary with prenatal and postnatal age (Osborne and DeGeorge 1959), sex (Osborne and DeGeorge 1959), zygosity (Potter 1963), social class (Lilienfeld and Pasamanick 1955), and so on. The interaction of these factors will have had a chance to alter substantially the composition of the twin population by the end of the preschool period. Osborne and DeGeorge (1959), for example, after giving an excellent review of the literature, contend the death rate in very early fetal life is high among males—much higher than among females and although it is much reduced, it continues to be relatively high in the postnatal period (Wilson and Jones 1931). The relative incidence of the sexes changes with age—even through the prenatal and at least early post-natal period more males than females die (Osborne and DeGeorge 1959; Potter 1963). Too, the incidence of death, in the later postnatal period, of males from opposite-sex fraternal pairs and, for that matter, of male fraternals generally, continues to remain high relative to that of females. The excess of females over males in the twin population naturally rises with age. Bernstein (1948) reported no great sex

difference in survival rate in MZ's but a substantial one among fraternals, whether from same- or opposite-sex pairs. Potter (1963), however, reporting on the fetal and prenatal period, did describe a sex
difference in mortality rate among the MZ's in this population. Stocks
and Karn (1933) state that more impairment of later health was noted
among opposite-sex fraternals, a trend to which those data reviewed
by Osborne and DeGeorge (1959) tend to lend some support.

One of the observations that intrigued us, when the territory
around Chicago was canvassed for twins who met our many specifications, was that the search had to continue over half a year longer to
fill out our group of eighteen pairs of presumably DZSSm's than to
locate the subjects for the other same-sex groups. At first, it was
thought the rarity of the DZSSm's might be a chance occurrence, but
when we read Osborne and DeGeorge's (1959) comments, it became
apparent that ours was probably not a surprising finding, although its
causes may not be too clear. Because the death rate among male twins
is considerably higher than among female, this would reduce the
number of males available. Secondly, the mothers of our fraternal
twins tended to be older, on the average, than the mothers of MZ's
and apparently had more difficulty conceiving. If difficult conceptions are correlated with later lack of vigor in the offspring, this could
further reduce the probability of postnatal survival among fraternals,
as well as, doubtless, influence the pattern of the care our subjects
received. It is barely possible, too, rarity was related to the morbidity
effects of some kind of prenatal exchange that became evident later
(Booth *et al.* 1957; Nicholas, Jenkins, and Marsh 1957; Osborne
and DeGeorge 1957; Chown, Lewis, and Bowman 1963). The effects of a possible chimerism (which at present is believed to be
very rare) has not been extensively explored, and the effects of
hormonal complications are, as mentioned earlier, beginning to receive more attention. Related, possibly, to this issue is Osborne and
DeGeorge's (1957) finding that fraternals discordant in the ABO
blood character survive less well than do those who do not so differ.

It is suspected that social factors, too, might have been operating to
complicate the search for DZSSm's. Parents may have been unwilling,
for instance, to permit their children to participate in the study if the
latter were quite different or difficult. Osborne and DeGeorge (1959)
noted that, even among the adults they canvassed, the fraternals were
less willing to serve as subjects in their experiment and male pairs

were more difficult to lure than female. It is to be expected that the twins or their parents would tend to be particularly resistant when psychological differences were being investigated. As mentioned earlier, it was noted that when identicals were compared (one must remember twin pair members are compared unmercifully), the emphasis seemed to tend to be on likeness and comments were usually favorable, whereas in the case of fraternals, the emphasis in comparisons was on difference, with often an unflattering implication for one of the pair members. This trend could well cause fraternals to be less inclined than identicals to participate in an investigation in which they would expect to be contrasted. Actually we do not know how many twin pairs refused us, because the schools scouted for us and probably reported only those pairs known to be willing to cooperate. We were aware of refusal to cooperate on the part of only one located pair, and this may not be a good indication of the resistance the schools encountered but did not make known to us. The above types of selection could color uncomfortably for us the sample of twin relations and attitudes available for observation and this differentially as far as twin zygosity and sex types are concerned.

It seems desirable to name a few more of the selective influences. It should not be overlooked, for instance, that our child subjects were normal enough to be enrolled in a public school, a state of affairs eliminating all seriously retarded children and this differentially—i.e., if there should be more defectives among one type of twin in the general twin population, this fact would be largely concealed. The complex nationality variable, too, may have slithered in, although there is no reason to suspect it may be clouding the meaning of the twin group differences observed.

Since our subjects were the only children in their families and were five or six years of age, it is clear the study is dealing essentially with first-borns, a status that usually has certain biological as well as parental attitude correlates. The control of birth order facilitates the interpretation of twin group differences but makes difficult the interpretation of the results of the twin-singleton comparisons. The fact that no viable sibling arrived during the five or six years after the twins, who were hence essentially first-borns, suggests that our population may result from more difficult conceptions or may be drawn from cultural groups that favor wide spacing between sibs. These two forces may have operated differently in the two zygosity groups.

Twins from Catholic families, too, would probably not be conspicuously represented among our subjects. The Catholic group would also have been studied by us in reduced numbers because all subjects were enrolled in public, as opposed to parochial, schools. In fact, we would probably have failed to locate twins in any special school, or twins separated from each other by being entered in different educational institutions. If the most divergent or difficult pair members are typically the twins who are separated, these diverse twins might not have been recognized as twins by our scouts, and then, by our failing to contact these deviates, we would have reduced the overall variance in our population, and possibly also differentially, as far as zygosity groups are concerned. Our subjects, both singletons and twins, having been drawn from intact families, probably escaped the stresses of broken homes and might have had relatively uniform home structures. If there were no interaction effects between twin type and broken home, then there might be little occasion for worry, but it is suspected there is some interaction between the variables named. A similar point can be made about using only urban dwellers. Whether there was interaction between twin type and place of residence is not known but, since fraternal twinning seems to vary some with poverty level and social class (Guttmacher 1939, 1958), we may with our many controls have restricted the variance in the fraternal group more than for the identical group.

Many other possible selective mechanisms could be mentioned, but time will not be taken to call attention to them, as it was desired by giving merely a generous sample of them to point up the problem that we and, for that matter, most other investigators have had to face. It must be emphasized, then, that when general statements are made, they concern only the population studied. How broadly the relations described may obtain is a question. The manner of selecting subjects doubtless limited the range of physical, intellectual, and personality characteristics available for study and thus may have given the impression of much less inter- and intratwin group variance than there is generally. The differential selection as far as twin subgroups are concerned has been troublesome. At the same time the various controls have kept rather low the probability of coloring the results by such irrelevant variables as age, social class, sex, race, family complexity and intactness, medical care, school opportunity, type or place of residence, language factors, and so forth. Whether the procedures employed have succeeded in clarifying the group difference picture rather than clouding it is not apparent. At any rate, it will probably take a massive basic influence, either biological or social, to show clearly through the clouding.

Up to this point, we have tried to make clear: (1) the extensiveness of the problem of sampling; (2) the difficulty of twin type diagnosis; (3) the openness of the question of the nature of twin types; (4) the inadequacy, for our purposes, of such a rule as Weinberg's (1901, 1902), which ignores the problem of differential prenatal and postnatal survival among twins of various types; (5) the need for intensive studies of both short- and long-time effects of mutual circulation, or of chimerism, as well as of the physiological interaction with the mother of fraternal twins differing in blood type; (6) the relation of prematurity to twinning; (7) the probable durability of some of the early effects of twinning and the possible illumination through these of various aspects of growth; (8) the need for a more detailed analysis of the dynamics of twinning and twin development, as much of the work to date has dealt with the end points of long chains of causal events and has left the enormous area of intermediate processes undescribed and unaccounted for. Extensive recent work on factors conditioning ovulation and the control of certain forms of sterility is fortunately doing much to fill in the picture (see, for example, Hartman and Leatham 1963; Donini, Puzzuoli, and Matezemolo 1964; Gemzell and Kjessler 1964; and Gemzell 1965).

DIAGNOSIS OF ZYGOSITY

General Program

As pointed out in the previous sections, no certain diagnosis of zygosity can be made in all cases, although the probability of the diagnosis being correct can be very high when certain serological methods (Gottesman 1963) and detailed examinations of birth membranes (Potter 1963) are employed, and probability considerations are taken into account (see Smith and Penrose 1955; Sutton, Clark, and Schull 1955). Unfortunately, since our subjects were not seen at birth, were young, and were in no sense captive, we were not able, except in a few cases, to employ these methods and had to rely on the comparison of the co-twins on a variety of readily observable body traits. In fact, the initial diagnosis was an impressionistic or subjective one. About seventy-five anatomical details were noted in our inspection for essential likeness or difference of pair members and upon these details the initial classifications were based. For those complexes or details for which a quantitative score was obtainable—such as height, finger ridge and fingertip pattern count—an effort was made to find the boundary score that best served to discriminate between the initial putative monozygotic and dizygotic groups. Since the boundary scores found to be the most discriminating were in essential agreement with those reported by other investigators studying twins, they helped some in arriving at the co-twin "concordance" picture (this procedure is of course somewhat circular). To reduce the detail observed to a small enough number of categories or body complexes —individual differences that are known to be influenced strongly by the genes—the features were grouped into the items listed below. On these complexes the children were judged as essentially similar or concordant, or dissimilar or discordant. Table 4 presents a summary of the trends of the concordance scores for twin pair members in various subgroups. These scores, then, represent a simple count of trait complexes or qualities with strong penetrance from a selected list on which pair members were sufficiently similar for us to feel justified in classifying them as very highly similar. There were usually thirteen "traits" or items observed, but only twelve were used for the DZO's, sex similarity being omitted since inclusion in this group was contingent on the pair members' differences in sex. About nine of the complexes on which the twins were systematically compared had a substantial degree of genetic independence, and had been found useful by others in diagnosis. Of course, many details of physique and history, other than those named in Table 4, were observed, and possibly these swayed, when we were most uncertain, some of our final judgments relative to ovularity. The item complexes receiving most attention were: (1) pigmentation of the iris—major color, and color and size of the fleckings; (2) iris pattern—color and number and width of the bands (varying in color density or brightness); (3) hair color; (4) hair coarseness and form—whether curly, wavy, or straight; (5) form of the ear and ear size—width of the helix, form and size of the tragus and antitragus, size and shape of the lobe and the extent of its attachment; (6) front tooth form (this item was sometimes omitted because serious oral deformities made judgment impossible, or because some of our subjects, being of the proper age, had lost their first incisors and had not yet acquired the second (mother's reports); (7) skin texture and color—also tendency to freckle, tan, or burn; (8) fingerprint patterns; (9) Slater-Shields-Nixon-Allen (see Nixon 1956) linear discriminant function score for ridge counts; (10) Newman's ridge count scores (1930); (11) presence or absence of hairs on the backs of the middle section of the fingers; (12) height; and (13) sex. In addition to inspecting the children carefully, we asked the mothers about the tendency of the children to burn or tan when exposed to the sun, and if the co-twins' relative likeness or difference on any of the above traits was observed to shift as the youngsters grew older.

The children in a pair were stood side by side in good light and judgments were made of essential similarity or dissimilarity. For pigmentation or form items, as explained, we made an effort to discriminate difference rather than to score each individual on a scale. It was believed a finer discrimination could be achieved by judging simple difference than by trying to categorize in accordance with a scale such as Grieve and Morant's (1946) scale for eye pigmentation, which employs selected pictures of eyes for reference. A final all-or-none classification, like or unlike, was used in more than half of the items. In our estimates of the details of ear and tooth form, we were somewhat uneasy about stabilizing the boundaries of the category of "essential likeness." When judging the skin color, we based the assessments on the pigmentation of skin on an area of the head and neck not exposed to any great extent to the sun. Hair form, in the gross way it was judged, was the least useful item for the diagnosis of zygosity, since most of the subjects had straight hair.

Fingerprints

Using the Faurot Inkless Method, we fingerprinted each child. With very few exceptions, if enough prints were taken, satisfactory ridge counts and pattern diagnoses could be made. The tendency of some children to perspire on the slightest provocation was very troublesome, because perspiration tends to blur the print. Because the boys perspired less, it was much easier to obtain good prints from them than from the girls.

The ridge counts and the scores for dermatoglyphic pattern need description. The Slater-Shields-Nixon-Allen (Nixon 1956) linear discriminant method gives each finger two counts, i.e., the number of ridges from the core to the delta on each side of each of the fingers. If the finger ridge pattern is an arch, the two scores for the finger would be zero, since there would be no delta; if a loop, one count would be zero; and if a whorl, both scores would be non-zero. Slater's method (see Nixon 1956) analyzes the distribution of the count differences, and when the counts are converted to logarithms, it describes them in terms of the linear discriminant function. In the Allen adaptation of the Slater-Shields-Nixon procedure, the log for each of the twenty ridge counts (two scores for each finger of the individual increased by one) for the individual is determined and the logs for the comparable loci on the fingers in co-twins are subtracted from each other. (Allen made available to the author a very useful table.) The log differences from the twenty loci are summed and averaged for each pair of twins. This method, some believe, is better than most in that the comparison, instead of being made on a total hand basis (see Newman 1930, 1934), involves the estimation of likeness at each of the twenty specific loci and takes into account the function that best discriminates between zygosity groups on degree of co-twin likeness. Nixon (1956) states that this log difference measure differentiated well between serologically diagnosed zygosity groups. Both serological and dermal ridge analyses, which, along with skin grafting, undoubtedly are the best techniques available at present, have, of course, some limitations. Osborne and DeGeorge (1959), for instance, found that in five of their opposite-sex fraternal pairs (this was about a third of the pairs of this type in their population of subjects), the serological picture for six items was identical for the pair members. Hence, the estimate of the probability of monozygosity in these individuals based on the blood characteristics no doubt would have been very high, but opposite-sex co-twins cannot be identicals. Potter (1963), using a three-factor serological test along with sex and number of chorions, felt she was left with about 20 per cent of her subjects not finally diagnosed. The serological data, especially when they are used independently of parent blood analyses, must be interpreted with caution (Wiener and Luff 1940). But the serological analysis is probably the most satisfactory method available to date, especially if many blood factors are taken into account. But even a limited serological test was not available to us because our subjects were young and their parents tended to be loathe to give permission for the blood test. This was particularly true among the lower socioeconomic classes. Hence, we did not try to get blood tests on as many of the same-sex co-twins as we would have liked, but we did use all of our persuasive powers to obtain a serological examination on a limited number of twin pairs about whose zygosity diagnosis we were rather uncertain. Unfortunately, permission to make the blood test was obtained for only a very few pairs. We still feel in something of a quandary concerning the classification of about 6 per cent of the cases and are quite uncertain about 3 per cent. The diagnosis of the zygosity of female subjects proved more difficult for us than that of males. It is interesting that Wilson and Jones (1931) expressed uncertainty for about 8 per cent of their pair classifications, and Newman (1930) for about 5 per cent of his when finger prints alone were used for diagnosis. Of course, to what extent feelings of certainty or uncertainty are good indicators of success in diagnosis of zygosity is an open question (see Gottesman 1963). Several of the girl pairs seemed to exhibit mirror imaging in their prints. Using the standard method, then, gave them unduly high Nixon-Allen scores. This fact, together with the possibility that two pairs were misclassified, may account for the fact that the finger print scores of MZf's and DZSSf's differed less from each other than did those for the MZm's and DZSSm's.

The mean of the Nixon-Allen scores for the co-twins in our putative MZ group was 3.158; and for the DZSS's, 6.017 (Table 2). Parallel figures offered by Nixon (1956) for his two zygosity groups are 3.331, and 6.179. A class boundary of 4.5 discriminated well between our putative MZ and DZSS groups, i.e., 83 per cent of the MZ's fell below the point and 76 per cent of the DZSS's, above.

Since there are not as yet many studies conducted in the United States in which the Shields-Slater-Nixon-Allen procedure has been employed, there were not many data available from the literature that would enable us to determine whether our optimal discrimination level would be in essential agreement with that which others have noted. Hence we supplemented the analysis involving the Nixon score, with one based on the cruder, older, Newman (1930, 1937) ridge counts. (These two measures correlated +.77.)

The Newman procedure was at one time commonly employed, and the results from the investigations that used the procedure gave us a basis for some comparisons. Newman's method, as stated, has not been used frequently in the most recent twin studies, since its testing was fallible in the usual sense that the criterion for the zygosity groups to be discriminated by the scores was less adequate than that derived on the basis of blood tests, and the diagnostic procedure employed was in essence somewhat circular. Our classification was likewise somewhat circular, although it was supported by a more extensive array of genetic findings. Also the measures of ability and attitude, which are the major focus of the study, are relatively uncontaminated by the classification taped on physical items. The observations in the two series were in large part obtained by different judges and, therefore, were objective in the main. The psychological measures did not force the assessor or tester into co-twin comparisons, which happened in some judgments of physical likeness.

In the Newman procedure, ridges are counted in the usual way, but the largest count of the two for a given finger was taken to represent the finger. The counts were then weighted arbitrarily to keep very large scores on individual fingers from dominating the picture. In our study these arbitrarily weighted scores for the ten fingers were summed and the difference between this total, which represented the hand of one twin, was subtracted from the corresponding sum descriptive of the hand of the other twin. Both hands, singly or together, were compared for the two members of the twin pair, a total difference score being derived by simple subtraction of the co-twins' total scores. The group means of the ridge count differences in one of Newman's early studies (1930) were for his putative MZ and DZSS groups 3.44 and 22.46. In the Newman, Freeman, and Holzinger (1937) study of chiefly adults conducted later, the difference score for the MZ's was 5.31; for the DZSS, 22.3. Comparable figures for our subjects are 5.43 and 23.23 (Table 2). McArthur (1938), using essentially the Newman method, reported that the pair difference mean for the group judged to be MZ's was 5.88 and for the group judged to be DZSS's, 22.88. The three sets of data are gratifyingly similar.

The best discrimination of our two zygosity groups was achieved by a boundary line of ten, which is four units above that indicated by Newman in the first study mentioned above and about five points below the boundary described for the Newman, Freeman, and Holzinger (1937) study on adults. Eighty-three per cent of our MZ's scored ten or less and 82 per cent of the DZSS's scored above this mark.

The intra-class correlation for the Newman ridge counts between the twin pair members were as follows: MZ, .96; DZSS, .50. Parallel correlations obtained by Newman were .95 and .53, respectively.

A classification of the fingerprint pattern similarity was not easy. Dermatoglyphic categories used in classification were the usual ones —loop, arch, whorl, and composite—and, in addition, four transition forms suggested and described by Brodhage and Wendt (1951), were employed. We let our judgments about similarity be influenced by Brodhage and Wendt's system of estimating pattern relatedness. If, for instance, in two patterns being compared, one was a "pure" form and the other represented a transition from the pure form, a half credit for likeness was arbitrarily given. A loop, for example, in which only one ridge recurved was considered very similar to an arch and, hence, in our scoring for similarity, was arbitrarily given a half credit. A central pocket loop with a one-ridge core was considered very similar to a loop.

Since practically no two investigators have used exactly the same scheme for describing fingertip patterns, the literature was not very useful for comparison purposes. There was at that, however, a fair amount of agreement, considering all of the small methodological differences that prevailed. All of our alleged MZ pair members had similar fingertip patterns on six or more fingers (Table 3). [Stocks and Karn (1933) reported a similar finding]—89 per cent had similar patterns on seven or more fingers; and 63 per cent on eight or more. The comparable per cents for the presumed DZSS's were 50, 27, and 3. Fifty per cent of the DZSS's fell below the minimum for the MZ's; 28 per cent of the MZ's above the maximum for DZSS's. Similarity on seven or more fingers was taken as the level that best differentiated the zygosity groups. Slater and Shields (see Nixon 1956) reported 64 per cent of their MZ co-twins were alike on eight or more finger patterns —a statistic that agrees completely with the data from this study— whereas 27 per cent of the DZ's were. The difference mode for Slater and Shield's MZ subjects was two, and four for the DZ's,—again, figures with which our data tend to agree.

HEIGHT

The mean difference in height for the putative MZ's was .49 inches; for the DZSS, 1.62 inches. Rife (1933) noted a mean difference for his assumed MZ's of .41 and of 2.00 for the DZSS. Newman, Freeman, and Holzinger (1937), whose subjects were mostly adults, noted a mean difference of .66 inches in height in identical co-twins and of 1.72 in the DZSS's. These results are all impressively similar. Shields (1955) reported that all of his putative MZ co-twins (teen-age chiefly) differed by less than two inches in height, and 73 per cent by less than one inch; whereas 43 per cent of the DZ's differed by more than two inches, 23 per cent between one and two inches, and 34 per cent by less than one inch. Our corresponding per cents were 100, 83, 29, 40, and 31.

Metaphalangeal Hairs

Another physical characteristic on which we checked most of our same-sex subjects was for the presence or absence of metaphalangeal hairs. We had some difficulty making the judgments, because the hairs on the fingers of these young children tend to be sparse and very tiny indeed. But since a magnifying glass was employed and each finger was held against a sharply contrasting uniform background, we finally were reasonably sure of our judgments. Two individuals checked each others' observations when there was doubt as to the presence or absence of the hairs.

Birth Membranes

Encouraged by the findings of Potter (1963) and others, we had hoped to receive some help in diagnosis from information on birth membranes. Hence, we wrote to each hospital where one or more of our twin pairs was delivered for information regarding the nature of the secundines—i.e., one amnion, one chorion; two amnions, but one chorion; two amnions and two chorions. We also asked about the amount of overlap of the placental discs, about the degree of anastamosis of geminal blood vessels in the placenta, about birth weight and birth length, and whether the diagnosis of zygosity was made at birth and its basis. Only about two-thirds of the hospitals replied or had any data to offer us. And the descriptive verbiage used in the reports—in spite of the questionnaire form we supplied indicating the categories—was so varied that we felt a systematic use of the hospital data could not be made. Nor did it sway substantially any of our decisions about the zygosity of our subjects. Fortunately, it was discovered that the birth weight reported by the hospital and by the mother agreed almost invariably and, hence, the latter was employed with comfort when no hospital report was available to us.

INCOMPLETENESS OF DATA

In a few cases studied eight years before our major effort was made, we did not have the full quota of data for zygosity determination that we later employed. Although two of these pairs were recontacted and reobserved, several of the pairs studied in the earlier period could not be located. Those subjects studied who were clearly different in pigmentation or were opposite in sex were retained because we felt sure of our earlier diagnosis of zygosity. In fact, any clear-cut difference in pigmentation in these cases was taken as an indication of biovularity, although we remember full well that the same individual may have one blue and one brown eye. Only one pair had to be dropped because it was felt data were inadequate for diagnosis. Judgment data on metaphalangeal hairs are sometimes missing because in the very early stages of the study the trait was not observed.

CONCORDANCE OF PAIR MEMBERS

The modal concordance score for the MZ's was, when the data were complete, eleven (out of the possible twelve listed earlier), and for all but two pair, the score was ten or more (Table 4). The girls appeared more similar to us than did the boys, a condition Osborne and DeGeorge (1959) also observed, although concordance scores of the sexes are about the same. Of course, since the various dermatographic measures and those dealing with pigmentation in various tissues tend to be substantially intercorrelated or linked, the difference of the two zygosity groups in concordance probably gave the impression of greater intragroup similarity than might scores based solely on more nearly genetically independent characteristics. For the items recorded, 95 per cent were concordant for the MZm's and 45 per cent for the DZSSm's, 93 per cent for the MZf's and 41 per cent for the DZSSf's. The per cent of concordance was less for the items in the DZOS pairs but, of course, here a sex as well as zygosity difference obtained. The concordance method, since it does not take into account the probability of occurrence of the "traits," may underestimate genetic likeness.

NATURE OF INSTRUMENTS AND TYPES OF DATA

Subgroups, Age and Social Class

As Table 1 indicates, there are six subgroups of twin subjects. The tables give the maximum number of subjects in each group as well as other identifying information. Where the data are incomplete, this will be indicated as we go along. The code to be used in referring to twin subgroups has been described.

The subgroups did not differ significantly, on the average, in age. But, as is apparent from Table 1, the frequency of representation of the various social classes was not the same in each subgroup. Social class was first estimated on the basis of the father's occupation, as judged according to the Minnesota Scale (Goodenough and Anderson 1931), which has seven levels. One of these levels—the fourth— was ignored, since it deals with rural occupations, whereas our subjects were all urban or suburban children. Later, to simplify further for the sake of our analysis of variance approach, the six classes were collapsed into three since our subjects were not numerous. Our Class I included Groups I and II on the Minnesota Scale; our Class II, Minnesota Group III; and our Class III included Minnesota Groups V, VI, and VII. (See Table 1, footnote, for the inclusions for the three socioeconomic groups.)

A brief, general description of the instruments used will be given here to sketch the major outlines of the program. But much of the relevant detail about the tools will be offered when results from the analyses involving specific instruments are set forth.

Interview with the Children

The same examiner interviewed all of the children for a half hour or more, while the children played with the toys supplied. The questions posed, since we were interested in twin interactions and social adjustment, concerned playmates and playmate choices, what was enjoyed in being a twin and what was found trying, how much association there was with the sib, and the quality of the relationship. (See Koch 1956*a*, 1960 for details concerning interview questions.)

INTERVIEW WITH THE MOTHERS OF THE TWINS

To procure information on the early development of our subjects, most of the mothers of the children were asked about the latters' behavioral and physical development; the twins' relations with each other and with other children; their order of arrival at birth; their birth weight, and any difficulties experienced on advent, as well as in the early weeks of life; the family alignment; the mother's age at marriage and at the time of birth of the twins. Special questioning was also directed toward getting a picture of the twins' hand preference development, the tendency to stutter, if there was any, and the general course of progress in speech learning. Information was also garnered on the twins' disease history: their possession of congenital physical defects, if any; persistence and stability of various physical and behavioral differences or likenesses in the infancy and preschool period; stability and nature of dominance in the pair. Most of the mothers were recontacted by phone after a period of one or two years following the critical testing and questioned on any developments of interest in this period. A year or two after the test period, queries were made to determine the stability or instability over this early school age period of co-twin likenesses and differences, especially in those physical traits used in the diagnosis of zygosity.

INTERVIEW WITH THE TEACHERS OF THE TWINS

The interview with the teachers aimed to discover school policy about the placement of twins in different classes; leadership of the child in the pair at school; the twins' early reaction to school; the relative abilities of the children in various school subjects or activities, and their response to this state of affairs; their responsiveness to other classmates; and the children's health record and school attendance.

PRIMARY MENTAL ABILITIES TEST

In addition to being interviewed, the twins were tested individually by the Thurstone (1946) Primary Mental Abilities Test (PMA). This instrument, which taps several different and important abilities, provided us with data that were of interest not only in and of themselves but also for the understanding of the social relations of twin pair members. Twins may be highly influenced, for instance, in their attitudes by their relative ability status in some area. And the responses others make to the twins may be much affected by the twins respective abilities. If one twin is less able than the other, he not only tends to discover this for himself, but he presumably will not escape hearing about it from others, a condition that is not likely to bolster his self-respect any. If the child finds he cannot keep up with his twin in competition, he is inclined to activate all sorts of defenses, some of which may not be particularly constructive. On the other hand, efforts on the part of the adults to treat twins alike when they are basically different can also have devastating effects.

CHILDREN'S APPERCEPTION TEST

The Children's Apperception Test (CAT), (Bellak and Bellak 1950) the responses to which were tape-recorded, was given to all subjects—twins and their singleton matches—by one examiner in the hope that this procedure would provide relatively uniform data for the analysis of certain aspects of language skill, as well as for reflecting family attitudes and general attitudes of anxiety and hostility. We would like to know, for instance, whether twins, since they are so close to each other, are less involved with their parents or other adults than are singletons.

EXPERIMENTER AND TESTER CONTROL

The fingerprints, PMA, and detection of digital hairs for any given child were the responsibility of one person. In the whole twin study two examiners were employed for these tasks, one making about two-thirds of the examinations, the other, about one-third. Each examiner tested about the same proportion of subjects from the various twin groups. Interviewing the child, mother, and teacher, and giving and tape-recording the CAT were the responsibility of another investigator, who was retained throughout the study. This procedure, of course, does not eliminate tester bias but it does tend to keep it constant. All scorings of the CAT protocols were done by one scorer. Apparent group difference trends are, hence, not likely to be the result of examiner personality or slight differences in testing or scoring methods. Since all the examiners were women, the boys may have been handicapped, or even favored. Even the teachers, all of whom were women, said they had more difficulty in assessing certain traits in males—i.e., they felt they had more success discriminating differences in their own kind. Since no one teacher judged more than one pair of twins, it is unlikely teacher bias determined group trends in the results.

TEACHERS' RATINGS AND RATING COMPLEXES

To help us get some idea of the twins' generalized social attitudes and behaviors, their teachers generously agreed to rate them on about 60 traits exhibited in school behavior. Items from the Fels Behavior Rating Scale (see Richards and Powell 1941 for an analysis of the instrument) and the University of California Rating Scale for Nursery School Children developed by Conrad (1933) were used to guide the teachers' assessments. See Table 72 for information about the items we drew from the two instruments mentioned. The ratings were done by checking a line scale. The checks were converted to scores on a nine-point scale, and these, in turn, were normalized, using the standards developed in one of my studies (1955) of singleton siblings. The scale means were 4.00 and the sigma value of the distributions, 1.00 (see Koch 1955).

Most of the teachers were unwilling to attempt any evaluation of the traits until they had observed the children for a while with the qualities in mind that were to be judged. The teachers' intensive observations extended typically over a period of about two to eight weeks. The total contact with the child judged was never less than three months. In the main, the judgments seemed to have been made thoughtfully and conscientiously.

To escape undue fractionation of description, five complexes of ratings were derived from a study of interrating correlation clusters. The normalized ratings for groups of six to eight traits that clustered were then summed and averaged to yield the complex score. These scores are evaluated in chapters 4 and 6. The trait complexes are labelled "involvement with adults," "involvement with children," "masculinity in attitude," "femininity in attitude," and "emotionality and tension."

CHAPTER II

Some Physical Characteristics of Twins and Matched Singletons

PROBLEMS

As explained earlier, the acquisition of data on the physical aspects and development of twins is not a major concern of the present investigation. But even the limited information of this type that was gathered proved useful at times in interpreting twins' psychological relations, which are the core interests of the study, and assisted in giving occasionally a more theoretical setting for some psychological findings than heretofore.

Below are a few illustrations of relevant issues: (1) What is the extent of prematurity among twins when medical care has been good? If the variation of the incidence of prematurity with social class is controlled, do twins still exhibit a much higher frequency of premature births than do singletons? If this is true, then neglect or incompetent medical practice can probably be ruled out as major determinants of the early births of twins. (2) Is prematurity much of a hazard or does at least a mild degree of prematurity, everything considered, seem to safeguard twins against certain obstetrical complications, perhaps, or exposure to the effects of such disorders as toxemia, eclampsia, or hydramnios, which often occur late in a pregnancy? If this is correct, then fewer mental and physical complications should occur in the mildly premature than in the term group. Twins are often alleged to tend to be rather small. Is this so and how durable is the size lack, if any? Is there anything in the prematurity complex, either as

25

cause or effect, that can account for the somewhat smaller size? Is the smaller size a result, for example, of merely getting a slow start, which can be overcome in due time, or the result of some effect at a critical period that can not be adequately compensated? Our data may at least indicate whether the effects of twinning on size tend to be abiding through the preschool period. It may also be useful to know if the age of the mother at the time her twins are born and/or her difficulty in conceiving them is correlated with their birth weight, congenital defects, later size, and health. On these points our data cast some light. Does the picture vary with type of twin? The course of prenatal and postnatal physical development of OS twins needs more attention. Although the phenomenon of the freemartin is believed not to occur in human twins, one may ask whether the male fetus in the OS pair appropriates more of the nutriment so that, as a result, the female gets a poor start and has durable handicaps, whereas the male has at least a normally favorable inauguration. If mutual circulation is the source of certain major complications in twins, then identicals should show these more than fraternals. Again on this point our data should be illuminating.

PROCEDURES

To help ferret out answers to some of the questions presented, we have, among other methods, compared twins of various types with each other on the basis of their birth weight, as well as on height and weight at five to six years (Tables 5 and 6). The latter measures were also contrasted with those for matched singletons (Tables 7, 8, and 9). We have, in addition, investigated the incidence of prematurity and physical defect (Tables 7, 10, 11 and 12) but for twins only. Intertwin group comparisons of birth weight, and later height and weight, were made on the basis of a three-way analysis of variance technique involving zygosity, sex, and social class variables (Table 5). (See Scheffé 1959, pp. 98 ff. for a description of the procedure employed.) The twin-singleton difference used when the two groups were contrasted was the difference between the mean for the pair of twins and the mean for two or four singletons who were individually matched with the former (see p. 5). An analysis of variance, employing the confidence bounds for linear combinations of means suggested by Scheffé, of the differences between the twins from same-sex pairs and matched singletons yielded a gauge of the influence of zygosity and sex variables (Table 9). For the DZOS twin-matched-singleton comparison a simple *t*-test appropriate for matched groups was made for the single sex groups derived from the opposite-sex pairs. The score for each twin subject was related to the mean of the scores of four singletons selected to match him individually. A two-way analysis of variance (sex of sib and social class) was used to compare the scores of the DZOSm's with the pair mean scores for the DZSSm's. A similar program was followed in comparable groups of girl twins. This procedure, although exacting, was employed because the DZOSm's and DZOSf's are related biologically—i.e., they are sibs as well as representatives of the two sexes—whereas the DZSSm's and the DZSSf's are biologically independent sex groups. The general program just described will be used to study differences between fraternal twins from same- and opposite-sex pairs when the measures characterizing the groups to be compared permit an analysis of variance procedure to be applied.

BIRTH SIZE—INTERTWIN GROUP COMPARISONS

We should ask here whether the variables of zygosity in twins—their sex, the sex combination (whether same or different) in the pair—and social class are related to birth size. Also the question of the incidence of prematurity and defect in twin populations of different types is a focal one.

Tables 5 and 6 reveal that no simple zygosity group differences in birth weight are apparent in our data when social class is controlled, although a consistent sex difference in favor of the boys is seen, as well as a significant interaction between zygosity and class. The DZSS twins from the lowest social class averaged heavier than did those from the other social groups, whereas the MZ's and the DZOS's of both sexes from the lowest class, as expected, had the lowest weight. The first is a strange configuration and we do not know what it means. Of course, one can always resort to the hypothesis of a chance difference. But it is possible that selective mechanisms are at work—that when the medical, nutritional, and other handicaps which tend to be commoner in the lower social strata are added to the biological ones, which the rarity of the DZSSm group suggests only the fittest among the group survive. Hence the DZSS's from the lower class might be larger than the DZSS's from the upper class who survived in part because of superior care when they were really less robust. Lilienfeld and Pasamanick (1955) suggest a similar mechanism to account for the increase of MZm's in the upper class group in the general twin population in recent years. The fact that at birth the girl subjects seemed slightly less heavy than the boys is probably a reflection of a sex-difference trend found among singletons even at birth as well as at most ages (see Karn and Penrose 1952 for a parallel finding).

PREMATURITY IN TWINS

We have no satisfactory matched singleton birth-weight data with which to compare the twins, but the incidence of prematurity (57 per cent, see Table 7) in our group is about seven times as great as that which Potter (1963) claims for her population of single-borns. The incidence of prematurity among her twin subjects was 55 per cent; among her singletons, about 8 per cent. Anderson (1956), reporting recently on a Scottish group of about 800 twins, stated that 58.6 per cent were early borns. The incidence of prematurity reported for populations similar to ours ranges from 23 to 70 per cent, but most is in the 52 to 58 per cent range. The estimates of the percentage of premature singletons in populations where hospital facilities are good and living conditions reasonably favorable are around 6 to 7. The frequency of occurrence of prematurity is, of course, a function of many variables, including the method of computing it.

About a third of our twins weighed under 4½ pounds at birth (Table 7). The fraternal twins from same-sex pairs exhibited a lesser (but not significantly so) prematurity rate, on the average, than did fraternal pairs with members of the opposite sex and probably less frequent extreme prematurity than did the MZ's (Table 7). Since the DZSSm group seemed least frequent in the total school population scoured, it is not unlikely that we are dealing only with the fittest among them—the ones who survived and were "normal." It is noteworthy that the DZSSm's also had fewer of the developmental, anatomical defects that we or the mothers were able to detect or report (Tables 10, 11, and 12). These included oral-dental, ocular, circulatory (incomplete ventricular septum), urogenital, and skeletal (club-foot) defects, and tumors. Probable nervous system defect, which might show itself more readily to us in low IQ, will receive more extensive comment in the next chapter. Of course, children severely deficient mentally or physically would not have been found in our group, because, as explained in chapter 1, only subjects enrolled in a regular class in the public schools were accepted as subjects.

A X^2 analysis indicated that prematurity was related to social class ($p = .01$), most early births occurring in the lowest class. (This agrees with the findings of Douglas and Mogford 1953, Lilienfeld and Pasamanick 1955, and Wiener 1962.) On the basis of a criterion of prematurity, which is a birth weight of under $5\frac{1}{2}$ pounds, more prematurity was found among girls than boys (Table 7), a fact we attributed, chiefly, to the smaller size of girls in general (see also Karn and Penrose 1952).

There were clearly more physical defects among the severely premature (Table 10), but there was a plentiful number among the term babies as well. The per cent of individuals with some, at least mild, defect in the three birth-weight groups—those under $4\frac{1}{2}$ pounds, between $4\frac{1}{2}$ and $5\frac{1}{2}$ pounds, and over $5\frac{1}{2}$ pounds—was, respectively, 41, 22, and 27. It is of some interest that, if one member in a pair was premature 75 per cent of the time, the other was also, thus suggesting fetal interaction of an unfavorable sort or exposure to the same complications. In a few cases, a difference in weight of several pounds occurred. The largest difference in co-twin birth weight in our twin population was $3\frac{1}{2}$ pounds, which occurred in a DZOS pair.

It is generally believed that twins put a strain on the mother and interfere with each other's development and that these conditions lie back of the high rate of premature birth. It is due comment, however, that Douglas and Mogford (1953) noted that the mothers of some of the prematures they studied tended to be shorter and lighter than the mothers of non-premature controls, but that the mothers of the prematures who caught up in size with singleton controls tended not to be shorter and lighter than the mothers of the controls. The above findings can be explained satisfactorily in either genetic or environmental terms, but they suggest that some babies may be small at birth not because their development is retarded but because their parents come from small stock. Congruent with this hypothesis are the observations of Drillien (1964) and Bookstaver (1951), who noted that twin prematures as a group did not have as high a death rate as singleton prematures of comparable birth weights. Some investigators (e.g., Drillien) believe there may be two types of prematures if birth weight is used as the criterion. It is thought that in some cases there might possibly be a genetic linkage between tendency to twinning and to small offspring. In this instance, the small offspring may be more mature at birth than is apparent according to the birth-weight criterion. The other type of prematures would be those resulting from unfavorable prenatal and postnatal conditions or mother inadequacy. Plotkin's (1958) finding of more individuals with type B blood among the early borns than among term controls also gives food for thought.

SOCIAL CLASS AND TWINNING

A relation between social class status and incidence of fraternal twinning was not found, as the literature might have led us to expect, although our method of locating twins might well have fogged this issue (see chapter 1 and Table 1). Or perhaps the fraternal twins from the lower classes were less willing to cooperate in our study; but on this point, of course, we have no relevant evidence.

TWINNING AND MOTHER'S AGE AT MARRIAGE AND AT BIRTH OF TWINS

It has been contended that twinning, among other variables, is related to the age of the mother. Specifically why they are related has not been well demonstrated. There is no evidence in our data of any substantial relation between mother's age at marriage and the zygosity or the sex of the twins, thus practically eliminating from the picture as influential the variable of cultural biases which determine age at marriage (Table 13). The age at marriage of the mothers of our twins apparently did not average higher or lower than that of mothers in the general population (see Glick's 1957 data for a comparison). In contrast is our finding that the zygosity of the twins and the age of mother at birth of her offspring, or the interval between her marriage and the advent of her twins, are significantly related (p, .05 — .01; Tables 13 and 14).

As others have noted (Greulich 1934; Guttmacher 1939; Yerushalmy and Sheerar 1940; Karn and Penrose 1952; Waterhouse 1953; Anon. 1965), the mothers of the fraternal twin subjects, especially those from the same-sex pairs, tended to be older when they gave birth to their children than were the mothers of the identicals (Table 13). Also the interval between the mother's age at marriage and at the birth of her twins was greater for mothers of fraternal than for mothers of identical of twins (Table 7). There was no significant difference, moreover, in age at marriage or at the birth of their twins for mothers of same-sex as opposed to opposite-sex fraternal twin pairs (Table 13). It does appear that something in the mother's physiology (probably a pituitary lack of some sort [Anon. 1965; Gemzell 1965]), which is more than the usual simple age-correlated processes, tends to be associated with the production of at least some fraternal twins. In the interview, the mothers of our fraternal twins often gave vivid reports concerning their efforts to conceive. In the main, their efforts seemed to have been persistent, varied, and well guided. Hence it appears improbable that the greater age of the mothers of the fraternals at the time of conception of their twins is in any way related to their motivation relative to child bearing. The stimulation of multiple births by the Gemzell (1965) or Donini, Puzzuoli, and Montezemolo (1964) treatment of sterile women of a certain type with certain gonadotrophins is relevant to our study. It is pertinent also that only fetuses generated by multiple ovulations were involved in the multiple births (Anon. 1965).

BIRTH WEIGHT OF TWINS, AND MOTHER'S AGE AT MARRIAGE AND AT BIRTH OF TWINS

Although the differences were not significant, the group with the most prematures in our study was also the group in which the interval between mother's age at marriage and her age at the advent of her first living babies, namely the twins, was the greatest. There is no evidence of a substantial correlation among our subjects between birth weight of offspring and mother's age when she married (Table 14), as the literature might have led us to anticipate. Thus it seems unlikely that any simple social-class differences in marriage age are significantly coloring twin birth weight trends. Apparently the older mothers were in many cases individuals who had tried long and hard to beget children. Then, possibly aided by some hormone treatment, they conceived (Anon. 1965; Gemzell and Kiessler 1964; Donini, Puzzuoli, and Montezemolo 1964; Gemzell 1965). Multiple ovulation may have resulted because the hormone treatment was not adequately controlled. If there should be a curvilinear relation between mother's age and multiple births, and we believe there may be—the very old and the very young mothers producing less adequate offspring—this may well not be revealed by our data, since only *rho's* were used because cases were few. Table 14 presents separately for each twin group the correlations between mother's age and birth weight of her offspring. The tendency for the MZ mothers to be relatively young should result in a slight positive relation between mother's age and birth weight of their babies, and the tendency of the mothers of fraternals to be older should result in a slight negative relation. Only one of the *rho's* in Table 14 was significant, but there is a slight trend in the pattern of the results that suggests that our hypothesis may have some foundation. It is also noteworthy that when the total twin population was considered, the older mothers delivered, with significantly greater frequency, babies who had some physical defect. Later in life, these children tended also to exhibit less good health than did the identicals.

GENETICS OF TWINNING

Since it would take us too far afield to review the evidence on the heredity issue, we must forego this program. Suffice it to say that it is a very important issue and difficult to resolve. It is generally believed familial trends in the female line occur in fraternal twinning (see Dahlberg 1926; Greulich 1934; Waterhouse 1950; Oettle 1953), whereas there is somewhat less convincing evidence of similar family trends in identical twinning. Albeit fraternal twinning is usually attributed to factors in the mother, some would like to hold factors in the father responsible for identicals, although there is not so much agreement on this point. Notwithstanding the fact many of the mothers of our subjects told us of the trends toward twinning in their families, we did not explore this question systematically.

BIRTH ORDER AND SIZE OF TWINS AT BIRTH AND LATER

One may well wonder whether there is any aspect of the twin himself that determines the order of his arrival at birth. Is it the individual who is in better condition, or larger, or the more active, who presents himself first at birth? About two-thirds of the time in all of our pairs (Table 7), the twin born first was the heavier of the two. The child who arrived first usually did so by just a few minutes, but in one instance it was by several hours. Moreover, 64 per cent of those born first were still heavier at school entrance (Table 8), but no similar trend was shown in height (49 per cent). The mean weight of the first-borns from same-sex pairs at school age tended to exceed slightly and rather consistently, but not significantly, that for second-borns (Table 8). Since the death rate among the twins in a pair who arrive last tends to be considerably higher than among the twins who arrive first (Bender 1952), we are, doubtless, dealing with a more highly selected population of second-borns than first-borns. Our second-borns, since they have survived, are probably among the stronger, better developed ones. This would reduce the size of the birth-order difference and would probably account for the small disparity observed. There was, moreover, no evidence of more prematurity among second-borns than first-borns (Table 7), except among the DZOS's, where we think a sex factor was operating. The OS pairs were interesting in that 64 per cent of the first arrivals were the heavier members of the pair, which is about the percentage obtained in the SS groups, but it was the male member of the OS pair who was delivered first 87 per cent of the time. (See Karn [1953] for a report of a similar finding; Potter's [1963] results, however, do not agree.) In only one case in our group was the firstborn both a female and the lighter member of the pair. Apparently something more than mere size—something such as placement, activeness, or vigor perhaps —was operating to contribute to the order of twin birth in the OS pairs. It is significant that the first-born did not tend to have the higher IQ (lower, if anything); but in same-sex pairs, he did tend to be judged the dominant co-twin, probably because of his greater size or vigor. (See Shields 1962 for a comparable observation.) Of course, in the OS twins other relations obtain, the girls who were usually second-born tending to be dominant at school age.

As indicated above, Potter (1963), studying a large population of newborn twins, did not note that in the OS pairs the male co-twin was born first more frequently than the female. The reason for this discrepancy between Potter's finding and ours is not clear. Perhaps the death rate among males born second is considerably higher than among males born first. Since we were dealing with school age children and only complete twin pairs, our population would then have included only the twosomes in which the male was strong enough to survive the infant and preschool years, and these males may have been chiefly the vigorous firstborns.

Twin Size at School Entrance

It is tremendously important to discover whether the handicap with which many twins start life persists. This is worthy of concern not only from a practical point of view but also from the point of view of the dynamics of growth. Do early brief derangements generally tend to have lasting effects or do only derangements of specific types have this effect? It would be puzzling indeed if we discovered that even twins who were normal in most respects at birth but were small tended to remain small. This might, among other things, suggest a genetic linkage between the two variables mentioned (see Douglas and Mogford 1953). The general optimism about outgrowing handicaps would be controverted. The notion that what happens very early in development is likely to be critical and to have abiding effects has registered in our thinking very slowly. Moreover, if there were any outgrowing to be done, we should have predicted that it would have occurred more frequently in weight than in height, weight being a function to a greater extent of environmental forces. Our data, which will be described in the next few paragraphs, seem to indicate a reverse trend, i.e., the thrust given by the genes is apparently obscured less. This trend might have been taken lightly and attributed to chance perhaps, had we not noted in the literature that twins tend to be described as slight, as both short and lean (see Stehle 1939).

Table 9 shows that, although our highly selected twin groups had lower mean weights than groups of parallel singletons, only the DZSSm's deviated from singletons significantly, according to the Scheffé estimates. Fraternal males from same-sex pairs tended at school entrance to be clearly lighter than singletons. All groups, however, veered in this direction. The girl twins in same-sex pairs fell only a little short of having significantly less poundage, on the average, than parallel singletons. The trend to remain small may, to a limited degree, relate to prematurity and whatever is involved in that complex. Hess, Mohr, and Bartelme (1934), Alm (1953), Shields (1962), Drillien (1964), and others all present data indicating that those born prematurely tend to remain relatively small. Alm (1953) checked his prematurely born male subjects, most of whom were not twins, when they were adults, and found they averaged both shorter and lighter than his full-term controls. This same tendency may well be apparent in our data, but it is probably muted some by our using only subjects normal enough to be in school.

At five to six years the MZm's and DZSSm's averaged significantly below the means for height for matched singletons (Tables 8 and 9), but none of the girl twin groups exhibited a substantial disparity from their controls. The girls' deviation, however, although slight, was always, in SS pairs, in the same direction—namely, lower than singletons. Although the weight trend, relative to singletons, of the OS twins was about the same as that of the SS twins, in height the former averaged slightly but not significantly taller. It is interesting that there is apparently a sex difference in degree of deviation. For this we have no explanation. It is also noteworthy that the DZSSm's, who averaged well at birth relative to the MZm's, fell distinctly below the latter in weight at five to six years (see Stocks and Karn [1933] for a similar finding).

Table 5 shows a significant zygosity and sex interaction in weight at five to six years. Although the MZm's were heavier at school entrance (see Table 5), there were no zygosity differences between girl twins who were members of same-sex pairs. Although the DZOSm's averaged heavier than the DZSSm's (Table 6), the DZOSf's again showed no essential difference from the DZSSf's. We have no explanation to offer unless, by some chance, the DZSSm's contained more pairs who differed in blood type and possibly, were handicapped physically. This is rank hunch. Osborne and DeGeorge (1957) found, when a blood type difference in the ABO fraction obtained, that developmental difficulties and even earlier death were prone to occur. The DZSSm's, it should be noted, received the lowest rating in health at school age (Tables 8, 15, and 16), but they did not exhibit a high incidence of physical defect at birth (Tables 10 and 11). It is true that the DZSSm's are the type that was difficult to locate and, hence, we suspect this group may have been subject to special hazards. What these are, other than maleness, is not clear. Of course, one must not overlook the question of the frequency of the type in the germ population. The group was highly selected, but since the DZSSm's weighed as much at birth as the MZm's when social class was controlled (Table 5), this variable seems not to have been a potent determinant of the pattern described.

Birth Order and Size of Twins at School Age

If one looks at the size at early school age of the first- and second-born twins, no significant mean differences in weight in the same-sex pairs are noted, although the slight difference is consistently in favor of the first-born (Table 8) just as it tended to be for birth weight (Table 7). The lack of a larger difference, the reader should be reminded, may be due to a muting caused by our having, probably, a more highly selected group of second-borns than first. The incidence of first-borns being heavier than second-borns was higher in all groups, both at birth (Table 7) and at the end of the preschool years (Table 8). There was no clearly similar trend for height. In the OS pairs the picture is obscured by the sex difference of the co-twins. Here, as mentioned earlier, almost all of the first arrivals were males. The OS boys at school age still had a slight advantage in weight over their sisters. Surprisingly, the DZSSm's, both first- and second-borns, were lighter (but not significantly) at five to six years than the DZSSf's (Table 8). This configuration suggests that in the DZSSm's we may be dealing with more than a simple sex difference. It is relevant to the sex relation described for the DZSS's that the MZm's and DZOSm's, first- and second-borns, outweighed significantly the females of their respective groups at school entrance (Table 8). In height the males in the SS pairs showed a slight but not significant tendency to be smaller than females, whereas those in the OS pairs tended to be taller.

Twin-singleton Differences in Size at School Age, Birth Order Controlled

Since it is generally believed that first-born singletons tend to be a bit smaller than the second-borns in their families, we controlled for birth order and compared the twins with first-born singletons only. The twins (who are all essentially first-borns in that they are the first viable offspring of their mothers) still averaged less in every group than did matched first-born singletons (Table 8). Only the twin-singleton differences in the same-sex pairs were significant, however. At any rate, it seems unlikely that the tendency for twins to weigh less than singletons has been misjudged because parity has not been adequately taken into account. The well-known tendency for second-born singletons to be heavier than first-borns is clearly shown in the data for boys but not for girls. In the matter of height at five to six years of age, no significant birth-order differences, either among twins or singletons, are apparent (Table 8).

Stability of Co-twin Relative Size in Same-sex Pairs

It was congruent with the rest of the findings relative to the stability of size differences that there was a tendency, except in the OS pairs where the usual sex differences in growth pattern showed themselves, for the relative status among co-twins to be maintained through the preschool years (see Table 8). The per cent of concordance in size status between birth size and that at school entrance varied, in the different groups, from .53 to .94. The average for the SS groups was .77. The tendency to concordance was not significantly less marked among MZ's than among the DZSS's, in whom gene differences could probably be expected to be more influential in determining the subject differences. Apparently, environmental forces playing early on the subjects can result in possibly lasting differences among the MZ's, even though these are slight. It is interesting that more of the girls maintained their size status relative to the sib than did the boy co-twins (Table 8).

Checking on the stability of a twin's size status within his group instead of within his pair, we correlated, for the various subgroups, weight at birth and at school entrance. The *rho's* for the MZm's and

MZf's were .42 and .44, respectively, whereas the comparable *rho's*
for the DZSSm's and DZSSf's were .14 and .15, levels that are clearly
insignificant. For the DZOSf's, a correlation of even a —.13 obtained
between birth weight and that at school entrance, whereas for the
DZOSm's a *rho* of —.43 was noted. Thus it appears that, with respect
to each other, the members of the identical and fraternal pairs tended
to maintain about the same stability in relative size (Table 8), but
with respect to the other twins in their groups, the identicals shifted
less in the preschool period than the fraternals did. It is doubtful that
the difference in correlation in the latter instance is owing to a simple
difference in group heterogeneity.

The intraclass correlations between pair members reveal as others
have found, a greater similarity in size between identical co-twins
than between the fraternal co-twins of the same sex (see Tables 7 and
8). The usual explanation is in terms of the greater genetic similarity
of the identical twins to each other. It should not be overlooked,
however, that the environments of identicals are also more similar
than those of fraternals. Our intraclass correlations agree well with
those of Newman, Freeman, and Holzinger (1937).

OCULAR DEFICIENCIES

Although we mentioned earlier that twin types may differ in incidence of defect, it would be well to take a more detailed look at this
problem. The high incidence (13 cases, 38 per cent) of those wearing
glasses in the DZOS group at five to six years of age is striking
(Tables 11 and 12), and the difference between the DZOS and DZSS
groups is significant at about the .001 level. The DZSS and MZ groups
did not differ significantly. Our twin groups generally, when compared with about 3,000 kindergarten and first-grade children enrolled
in similar schools and classes, all exhibited a greater frequency of
wearing glasses. The incidence of glasses among 3,000 controls was
4.39 per cent and the mean per cent per school class was 4.87; for the
DZOS's, the DZSS's, and the MZ's, the incidence was 38, 7, and 13
per cent, respectively. We do not know what lies back of these group
differences. It is barely possible that more of the DZSS and MZ
populations suffered eye damage sufficiently severe to prevent their
enrollment in the regular school classes. But this we doubt. (See

Stocks and Karn (1933) for observations on a similar finding of a relatively high percentage of eye defect in OS twins and in twins in general.) It is notable that if one member of a pair wore glasses or had an ocular problem, 44 per cent of the time the co-twin did also—i.e., whatever was responsible for the defect seemed to apply to both twins. There was no zygosity difference in this trend.

There is evidence that retrolental fibroplasia played a role in the above picture, that is, all defect was not the direct result of early birth or prenatal conditions. As explained earlier, our subjects were born in the era when at least the severely premature babies were kept for a time in chambers where the oxygen concentration and pressure was high (see Gregory 1957). It is significant in relation to this fact that the incidence of ocular deficiency in the subgroups tended to parallel that of the amount of prematurity in the group ($r = .83$). In keeping with this is Koch's (1964) observation that in three sets of thirty matched twins (matched in sex, age, social class, zygosity, family complexity, race, urban residence, and so on) the percentage of ocular deficiency in groups of different birth size (birth weight under 4½ pounds, 4½ to 5½ pounds, and over 5½ pounds) was, 17, 17, and 10 per cent, respectively.

GENERAL DEFECT

If we sum the physical defects we noted and the mothers reported, and compute the defect rate per child, it can be seen that the severely premature exhibited the highest incidence of serious difficulty (Table 10). The mildly premature and the term group seemed to fare about the same in the matter of defect. In fact, we are beginning to wonder whether mildly substandard weight at birth may not be a slight advantage to twins. This could spare the fetus certain obstetrical hazards. Slightly early birth may even spare them some involvement with maternal toxemia, eclampsia, and so forth, which are not uncommon in the late stages of pregnancy. To support the above hypothesis that mild prematurity may be, everything considered, slightly advantageous, it has been observed that the mean IQ's for the three birth-weight groups described above were, respectively, 99.6, 110.8, and 108. The mildly premature and term-born differ very slightly, the advantage being, however, with the former.

As usual, the boys in the same-sex pairs possessed more defect than did the girls (Tables 10 and 11), but the reverse, if anything, was true of the OS group. Apparently when competing with their brothers at the prenatal level, the girls in the OS pairs did not fare well. Although it is well known that the freemartin type of phenomenon does not occur in human beings (see Lillie 1916), it is desirable that someone explore thoroughly the question of the possibility of hormonal and even blood exchanges occurring in opposite-sex fraternals. Recent findings of a few chimeras should lend encouragement to such an exploration. The problem of twin-maternal-blood incompatibility also needs more study (Bookstaver 1951; Booth *et al.* 1957; Nicholas, Jenkins, and Marsh 1957; Chown, Lewis, and Bowman 1963).

HEALTH RATING

Since twins are known to be presented with more pre- and perinatal hazards than singletons, it seemed advisable to determine the relation of these experiences to the twins' later health.

The measure of health used in this study was a poor one, unfortunately, as we had no medical support. The measure of health employed was merely the teacher's estimate, based chiefly on attendance records and mothers' reports. There was no significant difference in these ratings between twins and singleton subjects at five to six years of age, although there is a slight hint that MZ's have better health than DZSS's (Tables 15 and 16). This is not out of line with some of the findings reported by Stocks and Karn (1933); Bender (1952); and Osborne and DeGeorge (1959).

Since the MZ's, some maintain (see Yerushalmy and Sheerar 1940), have a more difficult prenatal life and the pre- and perinatal mortality rates are alleged to be higher than those for fraternals (see Potter 1963), the intimation of less adequate health among the fraternal male subjects and DZOS's, if it could be demonstrated on repetition, would be intriguing. Of course, as explained in chapter 1, we may be dealing with differential or selective sampling effects in the various twin groups. There are, however, enough hints of findings of poorer health in the OS subjects by others (Wilson and Jones 1931; Stocks and Karn 1933; Bender 1952; and Osborne and DeGeorge 1959, pp. 57–58) to make the wisdom of ignoring the trend questionable. Lauterbach (1933) found the incidence of OS pairs among school age twins to be .30, whereas Osborne and DeGeorge (1959) noted an incidence of only .14 among their adult subjects. In the same two populations the ratios of the SSm's to all same-sex pairs were .48 and .37, respectively. Osborne and DeGeorge (1957) also report selective survival among fraternals, which these authors think depends on similarity or dissimilarity of ABO blood type in the co-twins. Twin subjects who are not concordant tend to have poorer health and a shorter survival period. More carefully gathered data, relatively free of population sampling defects, are greatly needed. Also, the question of the relation of the blood-type similarity and dissimilarity of mother and twins (other than on the Rh dimension) and the health and survival of the latter has had inadequate attention and is deserving of more detailed exploration.

SUMMARY

1. No simple zygosity-group differences in birth weight were apparent, although the interaction of zygosity and social class was significant. The DZSS group deviated from the expected trend for birth weight to be lowest in the lowest social class.

2. The lower the class the higher generally the prematurity rate, although one group did not show this pattern.

3. Girl twins tended to weigh less at birth than boys and to be more frequently classifiable as prematures based on a criterion of a birth weight of less than 5½ pounds.

4. The incidence of prematurity in our total population was 57 per cent—about seven times the rate noted by Potter (1963) and others in singletons. About a third of the twin subjects weighed under 4½ pounds at birth.

5. The fraternal twins from opposite-sex pairs showed more prematurity and more defect than did those from same-sex pairs, but the most severe degree of prematurity was not more frequent among the DZOS's than among the MZ's.

6. The children who were most premature at birth tended to exhibit the most physical defects.

7. If one member of a twin pair had a birth weight under 5½ pounds, the other tended to be premature also (75 per cent of the

cases). The co-twins in the population differed up to 3½ pounds in birth weight, however.

8. The mothers of the twins in the various subgroups did not differ in mean age at marriage, but they did differ in average age at the time of the arrival of their offspring, the mothers of the fraternal twins averaging older at the birth of their babies than did the mothers of the identicals. There were indications that the former tended to have more difficulty in conceiving. In the total population, the older mothers tended to deliver significantly more babies with physical defects.

9. There was a tendency for the first-born twin to be slightly heavier at birth, and even at school entrance, than the second-born.

10. In the DZOS pairs the male member was the first to be born in 87 per cent of the cases, even in several instances when the male was not the heavier co-twin. The high percentage however cannot be taken very seriously because the group was small.

11. Although all twin groups averaged less than first- and second-born matched singletons at the beginning of their elementary school years, only the DZSSm's were significantly lighter, whereas the MZm's and DZSSm's were both significantly shorter. In other words, the twin size handicap (probably due to prematurity and whatever is involved in that complex, including social factors) tended to persist. At school age, however, the girl twins did not fall significantly short in height or weight relative to matched singleton females, although the group averages for girls were consistently slightly below even those for first-born singletons. That the twin-singleton differences were not more marked is probably owing to the muting effect of our using only "normal" public school children.

12. At school age the MZm's averaged significantly heavier than the DZSSm's, but no similar zygosity difference was shown by the girls.

13. In same-sex twin pairs the size status between pair members present at birth tended to persist at least to school age, the consistency being greater in girls than boys. There was no notable zygosity difference in size status stability.

14. The intraclass correlations of birth weight, and weight and height at five to six years were, as others have found, substantially higher for identical than for fraternal twins.

15. When they were five to six years of age, the opposite-sex

fraternal pairs were wearing glasses with greater frequency than the other twin groups or singletons. Twins generally wore glasses more often than control singletons—in fact, about two to seven times as often, depending on the group. Among the fraternals the incidence of children wearing glasses was higher when the children had been prematures than when they had been term babies. There was evidence that retrolental fibroplasia was responsible for some of the eye defects observed.

16. In the same-sex pairs the boys exhibited more gross defect than did the girls. This was not true for the opposite-sex fraternal group.

17. Generally, the frequency of defect was positively associated with extreme prematurity at birth. Term MZ's showed a substantial number of abnormalities, however.

18. The teachers' ratings did not indicate any significant difference between the health of twins and singletons at school entrance. There was a suggestion in the data, however, that the identical males had better health than did the same-sex fraternal male pairs and the MZ's than did the DZOS's.

CHAPTER III

Primary Mental Abilities

There is probably little question but that twins, if an unselected sample is drawn, will have on the average a lower IQ than singletons (see Day 1932; Davis 1937; Rosanoff, Handy, and Plesset 1937; Benton 1940; Allen and Kallman 1955; Drillien 1961; Wiener 1962; and Drillien 1964). And the many twins whose very early demise bars them from being involved in a study such as ours must also be remembered (see Bender 1952; Record, Gibson, and McKeown 1952; Lillienfeld and Pasamanick 1955; Knobloch *et al.* 1956; Lilienfeld and Pasamanick 1956; and Osborne and DeGeorge 1959). At any rate, damage and especially injury involving the nervous system, which usually cannot be repaired, is not exactly rare even among viable twins. But investigations dealing with school children will have eliminated from consideration, as did ours, most of those individuals who have suffered substantial degrees of physical impairment. Hence, we are merely asking whether, in a highly selected group of "normal" twins, there are still to be seen sequelae of prematurity and of mild, early developmental or obstetrical complications. If there are seque-lae, we should expect them to be more frequent in males, because, as was expounded in the previous chapter, males appear to have a more difficult time generally getting started in life and seem subject to more trauma (see chapter 2).

Surprisingly little is known about the frequency of mild impair-ments. Yet schools need to be alerted to the possible special needs of

44

twins, for if there are nervous system disturbances, for instance, these may not be disclosed merely in slower learning. Even in the area of ability there may be need for explanation of differential skills—perceptual-motor *vs.* mathematical skills (see Graham *et al.* (1963). It is desirable also for the interpretation of many phenomena associated with twinning (such as speech-learning difficulties and inequalities that occur even among identical co-twins) to know to what extent intelligence level is contributing to the picture.

METHODS AND INSTRUMENTS

The "intelligence" test we used, the Primary Mental Abilities Test (PMA) (see Thurstone, *et al.* 1946), contains five subtests that, as studies by the Thurstones and by Meyers, *et al.* (1962) give evidence, tap rather different abilities. The tests are designated verbal (V), perceptual (P), quantitative (Q), motor (M), and spatial (S). Because twins are alleged to have speech and language learning difficulties, and, because, among other things, some may be the victims of slight brain impairment, we were especially interested in contrasting the twins' performance with the singletons' on the verbal test, a cognitive-semantic test, as opposed to the perceptual speed and motor tests, in which at least those with mild brain damage may even excel (see Ernhart *et al.* 1963; also Graham *et al.* 1963). Intertwin, as well as twin-singleton comparisons, may be very revealing.

Unfortunately, the singletons available to us for comparison with the twins were tested on the PMA in small groups by the schools in which they were enrolled—this not by our design—whereas our twins were tested individually. Hence, we do not feel justified, without proper reservations, in comparing our twin and singleton subjects —i.e., the testing conditions seem to us clearly to favor the twins, particularly in the motor and perceptual tests, which are not only timed tests, and thus sensitive to disturbances and distractions, but which also demand auditory discriminations that can be less effectively achieved in a room in which confreres are functioning as young children usually do. Despite the complications just described, we decided to use our data for twin-singleton comparisons. It seemed evident that, if other conditions were comparable, we would have every reason to expect our twins to score somewhat higher than matched singletons. But if the twins did not excel, notwithstanding their being favored by the testing conditions, the suspicion is justified that under strictly comparable conditions the twins would have averaged lower than singletons. When, as occurred in a number of instances, the twin subjects not only did not score higher than did the control groups of singletons, but even lower (as in the Verbal section; see Table 18), we were willing to accede to the view that our twins were, on the average, slightly less competent, for some reason, in whatever skills or abilities were tapped by the PMA.

Since all of our twin subjects were examined singly and by one of two examiners, we feel safe in at least comparing the twin subgroups. Although, as explained in chapter 1, we think we have controlled in the intertwin comparisons the biasing owing to the unique characteristics of each examiner, we are more inclined to be worried about the possibility of a constant bias such as might stem from the fact that the examiners were both women. Perhaps our male subjects would have responded with more enthusiasm to a male examiner. All singletons, let it be said, were also tested by women, but the tests were given and scored by a dozen or so different, but well-trained, examiners. We were permitted to do a limited amount of checking the scoring, which convinced us the scoring was carefully done.

INTERTWIN GROUP COMPARISONS

If a comparison of the various geminal groups whose members were identical in sex is made by a three-way analysis of variance study involving zygosity, sex, and socioeconomic class (see Scheffé 1959 p. 98 ff.), it will be noted (Table 17) that the MZ's, both male and female, averaged slightly lower than did the comparable DZSS's, not only on the verbal subtest but on the total test as well. Social-class group disparities in performance on all of the subtests but the spatial were significant, the upper and middle classes performing better than the lowest. This influence of social class was divorced from that of other variables by our analysis of variance procedure. It is felt, hence, that the effects of zygosity and sex have not been masked. There were no significant zygosity group differences observed for the P, Q, and S subtests. The rather consistently low performance, relative to the other twins, of the MZ's, especially the MZm's, is, however, one of our most conspicuous findings. What it may mean will be discussed shortly.

The effect among the fraternals of the agreement or lack of agreement of sex of the co-twins is brought into focus by juxtaposing the DZSS and DZOS groups. The comparison was made separately for the two sexes and a two-way analysis of variance procedure (sex of sib and social class) was used. No marked group divergences were uncovered here; social class disparities only were apparent and even these in only the total, V, and P test means. In the main, as in the comparison of zygotic groups whose pair members were identical in sex, the lower the class the lower the test performance. The upper and middle classes differed little, however.

PAIR-MEMBER LIKENESS

Although we have no intention in this monograph of getting into a discussion of the heredity-environment problem, let us merely report here the intraclass *r*'s for the PMA-total test IQ for the identical pairs, fraternal same-sex pairs, and fraternal opposite-sex pairs. These *r*'s are, respectively, .79, .45, and .52.

It is worth noting that Shields (1962), for his identical and fraternal pairs (age range 8 to 59 years) whose members were not separated and who were tested on the Synonym Section of the Raven Mill Hill Vocabulary Scale and Dominoes Intelligence Test, obtained intraclass *r*'s of .76 and .51 respectively. Newman, Freeman, and Holzinger (1937), for subjects ranging from middle elementary school age to adulthood, stated their intraclass *r*'s (age partialled out) for identicals and fraternals in the case of the Stanford-Binet IQ to be .88 and .63, respectively, and in the case of the Otis Test IQ, .92 and .62, respectively. To account for the likenesses and slight differences in merely these three sets of findings would necessitate a detailed examination of the instruments used, the nature of the groups studied, and many statistical considerations. This we shall forego. Suffice it to say that there is considerable similarity in the results, in spite of the major methodological differences. There are many other relevant sets of findings that are also similar. Hence the suggestion is strong that genetic factors tend to play a role in determining individual differences in performance on standard tests of intelligence, but parallelism in twins in impairment and experience also deserves consideration.

TWIN-SINGLETON COMPARISONS

If twin and singleton subjects are juxtaposed (Table 18), it is apparent that the MZm's ranked significantly lower than matched singletons, not only on the basis of their IQ's on the total test but also on the quotient scores on the V, Q, and S subtests, which provide the tasks in the test that probably demand the most symbolic thinking. The MZf's, in contrast to the MZm's, averaged significantly below singletons only on the V test. On the P test the twins scored above singletons. The difference on the P test between twins and the singleton controls were significant in three groups, and a deviation in the same direction in three others was apparent. All differences favored the twins, as had been anticipated on the basis of the conditions under which the test was administered. The same-sex fraternal groups deviated negatively from singleton controls to a significant degree in performance on the V test, whereas the DZOS's deviated in the same direction but not significantly. In fact, there was only one marked difference (test P for DZOSm's) between the DZOS's and the matched singleton controls, and this difference was favorable to the twins, an observation that particularly impressed us since the prematurity rate in this twin group was relatively high.

When twin-singleton group differences were analyzed from the point of view of zygosity and sex effects, the only significant finding was that the twin boys fell more noticeably below singleton males on the verbal test than did twin girls below singleton females.

We felt that the effect of different testing conditions, as explained above, is most clearly apparent in the P subtest results and is responsible for the higher means earned here by all of the twin groups, as compared with singletons. It may be erroneous, however, to attribute all P test advantage to testing conditions, since we may be witnessing what Graham *et al.* (1963) observed in their follow-up investigation of babies who were anoxic at birth or who were faced with obstetrical difficulties. The latter, perhaps as a result of compensatory mechanisms, excelled the non-traumatized controls in perceptual and motor test performance but scored lower in the tasks that required more of the semantic-conceptual type of mental activity.

The relatively poor performance of all twin groups on the V subtest puzzles us. This is essentially a vocabulary and general information test. We wonder whether, in addition to the physical hazards twins experience (see chapter 2), we could be dealing here, in part, with a social influence. For example, since twins can and do entertain each other, they may have fewer playful contacts with their parents in their early months or years. Also all twin groups listed more playmates of their own age than did comparable singletons. If twins typically do have a less varied playmate group than singletons, this could restrict the range of information and concepts to which the former would be exposed early in life. And the playmates listed by co-twins are virtually the same individuals, especially in the case of same-sex pairs, thus further restricting the variety of children with whom the twins would have commerce. Singleton sibs tend to be exposed to each others' friends, even though the age gap between them may be considerable. The playmates of the older sib, moreover, because the children tend to be upward striving, tend to be much admired and imitated by the younger sib. Thus, the variety of associates of singletons will clearly be greater than that of twins. The greater diversity of the singletons' associates probably extends their horizons beyond the range of twins whose playmates tend to be mostly of their own age and overlapping in identity with those of the twin sib. It is probably of some relevance in relation to the above hypothesis that the DZOS's who, according to the interview, played least with each other and each other's friends, and who, being of opposite sexes, exposed each other to greater diversity in playmates than was true of the other twin groups, did not differ significantly from singletons in their performance on the V test. This is especially implicative, since the incidence of prematurity was high in this DZOS group, a consideration that might lead one to expect the group to score relatively lower on the V test than the same-sex fraternals or singletons.

DISCUSSION

Our findings, in that they suggest that twins in general achieve in intellectual tasks on the average somewhat below singletons, are corroborated by those of other investigators. Day (1932), for instance, using the Minnesota Preschool Test for assessing twins and the Kuhlmann Test for assessing singletons, discovered that her preschool twins averaged about ten points lower than singletons and that the deficiency of the former was apparent on both the verbal and nonverbal sections of the instrument.

Davis (1937), using the Pintner-Cunningham Test for both her 5½ and 6½ year-old singletons and twins and the Pressey Test for the 9½ year olds, reported that the twins exhibited a lower mean IQ than singletons at all three age levels. This is noteworthy, since even the expected selective elimination of the least capable twins from the public schools as they reach the more difficult levels apparently did not bring the latter's test average to the singleton level by the mid-elementary school years.

Other recent investigations dealing with prematures (e.g., Asher and Roberts 1949; Douglas and Mogford 1953; Drillien 1964)—and this indeed most twins are—noted a consistent, small inferiority of their subjects in school performance and in IQ. Our own data indicate that the severely premature fall below term and slightly prematurely born individuals in IQ.

All of the above findings, then, provide convincing evidence that twins, as compared with matched singletons, tend in their intellectual development to show some handicap. That this is rooted in the slight, albeit abiding effects of early pathology seems not unlikely. Whether this impairment is the sole origin of the twins' less favorable status is the question. Another, at least supplementary interpretation—namely, that twins tend to have less broad experience—was described earlier in the chapter.

The observation that all of our twin groups averaged below singletons on the V test and not typically on the other subtests of the PMA suggests that we have here a unique twin-singleton type of disparity, whatever the specific dynamics are. Social class differences weighed heavily as a conditioner of performance on the V test; but this fact cannot account for the intertwin group and twin-singleton differences in score because, by our analysis of variance design (Scheffé 1959, p. 98 ff.), we isolated social class in intertwin comparison, and in the twin-singleton contrast, a matched group procedure was employed to discount the class variable. The matching, let it be recalled, was on the basis of age, sex, sex of sib, and social class as well as on about six other characteristics on which the inclusion of a child in the total sibling study was contingent. We were careful to include in each of the comparative groups of singletons the same number of subjects with sibs who differed from them in age by less than two years, two to four, and four to six years, both in the younger and older directions. This stratified sampling procedure, which was followed throughout the study, insured comparability among singleton groups at least along the sib-age difference and birth-order dimensions, and provided a wide variety of singleton types. Of course, it should be remembered that children from larger than two-child families were not participants in the investigation either among twins or singletons, and they might have performed quite differently from the population observed. Unfortunately we did not have enough subjects to study systematically the twins in relation to singletons representing different birth orders and spacings. The matched singleton group was a substantial one, however. As the reader will recall, for each same-sex pair there were four singleton matches and for the DZOS twins each subject was matched individually on all of the above-mentioned characteristics by four singletons who, among other aspects, had a sib opposite to him in sex.

We have wondered, since social class differences in our data were generally large, whether we might see some similar influence at work to determine certain twin-singleton differences. Does being a twin, for instance, result in restriction of experiences, especially in language and, accordingly, in vocabulary as well as information? Since the most uniform lack among our twins was in the V test performance, this would be congruent with the hypothesis, circumstantial evidence for which was marshalled in the previous section, page 49, that twins may be less widely experienced than singletons. It has seemed well to probe this question further and, accordingly, to examine in some detail the language behavior of twins. This will be done in chapter 4.

SUMMARY

1. Among our subjects significant intertwin group differences were most uniform in the social class variable, the subjects from the lowest class performing least effectively on all subtests of the PMA but the spatial.

2. On the perceptual test, the girl twins tended to average higher than the boys.

3. The scores of the MZ's on the V subtest and the total test averaged significantly below those of the DZSS's and DZOS's. The MZm group, moreover, on all tests but the P had a mean quotient score that was significantly lower than that of the matched singletons.

4. The fraternal twins with same- or opposite-sex sibs tended not to differ significantly from each other in performance on the PMA.

5. The intraclass r's for the MZ, DZSS, and DZOS groups in the PMA total test IQ were, respectively, .79, .45, and .52.

6. Twins from same-sex pairs averaged significantly below matched singleton controls on the V test. Even the DZOS's showed the same trend but not so markedly.

7. The MZf's, in contrast to male identicals, were generally not so retarded, falling significantly below controls only on the V test and even excelling the latter on the P test, although here the testing conditions particularly favored the twins.

8. With one exception (DZOSm's on the P test), the DZOS's did not differ significantly from the singleton controls in their performance on any subtest.

9. The same-sex fraternals, male and female, did, on the other hand, deviate significantly in a negative direction from the matched singletons on the V test. The DZSSf's, in contrast, excelled the matched singletons on the P test, probably because they were favored by the testing conditions.

10. The only significant difference in magnitude of twin-singleton disparity was apparent in the sex group performance on the V test. Here, male twins were more inferior relative to singleton males than female twins were to singleton females.

CHAPTER IV

Language Abilities of Twins

HYPOTHESES

The belief is current that twins, for some reason, have unique difficulty in learning to speak (Day 1932; Davis 1937). For this "fact" a
variety of explanations have been offered. It is conjectured: (1) that
retardation in language performance is caused by general mental
retardation, owing perhaps to pre- and perinatal central nervous system damage; (2) that poor performance sometimes stems from pre-
and perinatal injury to the muscles, skeleton, and peripheral nerves
involved in speech; (3) that twins have less incentive to learn to
speak, understanding so well each other's gestures and habits; and (4)
that twins, because of their dependence on each other and of the way
in which they are treated, tend to have the range of their experiences
curtailed, important among which are language experiences with
adults and older children. The twins serve as poor speech models to
each other. These explanations, it should be understood, are not necessarily mutually exclusive. Our evidence bearing on these theories
will be discussed after the pro's and con's of the instruments used to
describe language achievement of various sorts have been reviewed.

MEASURES OF VARIOUS ASPECTS OF LANGUAGE PERFORMANCE

To judge the quality of the twins' performance in speech form, an
attempt was made to obtain four indicators of status in language form

achievement at different developmental stages. One dealt with the twins' general progress in spoken language up to school entrance. This indicator was an estimate made by the twins' mother in an interview. Another was an assessment made by their teachers of the twins' phonological, morphological, and syntactical form at a time when the twins were probably being exposed to more verbal stimulation than previously, were having speech correction experience perhaps, and were probably being surrounded by a richer social environment than had presented itself in their preschool years. The rating procedure the teachers employed is described in chapter 1, as is the normalization of the raw scores. The teachers, no doubt, had, like the mothers, the usual difficulties of raters, although the teachers' judgments, in one sense, probably had a better basis of reference than the mothers', because the teachers had daily contact with so many children of the twins' age and heard the latter group hold forth under circumstances similar to that which obtained for many singletons. The teachers' ratings also were little influenced by memories of the twins' earlier behavior, as were the mothers', and better described the children's performance level after entering school. The ratings were carefully made in the main. The teachers were instructed about some of the problems of rating and ways of circumventing them, and were encouraged to observe the twins for a considerable period before forming a final opinion. Doubtless both the teachers and mothers, but especially the latter, did not make due allowance for the prematurity of many of the subjects they appraised, and based their judgments on the child's chronological age. Hence it is thought that the twins, particularly in their early preschool years, may have been conservatively appraised. Lastly it should be appreciated, in the case of both mothers and teachers, that at least each pair of twins tended to be assessed by a different judge. To correct in part for the problem of variability of rater standard, since in some cases the co-twins were judged by different teachers one judge, K, judged the phonological, morphological, syntactic form exhibited in all tape recordings of the stories the children told in the Children's Apperception Test (Bellak and Bellak 1950). A seven-point scale of general merit was employed, a score of one indicating the highest level of merit, and seven, the lowest. In extremely deviate subjects, however, it is doubtful that the scale permitted adequate description. There is a question also whether a judge can make as discriminating assessments from a tape recording as from direct apprehension of children's speech, although in one sense he may do better, for he is forced to rely more on auditory cues. This limitation (or advantage) needs to be kept in mind, as well as the fact that, since the stories told by the children varied greatly in length, the language samples assessed by *K* were not only limited but far from constant from child to child. The ratings, moreover, were made over a period of several years during which time *K*'s standard might have shifted. Occasional rescorings were done, however, to keep this difficulty to a minimum. A standardized test of the sort Stinchfield (1921, 1923), Wellman *et al.* (1931), Templin (1957), and Berko (1958) developed probably should have been used. Of our various ratings, *K*'s should describe the child's highest level of attainment and be least colored by a halo effect or the judge's knowledge of the subject's performance at some earlier period in his development.

Our fourth measure was a relatively objective one of degree of mastery of one aspect of language which, it was thought, would be highly correlated with achievement in phonetics and phonemics. This measure was one of morphological and syntactical form. It was probably more subject to social influences than were the gauges of articulation and less to fortuitous physiological handicaps. The number of morphological-syntactical errors made by a child was determined when we employed a sample of four hundred consecutive words that he used in telling stories about the CAT pictures. The material to be scored was drawn as far as possible from the same stories to provide some control over vocabulary. Little, of course, is known about the effect of various types of language samples upon the error count. Perhaps the child tends to use those words and forms he handles best (Day 1932). Such a tendency might distort some of the picture of his achievement that we obtained from a very limited sample of his verbal output in the story-telling. To control the examiner-variable, all morphology and syntax scorings were made by a single examiner.

The following types of morphological-syntactical errors were counted: lack of agreement of subject and predicate in number; faulty case; incorrect plural forms; improper forms of tense, pronouns, adjectives, adverbs and prepositions; faulty word order and sentence structure; incomplete sentences or omission of essential words; confused references; and garbled or misused words.

Because the training needed to assess a protocol properly was long and taxing, no second judge was employed, except in the early stages of the training, when two judges scored the same material until there was essential agreement on the rules to be followed. Because the scoring was difficult, one judge scored all protocols twice to insure the maintenance of consistency in procedure throughout the assessments. The r between the first and second counts of 116 records was .97 (Table 19). When a corrected split-half method of gauging score reliability was employed, the estimate of the reliability for the total test (n = 164, Spearman-Brown estimate) was .92 (Table 19).

INTERVIEW WITH THE MOTHERS OF THE TWINS

Ours not being a strictly longitudinal study, we had to be content to question the mothers about their children's early speech development. Although it seems reasonable to expect the mothers, and, for that matter, the teachers, as well as Judge K to have in varying degrees difficulties which are typical for raters, it is probably unlikely these distorting forces would operate more in appraisals for one group of twins than for another and thus obscure intertwin group differences. We had confidence to a degree in the mothers' reports, despite the fact that they were not trained observers, because these women did know their children well and only a global type of appraisal of the child's general development in speech (normal vs. delayed) was requested of them. Whether all mothers were familiar with the current belief that twins tend to have speech difficulties was not known, but we are sure most had this information. Although one can only speculate on the effect of this knowledge on the mothers' and teachers' judgments, we suspect it might have made it relatively easy for the judges to admit retardation in speech learning and achievement, or, possibly, even to see it when there was little present. At any rate, their information on the matter, it seems likely, would have made both the mothers and teachers more than normally observant of the twins' language efforts.

Since the mothers of the singleton subjects were not interviewed, assessments of the twins based on mothers' judgments cannot be compared directly with those of non-twins, as was possible for several of the other measures. Of course, implied in the mothers' appraisal is some sort of singleton standard. When a mother told us, for instance, that her twins were slow or very retarded in beginning to talk, this meant she thought their rate of progress was lower than children ordinarily exhibit.

The mothers were questioned as to: when the twins spoke their first word and their first sentence; whether the children were markedly delayed in their use of speech; whether baby talk was unduly persistent; whether the children for a considerable period seemed to have a language of their own; whether at any time they stuttered; also whether they were lefthanded; were reticent; or seldom spoke to adults; were read to much or little; had many child companions, and so forth. We also inquired about how the twin pair members usually communicated with each other. The mothers were interrogated until it was felt that the best information they could give us had been obtained.

INTERRELATIONS OF THE MEASURES OF SPEECH FORM

Unfortunately we have no estimates of the reliability of the judgments the mothers made, although the internal consistency in their reports was always attended to and intensive questioning did help to clear up discrepancies. Also the mothers', the teachers', and K's judgments of the children at school age could be roughly compared and serve as a sort of check on each other, even though the period and the behaviors emphasized differed somewhat. The interjudge r's are for the mothers' and teachers' assessments, $-.55$; mothers' and experimenter K's, $.73$; teachers' and experimenter K's, $-.49$ (Table 20). The r's between syntax error counts and mothers' assessments of general defect in phonetic and morphological structure, teachers' ratings, and K's judgments were, respectively, $.37$, $-.35$, and $.38$ (Table 20). The intercorrelations are based on the total twin group of 164 to 169 subjects. The negative correlations stem from the fact that one measure in the related pair stressed errors and failure, the other, merit or excellence. The intercorrelations were also derived for the homogeneous zygosity and sex subgroups, but only the data for the total group of subjects will be presented here. When any subgroup r's give an essentially different picture from that which the total group portrays, they will receive comment. For example, the inter-measure r's tended to be higher for the MZ's, male and female, than for the total group, although a similar relation did not hold for the fraternals. The conjecture that the differences here might stem from a greater heterogeneity among the identicals than the fraternals is not supported by attention to group sigmas. The greater co-twin similarities in many qualities among the MZ's seem a more likely cause. There is reason to suspect that a somewhat more massive merit-limiting factor was operative among identicals than fraternals. Such a factor might be brain impairment in some subjects.

A correlation coefficient of approximately .15 (Table 20) would be significant in the case of the total group. Let us remind the reader again that he will need to pay attention to the footnotes to Table 20, which explain the signs of the correlations. Some of the measures, as mentioned earlier, concentrated on the limitations of performance, others on those of merit.

Clearly, the judgments of phonological skill, although they were based on different traits and on behavior samples varying in scope, as well as representing somewhat different developmental levels, all correlated to a considerable degree (Table 20). Understandably, the various ratings of speech form correlated somewhat better with each other than they did with the objective morphological score (syntax error count), which described a more limited aspect of speech behavior. We believe that the two areas of language learning may overlap greatly in the child's early years but reach their ceilings at different times. The child goes on learning the nuances of syntax and morphology long after he has mastered phonetic patterns to a generally acceptable level. This also may account in part for the lower r's between the syntax error counts and the phonetic ratings.

INTERTWIN GROUP DIFFERENCES IN VARIOUS ASPECTS OF SPEECH FORM

In 29 per cent of the children, the mothers stated that marked delay in beginning to talk had been characteristic, and in 40 per cent that there was undue persistence of baby talk. These figures, although based on the rather nebulous norm each mother had in mind, still justify the suspicion that speech development among many of the twin pairs studied was slow. This is in line with Day's (1932) and Davis' (1937) finding that development among twins toward good articulatory form tends to proceed at a retarded rate, the retardation, according to Davis, being the more apparent the younger the children. According to the mothers' statements, there was significantly more delay in beginning speech among the MZ's (46 per cent) than among the DZSS's (16 per cent) ($X^2 = 12.9294$; $p = .01—.001$) or among the DZOS's (19 per cent) ($X^2 = 5.8259$; $p = .02—.01$). And persistent habits involving letter substitutions, omissions, and slurrings were reported as occurring more among the MZ's (53 per cent) than among the DZSS's (31 per cent) ($X^2 = 1.7389$; $p = .20—.10$), but less among the DZSS's, especially the girls, relative to the DZOS pairs (50 per cent) ($X^2 = 4.2812$; $p = .05—.02$).

The teachers' ratings of the children when the latter were five to six years of age, like the mothers' reports of performance in the preschool period, indicated the general speech form of the MZ's, especially the females' to be inferior to the DZSS's (Table 21), as well as, in the male, to be below at the 10 per cent level of significance that of matched singletons from appropriate same-sex sibships (Table 23). In the instance of K's ratings, the MZ and DZSS males did not differ significantly, but the MZf's and DZSSf's did so at the .01 level (Table 21). The largest MZ-DZSS differences, according to the teachers' and K's assessments, and to the syntax-morphology scores, occurred in the girls (Table 21)—i.e., the DZSSm's did not perform at a conspicuously higher level than did the MZm's, but the DZSSf's did speak better than their MZ counterparts. In fact, in general speech, the DZSSf's, to our surprise, were rated, on the average, slightly above the singleton controls. In K's ratings, the DZSSf's were judged superior to the singleton controls at near the .01 level of significance (Table 23). It should be mentioned that the fraternal girls in all three measures were appraised as better than fraternal boys (Tables 21 and 22), although not significantly so, whereas a sex difference was not very conspicuous among the MZ's. This twin-singleton picture, then, is consistent with the intertwin one, as far as speech form is concerned, with the MZ's and the same-sex male group among fraternal twins tending to perform relatively less well than matched singletons, and the DZSSf's and DZOS twins scoring similar to or slightly higher than their controls (Table 23). Without going into details, let it be said that, with surprisingly few exceptions (probably related to methodological differences), our results agree with those of Day (1932) and Davis (1937). They are also congruent with the findings from our study of singleton sibs (Koch 1956). Here we noted that the wider the sib spacing in age, the better the speech form at five to six years. Also the first-borns, who would have had more contact with adult models, tended to exhibit better speech than did second-borns. Although it is true our twins were first-borns, they did, nevertheless, have the twin sib as the most ubiquitous model in their very early speech-learning years and, hence, of all of our sib-age-spacing groups, could have been expected to have the most difficulty in mastering the language. It was no surprise to us that the MZ's and the fraternal boy pairs, the pairs who would have been together most in their very early life (young boys tend to be less sociable with others than girls [Jack 1934; Koch 1956 *a*]). would have had the poorest speech.

Talkativeness and Story Length

Some investigators have had the hypothesis that twins speak less frequently than do other children because they can communicate with their sib so well without speech. This, it is alleged, delays speech learning. Hence, in addition to garnering the data on various measures of speech form, we attempted to gauge the twins' inclination to speak and the amount of their practice with the skill by having the teacher rate them on talkativeness. The same procedure was followed for arriving at a normalized score, as was described for articulation. In fact, hereafter this procedure can be assumed in the teachers' ratings of any trait.

The other measure of language output employed was a count of the number of words utilized by the child in his telling of ten un-prompted stories in the CAT. The McCarthy (1930) rules for defining a word were followed. A story was considered finished when the subject stated, or indicated by gesture, that he was through, and before the experimenter began to question.[1] This word count was a rather reliable measure, whatever it assessed (Table 19). The two independent word counts made for eighty-three sets of stories by the same Experimenter and obtained to check the experimenter's consistency, correlated .99, and the counts made by two analysts on twelve records also correlated .99. The corrected split-half (alternate stories) *r* obtained on the basis of 167 records was .92. The score from a test

[1] Most of the details for the scoring of the items based on the CAT were worked out by Dr. Joan Swift. This material has not yet been published and, hence, no scoring manual is available. Should any investigator desire information on the treatment of a particular variable, this can be obtained either from Dr. Swift or the author.

and a retest made after a two-month interval in a group of fifty highly comparable children (our singleton controls chiefly) correlated .78.

We had the impression that when the teachers rated talkativeness, they were judging to a considerable extent spontaneous speech, volubility, and aggressiveness in speech; story length seemed to be more influenced by docility or attitudes of conformity in the child—i.e., the twins who told long stories tended to be obedient and tried to do conscientiously what they were requested to do by the examiner. At any rate, our surmise that the teachers' rating of talkativeness and the CAT story length may describe different qualities or motivations is supported by the fact that the word count and rating did not correlate significantly in the total group of twins ($r = .06$; Table 20). Since the former measure we know is rather reliable and there is evidence the latter is reasonably so, it seems unlikely that instrument unreliability is responsible for the low correlations.

There were no dependable intergeminal group differences in rated talkativeness nor in story length. Moreover, when the twins were compared on these measures with matched singletons, the data revealed no clearly significant twin-singleton differences (Table 23), except that the DZSSm's were judged less talkative than their singleton counterparts. As neither the teacher's rating of talkativeness nor the CAT story length correlated significantly with measures of speech form, it does not seem justifiable to attribute individual differences in deficiency in speech form in the total group chiefly to lack of practice in the use of language.

THE RELATION OF MEASURES OF LANGUAGE TO MEASURES OF SOCIAL CONTACTS AND ATTITUDES

Since practice with the sib may be practice without a good model, whereas extensive contact with others is more likely to supply a better one, one may wonder whether the SS boys were slightly below par in speech form because they were rather withdrawn and had fewer interactions with people other than the sib. To check on the range of the social contacts of our subjects, we developed a number of gauges. One we have called "closeness to the sib" (see chapter 6 for a detailed description). The second was the number of playmates the child listed when he was asked to do so in the interview. The third was the teachers' rating of gregariousness. All of these, unfortunately, deal only with the twins at five to six years. Two complex scores—one called "involvement with adults," and the other "involvement with children," and both described in detail in chapter 6—represent further efforts to estimate the extent of social contact and presumably the opportunity, at least, to hear acceptable speech at school age.

Although the correlations between talkativeness and CAT story length and measures of speech form were negligible (Table 20), those between talkativeness and measures of involvement with adults and children were of the magnitude of .45 and .48, respectively (Table 24). Indeed the measure of involvement with children correlated significantly and with appropriate sign with all the indexes of language and speech merit (Table 24). The r's for involvement with children were, if anything, slightly higher than those based on the scores for involvement with adults, a finding one might not expect if the view is correct that twins are deficient in language because they lack adequate contact with adults (who would be better speech models than children). Actually, moreover, we have no evidence that the twins lacked involvement with adults at school, as compared with singletons (see Table 25). In fact, there was a hint ($p = .10-.05$) that the MZf's, one of the groups relatively poor in speech form, were relatively more involved with adults at school than were matched singletons (Table 25).

If talkativeness or word count can in any sense be taken as a gauge of extent of practice in or frequency of the use of language, then, on the basis of the facts presented, it appears that the latter is not so important to differences in speech form as whatever it is that furnishes the dynamics of involvement with people (possible desire to please, to conform, need to be understood, effort to meet the standards of the group, etc.). The dynamics can, of course, be varied and devious and probably are. A dull child, whose speech as well as other accomplishments are meagre, may, for instance, be little involved with children because he has little to offer them, thus causing them to reject him or to be unaware of his presence, or he may not be mature enough to be interested in children. Or a child may be so entangled with his twin (who may well not be a good speech model) that he has little inclination for association with children or even adults. The r's between the scores for twin pair members in closeness and the measures of merit in speech or the extent of use of speech do not suggest that the latter attitude in the early school years has much to do, either positively or negatively, with individual differences in the acquisition of correct speech form by the members of our groups (Table 24). Like the child involvement score, the number of listed playmates did, however, have a significant, albeit very slight, relation to the ratings of general speech form (Table 24).

One may wonder whether the twins who had the least good speech —i.e., the MZ's of both sexes and DZSSm's—would also be the ones least involved with people. This does not seem to be the picture (Tables 26 and 27). Sex differences were generally consistent with the theory that association with people results in better speech, for girls tended to excel on both counts. But for the identicals, among whom the sexes did not differ conspicuously in speech form, the people-involvement differences of the sexes was considerable (Table 26). The group whose performance relations were not exactly as expected were the MZf's, who were much involved with their teachers (Table 26), but at the same time they were relatively poor in vocal products (Table 21). Possibly, the expected elevating effects of association with adults and others on merit in speech form is countered here somewhat by the depressing effects of a slightly lower IQ and possibly also by the very close relation of the pair members (which variable, in turn, may stem basically from the lower IQ).

The DZOS's, although not differing from the others in judged talkativeness, did show a slight tendency to tell longer stories (Tables 21 and 22). Their difference from the DZSS's was significant at the .10—.05 level of significance. The former also stood relatively high on the V test (Table 17). They did not deviate notably, however, from the DZSS's in speech form (Table 22). The former were less close to each other than the rest of the twins (Table 27), and the girls, at least, tended to be slightly but not quite significantly less involved with both adults and children than parallel singletons (Table 25). On the social involvement measures they did not deviate quite significantly from other twins.

That the DZOSm's differed so little from their sisters in speech variables is noteworthy, since girls generally tend to excel both in speech and socialization. We suspect this lack of a marked sex difference among the DZOS's may stem from the boys being stimulated by their sisters linguistically and by the general rivalry between these twins. Both, moreover, may have gone their own ways to some extent and hence were stimulated also by varied models.

What especially interested us, too, in view of various theories, was that, although the co-twins in the OS group were less close than other co-twins, there was no evidence that this increased their social contacts (Table 27). In fact, with the exception of the upper-class group, they listed even fewer playmates than did the other fraternal twins (Table 27), and they fell consistently below matched controls (Table 25). This, along with other observations, makes us very suspicious of the theory that twin closeness reduces interest in other people usually. It may even facilitate the latter. Unfortunately we did not tap the deeper levels of intimacy.

The consistency of the pattern of lesser adequacy in speech and language performance among the MZ's, and possibly among even the DZSSm's, made us query whether we are dealing basically with very mild mental retardation, even though ours is a highly selected group, rather than with a lack restricted merely to language. It is relevant that MZ's, according to the medical literature, are the group in whom developmental difficulties (especially those occurring very early in prenatal life and involving the central nervous system) tend to be greatest and the death rate highest (Potter 1963). Also the medical literature points to the greater hazards experienced in early development and at birth by males (see Osborne and DeGeorge 1959). It was, of course, the MZm's who were found most lacking in both performance on the PMA and on those language tests that were more highly correlated with the total PMA—i.e., tests of morphology, syntax, and coherence.

CORRELATIONS BETWEEN VARIOUS MEASURES OF SOCIAL BEHAVIOR AND ATTITUDE

That the various measures of so-called social stimulation, whatever they do describe, do not tend to tap the same experiences or qualities to a large extent is suggested by the relatively low intermeasure r's (Table 28). Only the social involvement, gregariousness, and popularity ratings, which may have been colored by a halo effect or inability on the part of the teachers to discriminate well between the traits, correlated significantly. The highest r—that of .75 (Table 28) between the rating on gregariousness and the measure of involvement with children—one may suspect of being somewhat spurious, because gregariousness was one of the six traits in the latter complex. The r of .47 between the scores on involvement with adults and with children (Table 28) does suggest, however, that we may be dealing with some sort of general sociability or social interest factor.

IMAGINATIVENESS AND COHERENCE IN STORY-TELLING

In addition to observing speech form and language output, it seemed advisable to investigate some qualitative aspects of language products to help evaluate the physical, as opposed to social, origin theories of the speech deficiency of some twins, although we believe the two influences to be interacting. One measure was selected which was thought might be especially sensitive to social influences, motivation, and experience range (this we have called thematic-descriptive, in short, TD); the other, one which might be more a reflection of "intellectual" caliber. The former index is one that mirrors the amount of meaning read into the CAT picture and probably reveals what might be called the imaginativeness or creativity of the child. It appeared to us that this indicator reflects a tendency to think beyond the present stimulus and to deal with more than simple static relationships. The measure was highly reliable (Table 19).

Although our analysis of variance study suggested that sex and social-class group differences obtained in the extent to which the children interpreted the CAT pictures (Table 21; females, as usual in language matters, did better than males and upper class children bettered lower), no significant zygosity group differences over and above the sex and social class ones were apparent. There was a hint, however, of a tendency (at about the .06—.07 level of significance) for the DZOS's, the group we thought might have more varied experience, and possibly be intellectually more able, to be more interpretative than the MZ's.

The T-D scores, however, correlated only slightly with those of speech form (Table 20), their conspicuous relations being with story-word count. Perhaps all this story-word count relation means is that more words are necessary to elaborate a story. But some children who merely enumerated systematically what the picture contained did run up a substantial word count. To our surprise, only the total PMA IQ and the subtest P quotient scores correlated with the T-D measure, and even these just barely significantly. This finding is not unlike that of Getzels and Jackson (1962) to the effect that IQ and creativity tend not to be highly correlated in the upper IQ ranges of the population.

The relations that the incoherence measure exhibited supported our conjecture that this indicator, in contrast to the T-D, might be tapping somewhat more formal intellectual abilities. The incoherence score, as expected, correlated slightly better with the measures of phonetic and syntax-morphology achievement (Table 20), and lower with measures of social interaction than did the T-D (Table 24). Also the MZ's, who are probably as a group the least able of our subjects, were the most incoherent (Table 21), whereas the DZOS's, who tended to rank relatively higher on the PMA (Table 17), were also inclined to score lower in incoherence (Table 20). Twins, on the whole, were distinguished less by incoherence than were parallel singletons (Table 23). In fact, several subgroups—e.g., the DZOS's and DZSSm's—tended to score higher in coherence, although our inability to keep the scorer constant from twin to singleton subjects, as we did in the T-D, could have resulted in obscuring any small differences between twins and singletons that may have existed. It is noteworthy that the T-D and incoherence measures, which reflect some of the more complex aspects of language, seem to exhibit, in the main, a pattern of relations in the twin groups rather similar to those which were apparent in the simpler language-form assays.

SUMMARY

1. In speech form in its phonetic, morphological, and syntactic aspects, as judged by teachers and one examiner, K, as well as by the PMA V-subtest score, the DZSSf's and DZOSf's tended to excel the MZ's, DZSSm's, and DZOSm's.

2. The zygosity group difference in speech form was largest and significant only for the girls.

3. The DZSSf's and DZOSf's slightly excelled in articulation even the matched singleton girls, whereas the twin boys, as stated above,

did not surpass their singleton counterparts. Indeed the twin boys scored below the singletons but not significantly. The twins, taken as a whole, did not perform conspicuously below their singleton controls.

4. The observation that MZ's were closer in their association than DZSS's, and DZSS's closer than the DZOS's is relevant to the above findings.

5. The MZm's were also judged less gregarious than the parallel DZ's. One may ask whether it was their greater closeness, lesser gregariousness, lower IQ, or all of these—since these forces may be interacting—that were responsible for the MZm's relatively inadequate speech performance.

6. Apropos of this question, it is significant that the MZf's, whose speech form, like the MZm's, tended to be relatively poor, were per contra judged high in people-involvement at school age. Thus it does not seem that any lack of involvement with people at this time can account completely for the less satisfactory speech form of the identical twins. What the early preschool experience of the MZf's had been was, of course, not known to us.

7. Fraternal girl twins from same-sex pairs had generally better speech form and told longer and more imaginative stories than did their male counterparts.

8. All of the male twin groups were judged less talkative on the average than matched singletons, although only the DZSSm's were rated significantly below. The twin girls showed no uniform trend.

9. The fact that the female groups who spoke relatively well tended to be closer to their sibs than were parallel boy twins is not consistent with the thesis that closeness in twins necessarily interferes with speech learning. Even with sex held constant, there is no convincing evidence of a relation between closeness at school age and merit in speech and language. A study of these variables in the early preschool years might, of course, yield different results.

10. The DZOSm's at five to six years listed fewer playmates than did the parallel females and gave evidence of the least sib closeness of all of the twin groups. These two characteristics of the DZOSm's—namely, few playmates and little closeness to the sib—one might not expect to occur together as they did, since, according to one theory, the lack of an especially warm relation to the sib is believed to encourage the child to associate with other children. The role of twin

closeness in their socialization may well need a different interpretation from what has been current. It is also possible, of course, that our measure of closeness, which is based on what the children themselves told us, needs reassessment.

11. Twin closeness in the early school years did not correlate significantly in the total twin group with the various measures of speech and language performance.

12. Social class seemed slightly but significantly related to story elaboration, PMA-V test, and incoherence and not at all to the simple phonetic-phonemic-syntactic skill with which this section deals chiefly.

13. The number of playmates the child listed when questioned at school age had barely significant correlations with measures of general speech form and no relations of significance with any of the CAT or PMA measures of language that were studied.

14. The indexes of involvement with children and ratings on gregariousness and popularity were consistently and significantly correlated with the language measures other than the CAT story length. Popularity, it is interesting to note, was not quite significantly correlated with talkativeness.

15. Involvement with adults, especially with teachers, did seem associated with rated talkativeness at school and a tendency to make fewer syntax errors, but not with the other measures of language. Indeed, involvement with children, whether as cause or effect, showed a stronger relationship to speech excellence than did the index of involvement with adults, who, of course, are expected to furnish the better speech model.

16. In the MZf group, the fewest significant r's occurred between language measures and measures of social interaction. No sex difference was apparent in the magnitude of the social-contact language-measure correlations involving the DZOS's. It seems, then, that in our like-sex groups social interaction differences and speech and language differences are more related in males than in females. Whether the magnitude of the difference in the coefficients of correlation described are due to lesser variability in females we do not know, but the usual trend is for the girls to be the less variable. In the DZOS's, sex differences in both language and social contact scores are not significant, but in both areas there is the hint of a tendency for the boys to perform less well than the girls.

DISCUSSION

Among all of the above relations, then, one can discover little that consistently supports, to the exclusion of all others, any one of the hypotheses elucidated earlier. The MZm co-twins, whose speech and language and PMA performances were relatively poor, had, congruently, a very close relation to each other. But the group was not significantly less involved at school with people than were singletons (Table 25), although they showed a slight trend in this negative direction in involvement with children (Table 25). On the other hand, the MZf's, whose speech form was also poor, had very close sibling relationships and were quite as involved with other people, both adults and children, as were other groups of twin girls (Table 26) and significantly more involved than matched singletons (Table 25). The DZOS twins, of all the groups, had the least close co-twin relationship (Tables 26 and 27) but their language development was rather comparable to that of the DZSS's (Table 22), who were apparently more dependent on each other. The somewhat better speech performance of twin girls, as contrasted with boys, was associated with greater social involvement, but the dissimilarity in speech merit of the male and female DZOS twins was associated with few differences in social behavior. There were differences in number of listed playmates, however, the girls naming more associates—there is even here a positive parallelism, in the main, between the speech and social interest and interaction variables. On the other hand, the MZf's, who were more gregarious and more involved with children than the MZm's, did not seem to excel the former significantly in phonemic and phonetic form. The girls, however, made fewer errors in syntax and told more imaginative stories.

It should be noted, since intelligence may be an important item in the twin picture, that if we rank the six twin groups on general or total test IQ (see Table 17), there is a good parallelism between this order and the one based on speech form achievement, as well as the one based on the imaginativeness and coherence exhibited in the CAT stories narrated. The MZm, MZf, and DZSSm's were uniformly somewhat low and the DZSSf's higher. Also, the same sort of group ranking based on syntax errors and word count correlated —.68 and —.66, respectively, with total IQ status. A similar type of correlation of PMA-V test quotient and total IQ scores and involvement with adults were, in contrast, —.13 and .07, and the correlation of the former with involvement with children was also insignificant. At any rate, because of the aforementioned correlations, even though they are based on few cases, we think it important that IQ differences not be ignored in interpreting intertwin group and twin-singleton differences. Although the twin groups in general tended to score relatively low on the PMA verbal test, it was only the MZm's who performed significantly below singletons on the total PMA (Table 18) and on the Q subtest, as well as on the V. Of course, as mentioned in chapter 3, had we had more nearly comparable testing conditions for twins and singletons, it is possible that more of the twin groups might have averaged clearly below singletons instead of marginally so.

In addition to IQ, it seems not improbable that an interacting complex of twin social-behavior trends may need consideration, but the relations here do not seem simple or clear cut. Twin closeness, for example, depending on the complex in which it is embedded, may be associated with withdrawal (MZm) or, on the contrary, with high level sociability (DZSSf). Also involvement with adults, probably depending on the motivations which determine the relationship, may be positively or negatively related with intelligence or speech skills. Indeed, it seems apparent that our twins, with the exception of the MZm's and possibly the DZSSm's, did not deviate negatively in speech form from matched singletons in either language or social attitudes described in this section. But, as has been implied, we are not yet ready to discount entirely the restriction of experience resulting from twin similarity in types of experience—it may be a factor to be reckoned with. We feel confident that not only are twins as a group closer to each other than are singleton sibs who differ in age, but also that identical co-twins, at least, are clearly more similar in interests and associates than are singleton sibs. This could be restricting. The twins' playmates are more likely to be the same age as the co-twins (see chapter 6) and to be the same individuals—i.e., the pair members tend to share the same friends—than are the associates of singleton sibs. Hence, even if there were no differences in the number of playmates listed by the children at school age, there could still be less diversity in the people represented among the twin associates and, thus, in the ideas and activities to which the twins could be exposed,

In their very early years, too, the social contacts of twins with others may have been much restricted. Such trends might be especially marked for MZ's. We have no material beyond the data on listed playmates (Tables 25, 26, and 27) that might be directly revealing, but these are at least not incongruent with our hypothesis. Apropos of the restricted experience range hypothesis, but not especially congruent with it, was the observation that twins were not, as a group, judged by their teachers as having more limited interests, nor as being less original than singletons (see chapter 6 and Tables 40, 42, and 56). Nevertheless, the MZm's and DZSSm's were the groups judged to be poorest in speech and the least communicative, as well as being the lowest on the PMA. The DZSSf's were, in contrast, rated higher than singletons in number of interests, originality, and competitiveness and scored slightly below the latter only on the V test (Table 18). These DZSSf's, significantly, were the group with probably the best speech and language achievement. They tended to rank highest as well on most of the measures of social behavior. It must be remembered, however, that measures of social behavior are not independent of IQ.

In summary, we feel certain that mild mental retardation in some members, even in our highly selected twin groups, is one factor responsible for the relatively lower speech skills and even child-involvement scores of at least one twin group, the MZm's, and possibly the DZSSm's as well. We do not know for sure whether constellations of social forces unique for twins tend to cut down the stimulation and experience range of some groups, especially in the early preschool years, Our data offer some suggestions that they might. But the fraternal girl twins and DZOS groups differed surprising little, if at all, from singletons, and sometimes they seemed favored. Why all of the twin groups averaged lower on the PMA verbal subtest, when, if anything, testing conditions favored them, is a question that still challenges us. An appealing hypothesis is that twins tend to have less varied associates, a condition that could result in less opportunity to acquire as wide a range of information as singletons typically absorb.

CHAPTER V

Hand Preference and Stuttering in Twins

Hand preference is no great educational issue at the present time: parents, in the main, whether with good reason or not, are being encouraged to adopt a laissez faire attitude. One of the main reasons for the laissez faire point of view is the fear that interference with manual preference may give rise to stuttering. This belief has, of course, its challengers. Since neither sinistrality nor stuttering is unique to twins, however, the main problem for this study is whether there is anything about twinning that facilitates sinistrality or stuttering or both.

Many believe lefthandedness occurs to an abnormal degree in twins and that this trait is associated in some way with stuttering (Travis and Johnson 1934; Hahn and Hawk 1943; Hildreth 1949a and b, 1950). Thus it seems important to observe the behavior of our subjects concerning both hand preference and stuttering.

MEASUREMENT OF HAND PREFERENCE

Our estimates of hand preference were based on several lines of evidence: (1) the mother's report of the course of development in her twins' hand preference; (2) the teacher's estimate of the child's status at the time he was being studied by us; (3) the general impression of two examiners who observed the child for a day; (4) the hand with which the child gripped the crayon when he was asked to draw a picture; and (5) the preference shown by the child when handling a suitcase full of toys while being interviewed. Attention was paid to the hand favored for the distant reaches, for the adjustments least involved in simple holding, and for those more frequently used in the relatively more difficult aspects of a manipulation. We did not attempt to get a precise measure of the "strength" of hand preference, because as a rule we were too occupied with the interview to make a detailed count. When a clear-cut preference was demonstrated in the manipulations, we ceased our observation since we were not attempting to get a graded measure; but when we were unsure of what the preference was, our recording became more detailed and precise. Fortunately there was a high degree of agreement among our various indicators of sinistrality. The doubtful cases were usually those children who, for some time as preschoolers, were sinistrals but whose hand preference was shifting toward the right, although it was not fully stabilized. A child in the lower level of this transition stage was classified as left. When his choices were predominantly right, the subject was classified as having a dextral preference. The subject's history was noted, however. Ours was an all-or-none type of classification, which, of course, belies the situation, since there are all degrees of preference.

INDICATORS OF STUTTERING

The notations on stuttering were of several sorts. The mothers in the interview were asked whether the child had stuttered with any consistency at any time in the preschool years and how long the tendency had lasted. The teachers were requested to rate the child on stuttering, and were questioned about the pattern of the tendency and the circumstances under which it occurred. The two examiners who had contact with the child also noted any instances of stuttering that occurred on the day the twins were tested and interviewed and the circumstances associated with the blocking, if these could be diagnosed.

LEFT PREFERENCE AMONG TWINS AND OTHERS

Forty-nine out of 176 S's on whom we had information were alleged by the mother to have exhibited a rather stable left preference at some time during the period up to seven years. This is about 28 per cent of the population (Table 29). It is interesting that Day (1932), likewise using twin subjects and mothers' reports as evidence of sinistrality, states that the incidence of a left trend among her preschoolers was 21 per cent. Possibly her figures are a bit lower than ours because the age range of the children in her study was more restricted than was that of our subjects. Her subjects also represent a generation in which a less laissez faire educational policy obtained with respect to the hand to be employed in a variety of socially important activities.

Lippman (1927), using singletons, estimated that 30 per cent of his subjects at twelve months favored the left hand when accepting something that was handed to them; Giesecke (1936) reported about 35 per cent of her infant subjects at twelve months took the more difficult reaches with their left hand; and Gesell (1931) stated that 32 per cent of his 18-month-old subjects scribbled and picked up objects more often with the left hand. Per contra, Updegraff (1932) and Hildreth (1948), paying attention to a variety of manual activities, noted that among the *preschool* children they observed 12.5 and 11.1 per cent, respectively, were sinistrals. These figures are rather similar to the estimate of sinistrality of 14.0 per cent in our Ss's who were assessed at the time they were five to six years old by their mother, teachers, and two examiners. Since we would have expected the incidence of sinistrality at the age represented by our subjects, who were slightly older than those of Updegraff and Hildreth, to be somewhat lower instead of higher, we have taken seriously the difference observed. It makes us suspect that there may be slightly more left-handedness in twins than singletons. The fact that our study was conducted a generation later than the investigations of Updegraff and of Hildreth may be responsible for the somewhat higher incidence of left-handedness among our subjects. In the present generation there has been a strong shift in educational policy relative to the matter of the control of hand preference. One study that compared the change in incidence of sinistrality in a given East Coast area (Carrothers 1947; Hildreth 1949*b*), assessed in 1932 and again in 1941 reported an increase in sinistrality of about 4 per cent during the decade. Since the mothers of our subjects, almost to a woman, insisted they did not interfere with their twins' manual activities as far as the hand used was concerned, we would have reason to expect our subjects to exhibit more left favoring than the subjects of Heinlein (1930), Updegraff

(1932), or Hildreth (1948) displayed, and to about the degree our results show. A questionnaire survey of Michigan schoolchildren made in 1945 indicated that about 8.2 per cent of the pupils were left-handed. This contrasts with Wile's (1934) estimate, based on a review of the older literature, that only 4 to 5 per cent of schoolchildren in taught skills favored the use of their left hand. At any rate, the educational situation described keeps us from being entirely sure, when we compare our data with those of other investigators who studied singletons, whether it is the effect of educational policy, other factors, or the effect of twinning that we are observing. Even if it is the influence of twinning, this can not be considered major if our results are valid, nor can the view, once held by some, that all sinistrality results from twinning receive any credence.

It is noteworthy in relation to the question of the inheritance of sinistrality that only in eight pairs were both members considered left-handed for a rather extended period before they were seven years old. Four of the pairs were identicals; four, fraternals. If sinistrality were chiefly a function of the genes, other than perhaps those which bias toward twinning, then, since the MZ's have the same genes, one would expect many more L-L pairs to be found among them than among the DZ's. Unfortunately our cases are too few to justify a significance estimate. When exploring this problem, Wilson and Jones (1932) summarized the literature and stated that in 4.5 per cent of the MZ pairs studied both members were reported left-handed and in only 1.8 per cent of the DZ pairs was this true. Our corresponding percentages were 11.4 and 7.5, when some sinistral behavior up to seven years was taken as the clue, and 2.8 and .9 per cent, respectively, when sinistrality at the early school age at which our subjects were observed was used as the basis for the estimates. The direction of group difference in our study and that reported by Wilson and Jones for the field is the same, the magnitude of our percentages deviating, no doubt, because of variations in the indicator of sinistrality employed and in the age of the children studied, as well as in the educational practices to which the groups surveyed were exposed.

Newman (1934) announced that 6 per cent of his MZ pairs of twin subjects included two left-handed individuals, whereas none of the DZ's exhibited this. Wilson and Jones (1932), Rife (1940), and Davis (1937), however, noted no significant zygosity differences. But, as has been said, we are impressed with the fact that all the reported findings indicate slightly more L-L pairs among the identicals. This trend, weak though it is, has consistency and should not be entirely overlooked. Newman, however, was more interested in the R-L pair phenomenon than the L-L; the former could not be attributed simply to heredity, he believed. Rather, he saw the R-L phenomenon as an effect of the mechanics of twinning. The fission, which could result in identical twins, he opined, would give rise to different metabolic gradients in one identical twin than in the other, if a strong, mid-line-periphery gradient had been organized before fission. Of course, following Newman's thinking perhaps, some have defended the view that twinning could result in a difference in hemispheral dominance in identical twins—dominance which would affect both manual activities and speech. Penfield and Roberts (1959), however, using the development of aphasia from a lesion in one of the cerebal hemispheres only as evidence of hemisphere dominance in speech, found no difference in the manual preference of S's who developed aphasia from a lesion in the left hemisphere from the preference of those who acquired aphasia from a lesion in the right hemisphere (if the cases in which the lesion developed very early in life were excluded). Of course, Penfield and Roberts' proviso could be a very relevant one from the point of view of the theory. At any rate, there is still a question as to whether the speech disturbance of stuttering and instability in manual dominance have the same or a related biological origin (see Travis and Johnson 1934).

It is pertinent to note that accounts of zygosity group differences in frequency of sinistrality vary greatly. For example, Dahlberg (1926), using throwing and cutting as indicators, and Newman (1934), using tapping, present data indicating about twice as many sinistrals among MZ's as DZ's (14.5 per cent *vs.* 7 per cent; and 12 per cent *vs.* 6 per cent, respectively); whereas Verschuer (1939), employing cutting with a scissors, hammering, and shuffling cards to diagnose preference, uncovered no significant disparity between zygosity groups. Siemens (1927) even noted more left favoring among DZ's than MZ's (22 *vs.* 11 per cent). Lauterbach (1933), heeding a divergence between two types of fraternals, stated that 12.7 per cent of the subjects in his opposite-sex fraternal groups favored the left, as did 18.7 per cent of the subjects from same-sex fraternal pairs. Hirsch's data (see Wilson and Jones 1932), on the other hand, suggest an opposite trend (22 per cent sinistrals among DZSS's and 6 per cent among DZOS's).

Wilson and Jones (1932), to add to the confusion, noted no disparity between the two types of fraternals. Our findings support the latter view of no significant zygosity or interfraternal group differences. In the analysis of our data for the MZ and DZSS subjects, for example, it was observed that when the twins were five to six years old, the percentage of sinistrals in the two groups was 15 and 13, respectively, whereas the incidence based on sinistral behavior displayed at some time in the years up to seven was, for the MZ's and DZSS's, 31 and 28 per cent, respectively. The ratios for our small DZOS group were for the two age periods 15 and 21. None of the differences is significant (Table 29).

There can be many causes for the divergent findings reported by different scientists. One would, for example, have reason to wonder to what extent the diagnosis of zygosity was correct. The statistical treatment of the data, too, has been uniformly poor. (This is no discredit to the investigators, as statistical tools have improved greatly in recent years and have made us much more cautious about generalization.) Also hand-preference estimates, since they vary with the means used to achieve diagnosis, as well as with age, IQ, era, culture, educational practice, sex, and other population characteristics, are not likely to be sufficiently comparable, unless these variables are controlled or discounted. They seldom are.

In accordance with diversity among findings, there has been a diversity of hypotheses offered to account for the findings. These will not be reviewed, since they are not likely to cast much light upon twin phenomena and would involve us in a great range of detail. Our results show no consistent difference in sinistrality between our various zygosity groups. Nor do we feel entirely certain of a twin-singleton difference, since we have no data from a strictly comparable singleton population. If there is a difference, we suspect it is not very large.

HYPOTHESIS RELATIVE TO LEFT PREFERENCE IN TWINS

We have a simple hypothesis to offer—perhaps no more well-founded than others—to account for what we suspect may be a slightly higher incidence of sinistrality among twins than singletons.

Let us stress that this should not be taken as any explanation of sinistrality generally. The hypothesis is in conformity with our findings and may help us to reconcile some of the divergent findings of others.

It is usually agreed that hand preference can be influenced in a major way by training and environmental pressures and that a dextral trend tends to increase with age in the early years at least (Jones 1931). We believe, accordingly, that one of the problems in dealing with twins is merely that of discovering whether there have been somewhat different educational and environmental pressures put upon them in the early months and years than upon singletons. Our suspicions about what these might be grew out of an observation reported by Dennis (1935) many years ago. Dennis observed in very great detail for about a year a pair of twins who were given as little social or environmental stimulation as possible, and who were kept, as far as could be managed, from any right- or left-disposing pressures. The cribs in which the twins spent most of their time stood side by side with a screen placed between them. When Dennis discovered a position preference was developing in his infant subjects, he alternated the cribs in which a given twin was placed. What impressed us was Dennis' observation that before the alternation was instituted and each child was fed by placing his bottle on a pillow at his side—in one case this was on the S's' left; in the other, on the right—a relatively strong position preference or "habit" was established in the infants in only two days at the age of 46 to 48 days. It occurred to us that if two days of such arrangements could be so effective in creating a posture preference in feeding, twins who were not protected from the development of a position habit, as were Dennis' subjects, might very well come to favor a given side. It seemed probable to us that in many homes the twins' cribs are placed side by side in their bedroom, or head to head, or foot to foot, and that a given twin will be deposited consistently in a given crib. Since other features of the environment could be more interesting than the sib—e.g., the ministering adult would usually approach a given twin from a given side, and the visual field on the "open" side would offer more of interest than that on the somewhat barred side—the direction of the early biasing of the individual co-twins would be different. Of course, once an inclination has been established, it has a tendency to persist and generalize. Dennis' babies even cried and showed signs of distress when their bottle did not have the location it had for only two previous days. A modern American parent, who has been taught not to interfere with hand preference, might even facilitate any apparent preference that develops.

LEFT PREFERENCE AND RESISTANCE, DOMINANCE, PREMATURITY, AND SEX OF CHILD

That so many of our subjects apparently showed some early temporary sinistrality but had taken on a right preference by school age, and, according to the mothers, without their being subjected to much pressure from the family, suggests that whatever the source of early biasing, it may well yield to the massive, persistent, direct, and indirect pressures provided by our right-handed society. Wilson and Jones (1932), Dennis (1935), Giesecke (1936), and others have commented on the great lability of manual behavior in infants and young children. Resistant children, and among these may be more boys than girls, may persist in their left preference (see Durost 1934; Wile 1934; Burt 1937), or their preference may even be strengthened by the arrangements that doting parents deliberately institute to make things convenient for the child who shows a laterality trend and voices his discomfort when exposed to situations not congruent with this. The hypothesis just recounted, then, is congruent with our findings that (1) no zygosity group difference existed (Table 29); (2) a sex group difference did exist (Table 29); and (3) the left-handed member of a R-L pair tended to be dominant, and more resistant and competitive (Table 30). This finding is not in agreement with that of Shields (1954, 1962).

We were in no position to test the hypothesis that is derived to explain why slightly more sinistrality tends to appear in twins than singletons, as most investigators agree it does. Let us say that we have a strong suspicion there may be some biological forces (see studies on brain tumors and lesions such as Critchley 1954; Ettlinger, Jackson, and Zangwill 1956; and Penfield and Roberts 1959) that can and do influence preference or laterality. But just how general and frequent these forces are is a major issue we are in no position to explore. To test our hypothesis relative to twins, several lines of observation would be helpful. Perhaps most relevant would be the observation of those consistent household arrangements and handling patterns that might favor a left bias in one twin and a right in the other. Does the mother approach the twins usually from different sides? Are the cribs placed (side by side, head to head, etc.) to provide more stimulation from the right for one and from the left for the other child? If the children have a dual stroller, is each seated with any consistency on a given side, thus resulting for the pair members in a different approach pattern from other people and in the laterality of the body members permitted the freer action? How are the high chairs placed at the table? How are the babies usually carried if they are both held at the same time? Is one nursed at one breast consistently, the other child, at the other breast? It will be important, too, to quantify preference strength and, if this shifts while development is being observed, to study the correlated conditions of the change (see Giesecke 1936 on spontaneous shifting in infants). Are parents more yielding to the resistant child or to the protests of male twins than females? Is the frailer twin more likely to be indulged in the matter of his laterality, or conversely, is it the more vigorous one whose protests bring results?

Shields (1954, 1962) believes the left-handed child in a twin pair, the members of which exhibit a different manual preference, tends to be biologically inferior and displays this in being more neurotic, less dominant, less aggressive, less intelligent, smaller, etc. If this were the rule, it would tend to favor but not establish as highly probable the theory of very early biological biasing as the force behind hand preference. Our own data do not lend support to Slater and Shield's finding. Among our subjects, we compared the left- and right-handed twin in the thirty-two pairs that contained such a combination with respect to birth size, birth order, height and weight at school entrance, IQ, tendency to stutter, tendency to speech disorders other than stuttering, teachers' ratings on competitiveness, activeness, involvement with children at school age, and mother's estimate of the child's dominance status in the pair (Table 30). In most of the measures, there were no significant differences between the right- and left-handed children in the mixed pairs. Sex, dominance within the twin pair (as mentioned earlier), and general competitiveness were the exceptions. The left-handed member of the pair tended to be reported as the dominant one (23 *vs.* 9) and to be rated as more competitive (at near the .05 significance level; Table 30). This same phenomenon may lie back of the observation that more males are left-handed in their early years. There is a general consensus in the view that males tend to be more resistant, combative, and aggressive individuals than females. In accordance with the above notion, males would not be expected to lend themselves so readily to dextral biasing, if it seemed to them like interference. We noted, in keeping with the hypothesis, more early sinistrality in males, but by five to six years, the sex difference in hand preference in our population had virtually disappeared (Table 29). The shift toward a right preference occurred chiefly in our DZSSm's. The MZm's, who seemed more resistant to change, were, however, our slowest learners, a fact that may account in part for their lesser lability in manual preference. The results of Gordon (1920), Oates (1929), Wile (1934), Burt (1937), Dart (1938), and Merrell (1957) would reinforce this hypothesis—i.e., more left-handedness was noted among retardates than normals. Since there are more retardates among twins, and brain damage, whatever its effects, is more common, it may even be that in this latter fact we shall find a partial basis for somewhat greater sinistrality among twins. It is of some relevance, although not supporting the foregoing hypothesis, that in our population neither severe prematurity nor a simple birth weight under 5½ pounds was significantly related to a left preference occurring some time in the preschool or early school years (Tables 31 and 32). More developmental studies, both of biological (brain) functions as well as behavior-biasing environmental forces, are desperately needed.

SUMMARY OF FINDINGS ON HAND PREFERENCE AND TWINNING

1. The findings of this study do not seem incongruent with the usual one—i.e., that there tend to be more sinistrals among twins than singletons—but our data are not critical on this point because a strictly comparable singleton group was not available to us.

2. No significant zygosity group disparity in the incidence of left preference was observed, either early or late, in the period before seven years.

3. In the preschool years the males exhibited a left preference more frequently than did females, but this sex difference seems to have

virtually disappeared in our twin population by the completion of first grade.

4. Approximately nine per cent of the twin pairs studied were composed of individuals both of whom at some time before seven years were thought to show a sinistral trend; but by five to six years in only about two per cent of the pairs were both members still left-handed. The L-L pairs were not noted in one zygosity group significantly more frequently than in the other, but there was a bare hint of more instances among the identicals, a tendency not uncommonly reported in the literature.

5. In the R-L pairs, the left-handed member tended to be judged more often the dominant member by the mother and was rated the more competitive by the teacher. There was no evidence, on the other hand, that the left-handed members in the R-L pairs were different from the dextral in birth weight, extent of involvement with children, activeness, or that they differed in birth order, or tendency to stutter, or to exhibit other forms of speech disorders.

We have presented a rather simple hypothesis that is not incongruent, at least, with most of the relationships observed. It is not offered to explain completely sinistrality but rather to account chiefly for the somewhat higher incidence of sinistrality alleged to occur in twins than in singletons and in male than in female twins. It may, however, have wider application. It is possible the hypothesis may in some way account for some of the conflicting findings reported in the literature, since it stresses simple, early biasing by the environment, biasing that can vary with the age of the subject, the era, the culture, and the educational practices current relative to the control of manual preference. The hypothesis assumes that no basically different mechanisms operate to produce sinistrality in twins than obtain among singletons, but that there is merely a slight difference in emphasis. The assumed unique pressures should apply to all twin types alike, but it may be yielded to, or resisted, perhaps to a different degree by males than by females, and by slow learners than by rapid ones. As a second hypothesis we would suggest that, since brain damage of various sorts and degrees is more common among twins than singletons and certain brain lesions have been shown to influence hand or paw preference (Jasper 1932; Hildreth 1949a and b, 1950a and b; and Penfield and Roberts 1959), the fact of more brain impairment in twins may result in more sinistrality among them. We do not see our twins as illuminating the problem of sinistrality particularly. For exploring more of the theories offered, there are better, more focused methods available.

THEORIES OF STUTTERING

The problem of stuttering is of interest not only in and of itself, but also because it becomes especially significant in twins owing to the possibly higher frequency of left-handedness in this population. It is justifiably contended that there is some sort of association between sinistrality and tendency to stutter. The nature of this association is still an unsettled question.

There are conflicting points of view, to be sure, in regard to whether there is indeed an association, as well as to the nature of the relation of the variables. Of course, most every one stutters on occasion. Hence we may find some grounds for disagreements among investigators, especially as the incidence of the behavior may vary partly on the basis of the criteria of stuttering used. Also, since the age, as well as other aspects of the population explored, seems to be related to the frequency of stuttering behavior, the variables need to be controlled or systematically varied when stutterers and non-stutterers are being compared, unless the variables are the focus of the investigation.

Since we do not have in our study an adequate singleton population for comparing the incidence of stuttering, our contrasts will have to be limited to those which our twin groups permit. We located twin pairs, one member of which was a sinistral and the other a dextral, to study the relation between sinistrality and stuttering. Here the twin pair members are, in one sense, excellent controls for each other (Table 30).

Before presenting data, let us mention a few hypotheses relative to the causes of the alleged association between stuttering and sinistrality. Some insist that the association is between simple left preference and stuttering, the conflict occurring at the cerebral level between speech and hand-control mechanisms that are thought to be closely related in structural base. Penfield and Roberts (1959), as mentioned earlier, question the theory, believing that manual and speech functions are biologically independent. Some theorists contend, in contrast to those who emphasize brain organization, that the effort to change a sinistral preference is critical (Ballard 1912; Travis 1931), because it produces environmental interference with biological controls, such as are implied in cerebral dominance. Some investigators maintain, on the other hand, that effort to alter laterality results merely in simple habit conflict; others, that the effort to change a child's preference gives rise to feelings of inferiority and frustration, since he must necessarily be corrected often. The emotional disturbance thus aroused is viewed as the cause of stuttering. The position is common also that ambidexterity, or lack of a clear-cut manual dominance, for whatever reasons (Ballard 1911), causes the confusion and the blocking of stuttering. Explanation then is interpreted (1) in terms of basic biological mechanisms (interference with cerebral dominance and biological manual control or lead patterns), or (2) in terms of psychosocial conflict that may develop personal status concerns, or (3) in terms of simple motor habit interference.

FINDINGS RELATIVE TO STUTTERING

As mentioned earlier, 49 of our 166 twin subjects exhibited a rather consistent, but usually temporary, sinistrality at some time in their lives up to seven years (Table 32). Nineteen subjects (about 11 per cent) had stuttered noticeably for a time in the same period, according to the mothers' reports (Table 33). Only seven subjects were alleged to have exhibited a left preference for some interval before seven years and to have in their history at least a period of consistent stuttering (Table 33). We do not know for sure whether the stuttering and sinistrality occurred at the same time in all of these subjects. Three of the children who both stuttered and had a left preference at some time were MZ's and four were DZ's. This fact is not particularly congruent with one of the above hypotheses, namely, the one assuming that the disturbance in metabolic gradients created by the fissioning that produces the MZ pair members results in both sinistrality and stuttering. Only two of our subjects were left-handed and stuttered consistently at the time they were kindergartners or first-graders (Table 34). This is 1.1 per cent of all twins on whom we had information and no more than would be expected on the basis of chance.

That there may be some relation between manual preference and speech disturbances is suggested, however, by the following: about 14 per cent of those who were sinistral at some time before seven years stuttered at some time, whereas the incidence of stutterers in the total right-handed twin population was 9.4 per cent. In other words, 32 per cent of the one-time stutterers were still sinistral in their early years in school, but in the non-stuttering population the comparable per cent was 12. Using a X^2 procedure we did find a significant ($p = .05$) relation between a left preference at school age and a history of stuttering for a period in the years up to seven (Table 33). The association of the speech and manual behaviors was not apparent after five years, since, as stated above, in our total twin population 1.1 per cent were left-handed stutterers in their early months in school. It may be of some interest that the two subjects who were left-handed stutterers at five to six years were born markedly prematurely. Are we seeing brain damage sequelae here? We can't tell with certainty. Our data, at any rate, generally lend support to the dozens of studies that show some sort of association in the development of left-handed-ness and stuttering, but the data do not illuminate the question of the mechanism of the association. Our findings, furthermore, suggest that both the speech and manual tendencies are not very firmly en-trenched during the preschool years, for in about half of the subjects who exhibited either the tendency to stutter or to prefer the left hand the inclination had disappeared by five to six years.

We have no evidence that there was more stuttering at any time among the MZ's than among the DZSS's. If anything, the reverse was true. The stuttering of the MZ's, however, was the more stable (see Tables 33 and 34). Quite apart from the possibility of more biological complications among them, one might have expected more stuttering in the MZ's because the children tend to be very close and might have imitated each other. Also more brain impairment is likely to occur among the MZ's. Since we did not demonstrate the expected relation between sinistrality and speech disturbance in older children, we are inclined to look for some of the causes of stuttering in older twins in their rivalry or in social stress rather than in the biological mecha-nisms of twinning itself. A case can be made against this view, how-ever.

We did not observe a strong sex difference in tendency to stutter, but still a hint of one did appear ($p = .10 - .20$) if the period up to seven years is taken into account. We noted that males tended to stutter more than females. This is the association usually reported. There was no evidence from our crude data that stuttering and prematurity, whether mild or extreme (birth weight under 4½ pounds), were significantly associated in our group, nor that there was more than a chance association between prematurity and sinistrality. The mean IQ of the stutterers was 107, which is about average for our population, but, viewed in relation to their twin sib, the stutterers tended to score slightly, but not significantly, lower on the intelligence test. This could be significant if the stress of rivalry lies back of some of the stuttering. Apropos of this view, the stutterers were rated by their teachers as generally more intense. We do not feel, as has been stated, that the study of our twin population has given us anything that particularly illuminates the problem of the mechanism of the association of sinistrality and stuttering, for this relation has been observed in non-twins. The data we have can probably be interpreted more easily in terms of social attitude variables than biological variables, but we regret having no refined information on brain trauma or hemisphere dominance. If we take Wallin's (1924) estimate of seven-tenths of one per cent for the incidence of stuttering in the school population, then the frequency among our twins is somewhat higher, but our subjects were young and we would be unwilling to assess their relative status on the basis of a comparison with an older group such as was represented in the population Wallin investigated.

It is probably worth reporting that, as for stuttering, we found no significant association between sinistrality—temporary in the pre-school years or relatively stable at school entrance—and the conglomerate of such faulty speech patterns as letter substitutions, omissions and misplacements, slurring, lisping, severe blocking, marked delay in learning to speak, or non-speech.

SUMMARY OF FINDINGS ON STUTTERING

1. About 11 per cent of the twins in the present investigation had stuttered noticeably at some time in their lives before seven years, but only about six per cent stuttered in their early years in school. This is high relative to findings such as those of Wallin (1924) or Travis and

Johnson (1934) or Parson (see Hahn and Hawk 1943) in school populations.

2. Stuttering and left preference were not associated above chance at school entrance, but of those S's who were still left-handed in their very early years in school, a more than chance proportion had undergone a period of stuttering at some time before they were six to seven years old.

3. More males tended to stutter than females.

4. The variables of stuttering and twin zygosity were not significantly related in the population studied.

5. Stuttering and neither mild nor extreme prematurity seemed to be correlated.

CHAPTER VI

Personality and Attitudes of Twins

PROBLEMS, PROCEDURES, AND INSTRUMENTS

PROBLEMS

This chapter will be concerned with such issues as the relation of the twins' attitudes toward their sib and their resultant general social effectiveness; the extent of their dependence on each other, as this bears upon their interest in other children; their general dominance or submissiveness in attitude, as this relates to the role the pair members play with respect to each other; the degree of their involvement with adults; the range of their interests generally; the desirability of separating the co-twins at school; the degree of success of their sex-role learning (especially as it may be contingent upon the sex similarity or difference of the sib).

Since twins are specimens, unique human forms, are they victims of others' curiosity and superficial attention? Are they often put on display and receive attention not especially sensitive to their feelings or needs? Do twins, in the main, come to like to display themselves generally or only under certain circumstances? Are they especially sensitive to any hint of lack? Does "equal" treatment tend to be meted out to the co-twins, whether or not the treatment is congruent with the needs of the individual pair members? What are the effects of "equal" treatment? Does this make the twins less rivalrous or less jealous than singletons, reduce competitiveness, and perhaps even ambition, or are the trends reversed? Is the rivalry aimed chiefly at

88

keeping abreast of, or outstripping the sib? How far does the attitude developed in relation to the sib spread? Is the twin typically exposed less to the varieties of life than the singleton? If the co-twins are similar in sex, does this make the learning of behavior congruent with what is expected of the sex easier or more difficult than with most singletons? Do the girls tend to be relatively more strongly feminine than singleton girls because of having chiefly feminine models and boys relatively less strongly masculine in behavior?

RESEARCH DESIGN AND PROCEDURES

Since the presentation of the data from the study of twin attitudes and social behavior may be difficult for the reader to follow, as there are many facets and many traits to be described, the description will usually proceed from a detailed examination of the question of whether various types of twins differ from each other, to the more general question of whether twins, as a group, tend to deviate from a sample of singletons matched with them individually in ten or so respects. The gemini, as will be remembered, were matched with singletons in age, sex, social class, family complexity and intactness, sex and number of sibs, race, neighborhood of residence, country of birth, residence in a city in the American Midwest, and enrollment in the public school. When the twins were compared with singletons on the basis of teachers' ratings, four singletons were chosen to match each pair of twins whose members were of the same sex, and four matches for each individual when the pair was composed of children unlike in sex. When the interview data and those from the CAT were used, each twin had only one singleton match. When twin-singleton relations were studied, the scores of the members from each of the like-sex pairs were averaged, as were those for the two or four singleton controls for the pair. An estimate of the significance of the difference between the means for the twin pairs and those for the groups of single-borns matching the pairs was then made, using statistics appropriate for matched groups. Since twin pair means or even individual scores here are matched sometimes with control averages based on four cases, questions might be raised relative to the use of the simple matched-pair formula. We could locate no formula strictly appropriate for our situation but were advised that our minor deviation from the basic assumption underlying the formula derivation probably will not influence the findings significantly.

Finally, a two-way analysis of variance of the twin-singleton differences for same-sex pairs was pursued to determine whether there were sex and zygosity group differences in relative magnitude of deviation of twins from matched singletons. For most twin-singleton comparisons, however, a simple *t*-test of the difference between matched group means was employed.

INTERVIEWS

The measures devised to describe the heterogeneity and similarity in social attitude and behavior were varied, ranging from an interview to the CAT (see chapter 1). Each child was interrogated separately for a half hour or so, while he played with the many small toys with which he was presented. It was essayed to cover each question with every child, the order and wording being usually the same for each individual, although an effort was made to maintain a spirit of informality. If it were obvious a subject did not understand a query, another wording from a standard series of substitutes was offered. The probings dealt with playmates and playmate preferences, attitudes toward being a twin, toward play with the sib, and toward the sib on such matters as his quarreling, bossiness, sharing of possessions, relative achievements, and affectional status with the parents. Questions dealing with the possessions, statuses, and qualities of the twin that were coveted were also explored. The children were asked, in addition, whether they desired separation from the sib at home or at school, and their reaction to their school placement as well as their teachers (see Koch 1956*a*, 1960).

Of course, with children of very early school age, one can never be sure the questions presented will be understood in the sense the interviewer had in mind. This is especially a matter for concern when estimates of magnitude are requested. All that can be said is that it seemed that the various twin subgroups did not differ particularly in set and, hence, can probably usefully be compared with each other, as well as with singleton controls. Also it should be emphasized that the responses and response trends noted essentially made sense. Thus the view can be defended that at least in a gross way the intergroup differences in what the children told us about themselves reflected actual trends. Since, moreover, the subjects soon discovered the examiner was not critical, there was little evidence of any powerful tendency on their part to give the responses they thought the examiner would approve. The responses were recorded verbatim, as far as this could be managed, if they were of a type involving more than a few words. If responses were not at first clear, probing continued until it was felt the interviewer understood in essence what the subject was trying to convey. All interviewing was conducted by one person.

The children, it is true, did differ considerably in their ability and willingness to communicate, but this was not so much of a problem at certain response levels as it might have been because the information requested usually required a very simple sort of answer—e.g., a yes or no; much or little. Naturally, when the reason for an attitude or response was requested, many of the children were unable to reply other than by reassertion, i.e., with such phrases as "because I do." Since there are selective factors that determine ability to discuss reasons for attitudes or practices, no effort has been made to provide here a systematic summary of the reasons stated. See Koch (1956a, 1960) for a sample of typical responses. Emphasis, instead, will be placed largely on the positive or negative affect verbalized by the twins relative to given issues. Most children of school age can tell whether or not they tend to like something and whether or not it was usual for them to react in a given simple way. Answers on these matters, it was felt, could generally be trusted. In these simple responses bearing on positive or negative affect, a virtually complete series could be obtained from our subjects. Data in table form are presented usually only for responses showing significant group differences. The instances where the group differences were insignificant will merely be listed. This procedure was dictated by the voluminous amount of data.

MEASURE OF CLOSENESS

Although the responses to the items in the interview will be dealt with singly, in the main, a measure of closeness based on a number of items and one of so-called sex preference were developed. We have already referred to these measures (chapter 5). The closeness score is merely a count of the items (out of twelve) in which the child's response was favorable to the sib. The child was asked whether: (1) he would rather play alone or with the sib; (2) he would rather play with others than with the sib; (3) he would prefer to go visiting alone or to have the sib accompany him; (4) he would rather have a bedroom of his own or share one with the sib; (5) he played much with his twin or little; (6) he would be happier with than without the sib; (7) he wanted the sib in his class at school; (8) he desired to dress like the sib; (9) he would prefer a twin to an older sib; (10) he would prefer a twin to a younger sib; (11) he quarrelled seldom or much with the sib; and (12) he liked being a twin. The corrected split-half reliability of the closeness score was .93.

SEX PREFERENCE SCORE AND OTHER MEASURES OF SEX-TYPICAL BEHAVIOR

The sex preference score was made up of the number of responses to six items in which the child showed or expressed a preference for his own sex. (1) Did he affirm that he preferred members of his own sex as playmates; (2) did he list more children of his own sex as playmates; (3) did he name as his favorite playmate a child of his own sex; (4) did he name as his best friend a child of his own sex; (5) did he say he preferred an infant of his own sex if a new one were to be added to the family; and (6) did he state that if the family were to be reconstituted he would prefer a sib of his own sex to one who differed. The corrected split-half reliability coefficient of the sex preference score was .95.

In addition to the alleged sex preference score, an assessment was obtained of the degree of conformity of the child's behavior with the sex behavior norms of young urban and suburban children in the American Midwest—i.e., the teachers were asked to rate the boys on sissiness and the girls on tomboyishness. The teachers also rated the children on many other traits, in a number of which our analysis revealed marked sex differences. The normalized ratings on six traits for each sex were then averaged to yield what was labeled a "masculinity in attitude" score, and the same procedure was followed to obtain a measure of "femininity in attitude." The mean of the distribution of normalized scores for all ratings was four; the sigma was one. The six traits on which twin boys were rated markedly higher than girls and which constituted the basis for the masculinity complex score were: resistance, moodiness, revengefulness, tendency to project blame, tendency to tease, and social apprehensiveness. The six traits on which girls received a significantly higher appraisal than boys were: affectionateness, tenacity (ability to stay with a task until finished), obedience, cheerfulness, responsibleness, and friendliness to children. The corrected split-half "reliability" coefficients for the masculinity and femininity attitude scores were .62 and .90, respectively.

The three gauges of sex characteristics detailed above, it was hoped, would yield us a sort of picture of the extent to which the child's behavior was sex typical, as well as the sex preference that he felt. Whether what he professed always agreed with his behavior and belief is a question, although we have no reason to suspect he was deliberately masking his attitude. That he sometimes protested too much, however, made us wonder whether he always understood his own basic feeling. It is of some interest in this connection that the sex preference score seemed to correlate insignificantly with the other measures designed to tap sex preference. The teachers found it difficult to judge sissiness and tomboyishness except in their more extreme manifestations. Thus the rating range was narrow and the rating distribution almost *J*-shaped, which probably accounts for the generally low relation between these assessments and those used to appraise social involvements and sex-typical behavior. The indicators dealing with sex-typical behavior and attitude yield some material of special interest when the effect of having a twin opposite in sex, as opposed to same, is studied.

OTHER COMPLEX SCORES

In addition to the masculinity and femininity complex scores, three other complexes were derived from the teachers' ratings not only because there was evidence that the traits selected overlapped but because it was thought the overlap might be a result, in part, of the teachers' inability to discriminate well between them. As in the case of the masculinity and femininity scores, the complexes are the means of the normalized ratings for six to eight traits found, in a study of trait intercorrelations, to cluster to some degree. These complex scores have been labeled "extent of involvement with adults," "extent of involvement with children," and "emotionality and tension." The measure of "involvement with adults" was the average of the normalized ratings on the following traits: friendliness to adults, tendency to seek adult attention, tendency to ask adult aid when in difficulty, responsiveness to adult encouragement and approval, tendency to tattle, and affectionateness. The corrected random split-half coefficient for this complex was .66. The complex score designated, "involvement with children," was the mean of the ratings on: friendliness to children, gregariousness, leadership in the peer group, cooperativeness in group activities, social confidence, and enthusiasm for group activities. The corrected split-half reliability coefficient was .86. The measure of emotionality and tension was the mean of the normalized ratings for the traits of excitability, intensity, slowness of recovery after upset, readiness to anger, "physical" apprehensiveness, flightiness, nervous habits, and activeness. The corrected split-half reliability coefficient for this score was .67. How much these so-called reliabilities for the complex scores reflect consistencies in the teacher or her lack of ability to discriminate between traits and how much they reflect consistency in the behavior of the children rated is a point that should be raised. Also some of the clusters, it should be appreciated, were rather weak ones.

MEASURES BASED ON THE CAT STORIES

In this chapter some of the content scores that may bear on questions of family and self attitudes will be presented, as will some reflecting perhaps general hostile interest and anxiety. The so-called hostility measure, for example, describes the extent of preoccupation of the child in his stories with hostile episodes or interpretations. By a hostile episode was meant an action by a character or an expressed attitude directed toward the damage, injury, annihilation, belittling, or ill fate of another. Each story was rated on a five-point scale and these scores for the ten stories were then summed. The scores could range from 0 to 50. They are reasonably reliable (r's for split-half and test-retest reliabilities were .85 and .75, respectively) and considering the youth of the population, stable as well (see Table 35). What they may tell about the child will be discussed shortly. All test-retest reliabilities were based on the scores of fifty subjects from our control group. The retest was given two months after the original testing. For computing the other reliability measures, extensive data from the total twin group were employed (see Table 35 for our findings relative to gauges of various forms of reliability for the CAT-based measures). We were especially careful to check consistency in the protocol analysis and scorer interpretations.

The CAT was, in fact, used only because it was felt the specific content produced probably would not, to a large degree, be the result of a desire in the subject to please the examiner and the measures would be relatively free of the halo effect or subjective biases that are always involved in ratings. An effort was made to escape, in part, the interpretation bias of the person who judged the protocol by making the scoring as objective as possible.

Although the reliabilities of the various CAT measures are usually acceptable (see Table 35), it is not assumed the validity has had much checking. The measure intercorrelations such as Table 36 presents are helpful in dealing with the problem of interpretation and will be discussed later in this chapter.

A second measure, derived from the CAT data in a fashion somewhat similar to the one on which hostility was based, deals with the child's preoccupation with catastrophe or danger. A count was made of how many stories out of ten described or mentioned at least one dangerous episode or catastrophe. These episodes include such happenings as an accident, deluge, storm, serious illness, failure, loss, and so forth. The incidents do not involve direct attack by a character on another character. Some would view these incidents as evidence, nevertheless, of indirect hostility and this meaning may well be defensible. But that this is a uniform or necessary interpretation can also be questioned with reason. It is interesting that the correlation of the catastrophe scores and teachers' ratings on hostility was insignificant ($r = -.04$; Table 37), whereas that between the catastrophe scores and the CAT hostility score was .48 (Table 36). The latter r, it appears, does not stem from the influence of story length, since the correlation between the hostility and catastrophe scores with the story length variable partialled out was .49 (see Table 36). The split-half reliability of the catastrophe score was .78 and the test-retest r

was .83 (Table 35). Hence, the low correlation with the teachers' ratings does not seem to be a function of merely a low reliability in the catastrophe score. Neither was the latter's correlation with the composite rating designated "emotionality and tension" significant ($r = .10$, Table 37). It had been suspected that the catastrophic episodes are evidence of the child's anxious concern with danger, but the above correlations raise doubts that this measure reflects in a major way general fear of danger or general anxiety. Perhaps the child with the high score enjoys courting danger, likes excitement, or has merely learned from viewing TV that stories usually involve such happenings.

A further, possibly more focused, indicator of the feeling a child might have that he was not the master of his fate—i.e., that he could not control forces—was the number of stories in which the outcome was unfavorable for the little or identification character. Still another estimate of the extent to which the world might be viewed as threatening was attempted by determining the number of stories in which at least one unpleasant event occurred. The split-half and test-retest reliabilities of the former measure were, respectively, .81 and .56, and for the latter measure, .84 and .88, respectively (Table 35).

We shall be using the story counts, such as that basic to the catastrophe score, as indicators of various sorts. The so-called tales that children of the age of our subjects tell vary a great deal in the length. Since, also, counts of specific episodes relevant to the attitude being tapped are very much a function of story length, an effort was made to reduce the effect of this probable volubility variable by using, instead of a relevant episode count, scores that were numerations of the stories in which there occurred one or more happenings possibly reflecting the attitude under study. It was thought, too, that the story count would be less heavily influenced by individual differences in linguistic skill and general ability than specific episode numerations and would thus obscure less individual differences in affect related to the content of interest. The measure, number of relevant episodes per one-hundred words, was tried and abandoned, as it seemed more unreliable than the story counts. But there is really no way of circumventing the difficulty of inequality between subjects in the product sample they provide for analysis.

In addition to the above tappings, a census was made of the number of stories in the CAT in which a mother figure and in which a father figure occurred. It was hoped these "parent mention" scores would give some idea of the extent of the child's involvement with parents in various ways. To portray the coloring of the parent-child relations, four separate counts were made—namely (1) the stories in which at least one episode describing a pleasant interaction between a parent and child figure occurred, and (2) the stories in which at least one unpleasant interaction took place. These positive and negative person-interaction scores were obtained for each of the two parents. Positive or pleasant episodes included any friendly, protective, cooperative, or favoring interaction between a parent and child figure or between a child and parent. The negative responses embraced any unfriendly, uncooperative, hostile, punishing, or thwarting interactions (see Table 35 for reliability estimates for these). These counts of various parent-child interactions seem, with the exception of the mother-child positive score, to have a rather low degree of test-retest reliability.

The intercorrelations of the various CAT-based measures, with and without story length partialled out, are presented in Table 36. Partialling out story length reduced the interitem correlations seven to eight points on the average, the maximum reduction being eighteen points. These partial correlations indicate our efforts by various scoring devices discount to some degree differences in volume of output were partly successful, as well as suggest that most of the CAT measures used reflect somewhat individual differences that are over and above mere volubility.

It is obvious, of course, the many of the intermeasure *r*'s are spurious, as the various counts do not yield entirely independent information—i.e., mother-mentions and mother-child plus and minus scores, or number of stories with unpleasant themes and number of stories involving catastrophic episodes. Only the hostility, catastrophe, negative outcome, mother- and father-mentions, and thematic-descriptive scores are relatively independent of each other structurally.

When the correlations between the CAT-based measures, as well as between these and various ratings or tests thought to be revealing of related qualities (Table 37) are studied, not much that is encouraging in the way of validation evidence is uncovered. For example, the teachers' assessment of the children's involvement with adults and the CAT scores that indicated the extent to which the stories revolved around parents are insignificantly correlated, as are the CAT-based hostility score and the teachers' ratings of the child's tendency to exhibit the acting-out type of hostility at school. Nor do we find any impressive relationship between the CAT-based scores labeled catastrophe, negative theme, negative outcome, and hostility and the teachers' ratings of emotionality and tension, although three of the measures were significantly, albeit slightly, associated with the teachers' assessments of intensity, as well as, surprisingly, with their judgments of cheerfulness.

Indeed, there are grounds for the suspicion that the CAT scores tend to gauge not so much the contents that their labels imply as they do individual differences in attitudes or skills which are more general, as well as covert—e.g., intelligence, imaginativeness, or language skills, general family interest, or extraversion. It is noteworthy that the PMA V-subtest quotient, as well as social class, are marginally but still significantly correlated with all of the CAT-based measures, except negative outcome (Table 37). Although unrelated to activeness, the number of playmates the child listed, twin closeness score, rated hostility, or the CAT-based measures did tend to correlate with ratings of child leadership, popularity, and social confidence. It was noted that, in keeping with the view the CAT items may measure drive, imaginativeness, and language skill, the T-D score correlated better with the CAT-based measures than did word count. The T-D score, moreover, was correlated with involvement with children, gregariousness, leadership, popularity, femininity of attitude, social confidence, intensity, cheerfulness, number of interests, and social class. It is to be observed that even negative theme, catastrophe, and hostility scores were related to a small degree to popularity, leadership, involvement with children, social class, cheerfulness, intensity, and number of interests. The elaboration of themes involving parent characters seems slightly related to IQ, PMA V-quotient, femininity of attitude, and favorable standing with peers. These latter CAT-based measures were not, on the other hand, correlated with the teachers' assessment of involvement with adults at school.

Although we feel sure some of the specific episodes in the CAT stories involving mother figures do reveal the child's unique feelings toward his own mother, it is doubtful that our simple counts differentiate dependably between specific affective reactions of individual children toward their parents. But it is of some interest that the children judged most feminine did tend to use mother figures more in their stories. In fact, it seems likely the parent scores, as explained above, may reveal general family interest or involvement rather than detailed differences in affect trend with respect to a specific parent. Mother- and father-mentions correlated .66, for example, mother-child plus and minus scores correlated .61; and father-child plus and minus scores, .52 (Table 36).

We are of the opinion that the *r*'s involving the T-D and hostility scores tend to be relatively higher than many of the others, partly because the score spread for these two measures was much greater than that for the other items. The score ranges for the father-child plus and minus items was, in contrast, very narrow and here the correlations tended to be correspondingly low.

SUMMARY OF OBSERVATIONS ON CAT-BASED MEASURES AND THEIR RELATIONSHIPS

1. Probably about half of all of the CAT-based measures correlated spuriously high with each other.

2. The CAT-measure intercorrelations (practically all of which are respectably significant) dropped, on the average, seven to eight points when story length was partialled out, the maximum drop being eighteen points. Two *r*'s, however, increased very slightly. These findings suggest that the measure relations were at least not solely functions of the child's volubility and its correlates.

3. The fact that the PMA V-subtest score correlated significantly with all but two of the CAT measures (one of the two lowest significant *r*'s was with word count) suggests that general intelligence, linguistic skill, or vocabulary may play a role in determining the CAT-based measure intercorrelations. The PMA V-subtest quotient was slightly more highly related to CAT measures than was the PMA total IQ.

4. The teachers' ratings on involvement with children, popularity, leadership, and gregariousness exhibited the most relationship with the CAT measures.

5. The inter-correlations described in (4) hint of a general social or peer interest factor. Since the mother- and father-mention scores correlated .66 and the mother-child and father-child negative, as well as positive scores, intercorrelated with one exception at .52 or above, it appears we may also be dealing with a family involvement factor.

6. The more feminine or effeminate the child, the more parent-

involved he tended to be in his stories; and, conversely, the more masculine, the less so involved.

7. The hostility gauge, which had a wider spread than did the other CAT-based measures, tended to exhibit the highest r's with the other indicators. The question is whether the greater spread in score or the content relationships are responsible for these larger r's between the hostility guage and the other CAT measures.

8. The hostility score was positively correlated with popularity, leadership, and gregariousness, as judged by the teachers. One may wonder whether the more aggressive, imaginative, and interesting children see life as more competitive or as more of a struggle, which they enjoy.

9. The teachers' ratings of child intensity did seem slightly related to the catastrophe, negative theme, and negative outcome scores. The various indicators, contentwise, point in the same direction. Hence, it seems reasonable to assume they provide some hints bearing on the interpretation of the measures.

10. The negative theme and outcome scores correlated just barely significantly with the estimate of involvement with adults, who were probably described as punishing or unrelenting. It is also possible the correlations reflect the fearful, conscientious child's concern with pleasing adults.

11. The twin-closeness score and the rating the child received on activeness were unrelated to any CAT-based measure. The number of playmates, however, intercorrelated barely significantly with the catastrophe and negative theme scores.

The above observation will govern our attempts to interpret the intertwin group and twin-singleton group likenesses and differences. It is suspected that the nebulous or general nature of the CAT-based measures underlies, in part, the fact of few significant group differences in these items. The use, except clinically, of such indices as we have described, in research involving the young child, seems to us at best hazardous and unrewarding.

LOCATION OF DATA AND STATISTICAL PROGRAMS

The mean and sigma of the mean for each subgroup for each of the measures of social attitude that provided a continuum are given in

Appendix A, Table 72. In the Appendix are presented the mean and sigma of the mean for each of the subgroups for the *differences* between the twin pairs' average score and the average of the scores for the group of two or four singletons who matched the pair. Groups to be compared were matched wherever possible—e.g., in the twin-singleton part of the study—but the various twin subgroups could not be matched in social class (Table 1) because the difficulty of locating the cases who met our many specifications was so great we had to press into service every case we could find. One type of procedure we used to discount the influence of class, or disengage it from other variables of interest to us, came from Scheffé (1959, pp. 98 ff., 112 ff.). This reference, as mentioned in a previous chapter, describes a model for a three-way analysis of variance procedure with one measure per cell. The three variables whose interrelationships were studied by using the Scheffé approach were zygosity, sex, and social class (here only the same-sex twin group differences were investigated). Sex-of-sib and social class were the variables whose relations were analyzed when the question of the effect of likeness or difference in sex of sib was focused. The analysis here was made separately for each sex.

See Welch (1947) and Bennet and Franklin (1954, p. 117) for a description of the procedure we followed in computing t when the groups set in contrast were unmatched and differed some in variance and number. If the aggregates compared were matched and the descriptive categories dichotomous, as many responses in the interview were, McNemar's formula (1947) was chosen as the procedure to be followed in deriving X^2's. When, however, the classification of responses involved more than two categories, a shift was made to Cochran's Q (1950).

MZ *VS.* DZSS TWINS

Problems

In the MZ-DZSS comparisons a central issue is whether presumably genetically identical individuals (MZ's), who in addition tend to have highly similar environments, tend to feel more similar to each other, as well as more different from other people than do DZSS twins who do not vary from singleton sibs in degree of gene likeness at least. In other words: (1) Are identical twins more similar in temperament and ability than are fraternal co-twins? (2) Do the identicals if they are more similar, for whatever reason, get on better with each other? (3) If they are more compatible and devoted to each other, does this interfere with or facilitate the building of good relations to others? (4) It is important to ask, too, whether identical twins, because of their similar appearance, tend to be dealt with differently from fraternal twins who are of the same sex. For example, in an informal count of comments made by the teachers to our request, "Tell me about the twins," it was apparent that in the case of identicals most of the statements described the twins' likeness, whereas in the case of the fraternals most of the remarks dealt with differences, with the inevitable implications of a less favorable evaluation of one of the pair. (If one is interested in exploring the effect on child personality of sib differences in age, twins can be taken as representing the condition of no disparity in this dimension.)

Twin-group differences may be difficult to interpret, however, since the children tend, for the reason of their usual highly similar appearance, to be particularly conspicuous and surrounded by a sort of halo and, more important, they will have had perhaps some pre- and perinatal experiences that singleton sibs cannot have. The latter two sets of factors may influence intertwin relations so as to mask the role of the genes and their correlates as well as the social effects of the typical sib age-difference complex witnessed in nontwins. Twin prematurity, for instance, although it is a function of identicalness in age among sibs, finds no strict parallel among brothers and sisters differing in age, yet it may have effects that obscure or blur the usual ones governing the social relations and attitudes of sibling pairs.

Intertwin Group Comparisons—Attitudes of Twins from Same-sex Pairs toward Each Other

If one heeds now what the children communicated in the interview, it is clear the MZ co-twins were more nearly one with each other than were the DZSS's (Table 38), although the latter, in turn, appeared closer than did twins opposite in sex. (For evidence supporting the foregoing assertion, see Tables 26 and 27; also Tables 38 and 39, as well as most of the observations that will be described in the next few paragraphs.) The identicals more often saw similarities between themselves and the sib than did fraternals from sib pairs whose members were like in sex. The MZm co-twins reported with greater frequency that they were dressed alike than did the DZSSm's. And the MZm's asserted that they enjoyed dressing alike because they thought it announced their twinness, a status they viewed as giving much distinction. Identical girls, at least, seemed more often to use each others' possessions freely, and they affirmed that they objected when this was done without permission less frequently than did the comparable fraternals. The monozygotics' interview responses indicated they played more together and with each others' friends than did the parallel dizygotics, and the MZ's, at least, stated they felt better accepted by the sib's friends. The MZf's also expressed less inclination to play alone than did the DZSSf's, and asserted more often that they preferred play with the sib to play alone.

It is significant in the light of the apparent greater closeness of the identicals that the members of the two zygosity groups listed essentially the same number of playmates on the average (Tables 26 and 27)—that is, the somewhat greater intimacy of the MZ co-twins did not appear, according to these data, to have much of a restricting effect on the children's association with others, as some have feared. Neither sex of identicals differed, moreover, from singleton controls in the number of playmates reported (Table 25). Whether the MZ's actually played with as many or as great a variety of children as did the DZSS's or matched singletons is another question. Indeed, the teachers described the MZm's, in comparison with the same-sex fraternal male pairs, as less gregariousness at school, less responsiveness to adults, and as less effective leaders (Table 40). It seems likely, however, that the teachers' impressions are based more on the twins' ability to influence or to insinuate themselves into the peer group than on the children's simple, friendly interest in their schoolmates. Relevant to this interpretation is the observation that, whereas the identicals tended to be assessed as less exhibitionistic, less insistent on their rights (Table 41), and less good leaders (Table 40), the measures of involvement with adults and children did not reveal any zygosity differences (Tables 26 and 27). The judged lesser gregariousness of the MZ males may have been due to their peers' reactions to them, since some of the MZ's, because of a slight intellectual lag, may have had less of interest to offer others. As a matter of fact, the males' slightly lower intelligence average may even have accounted partly for the sex difference in the pattern of relations noted. Although the identical girls, like the boys, were especially close—associated with and shared more with the sib—their greater intimacy did not seem to reduce significantly their social effectiveness. Indeed, compared with singletons, the identical girls were judged more sociable with children and even more effective socially (Table 42), a claim that can not, as has been said, be made for the MZm's.

If some of the MZm's seem to be socially more or less on the fringe, one might expect this to show itself in a greater professed preference for their own sex kind but in less exhibition of sex-typical behavior and attitude, since these children would have had less opportunity to learn the prevailing sex-group behavior code or would have learned it more slowly. This idea gets some support from the fact that MZm's scored significantly higher in professed preference for their own sex (Table 38) and in the greater number of male playmates they enumerated or fantasied than did the DZSSm's (Table 43); but the MZm's were described as not different in masculinity from the latter (Table 44), and compared with singletons, as even rather sissyish (Tables 42 and 45). The MZm's, in accordance with our anticipations were viewed as apparently lower in drive and as gentler than parallel fraternal twins or singletons (Tables 41 and 42). They were judged relative to DZSSm's, for example, as less exhibitionistic and insistent on their rights, less selfish, cruel, and indirect (Table 41), a pattern that, since it appears in both sexes, may well be attributable partly to the greater similarity of treatment that identical co-twins, as contrasted with fraternal, receive. The greater likeness in treatment meted out to the identicals is, doubtless, rooted not only in their similarity as physical and social stimuli (e.g., they can be scarcely told apart), but also in the educational-cultural derivatives from this (e.g., it is expected identicals will be dressed alike). The MZ's tend not only to resemble each other strongly and to be highly similar in ability and temperament, but they are also taught they are the "same," as some children told us, and similarity in behavior is rewarded. In fact, being an identical twin has much prestige value. All of these considerations may result for the MZ's in lesser rivalry and attention-seeking. The MZ co-twins, too, if they are more compatible (being genetically identical, etc.), may have less opportunity to learn the more active kind of defenses.

Although one cannot ignore the possibility that, since the MZm co-twins are so much alike, this reduces the spur to competition below that which obtains among the DZSSm's (see von Bracken 1934), nevertheless, the contingency that biological handicap may contribute to the trait pattern observed must also not be overlooked.

As mentioned above, the trend among the identical girls, as opposed to fraternal females, appears somewhat similar in many traits to that noted for the males, but it was not sufficiently marked to be classified as significant. The MZ girl co-twins were apparently slightly closer to each other than were the DZSSf's (Table 26), possibly less aggressive (Table 40) and more adult- or teacher-centered (Table 40). They were assessed, relative to the DZSSf's, for example, as more responsive to adults (Table 40), as well as less original, planful, final (Table 40), indirect, exhibitionistic, and insistent on their rights (Table 41). On the other hand, they were thought to be both more critical and resistant (Table 41) and their CAT stories had more negative outcomes (Table 46), traits which could be a function of lesser daring, greater dependence, and conscientiousness. These girls, as compared with matched nontwin sibs, were judged more responsible (Table 42), whereas the DZSSf's were not. This observation supports the hunch that the alleged criticalness in the MZf's mentioned above is chiefly that of the conscientious person.

The MZf's may present the picture sketched in the previous paragraph because they are somewhat more often the center of attention than are the DZSSf's, since they are thought particularly "cute," being alike, and are exhibited more. The DZSSf's are not without some of the conspicuousness of the MZf's but, doubtless, do not receive favorable attention to the same degree as do the identical girls. Comparisons made between the fraternal co-twins usually specify or imply a less favorable status for one of them.

In the main, however, likenesses between the two zygosity groups of girls are more notable than differences and neither group can be said to be lacking in social interest. The MZm's who, like the identical females, are typically very close to the sib and rather unaggressive, seem, in contrast, not to have achieved the level of socialization the MZf's have nor the level observed in singleton males (Table 42). The DZSSm's, on the other hand, do not seem to differ much from singletons in social behavior (Table 42). The DZSSm co-twins appear to go their own ways to a greater extent than do the MZm co-twins and to be more aggressive (Tables 40 and 41).

IDENTICAL TWINS AND SINGLETONS

To spell out the above statement further, let it be said that the MZm's, in contrast with matched singleton males, were assessed by their teachers as less gregarious, less competitive, less insistent on their rights, less given to alibiing, as well as being more sissyish (Table 42). These twin males seemed to be characterized by lower drive, less alertness, and by considerable anxiety and reserve. The reverse, however, appeared to obtain for the girls who, when set in contrast with matched singleton girls, were rated by their teachers as better leaders, on the average, as more friendly to adults and involved with children, more popular, less apprehensive in social situations, more responsible, possessed of a wider range of interests, less moody, and, correspondingly, more cheerful, as well as more feminine. And, congruently, the MZf's were rated significantly lower on masculinity in attitude than were matched singleton girls (Table 42).

The greater judged femininity of the identical girls (Table 42), relative to singletons, is a finding of some interest. Since the constant child companion of both twins was of their own sex, as were also their mother and their teacher—i.e., the chief figures of interest in their world were all female—this should favor feminine emphases in our quite young subjects. But why then were not the DZSSf's considered relatively as feminine as the MZf's (Table 42)? The femininity of the M2f's, besides being favored by the above-mentioned factors, was doubtless emphasized by the fact that, as a rule, they were very attractively and femininely groomed. It seems more likely, however, that the MZf co-twins may, because of greater similarity in ability, temperament, and treatment, have been less combative, a trait thought to be distinguishing of males and with which the masculinity complex score was accordingly heavily weighted. It is important to note that when MZf's and DZSSf's are compared directly with each other on our various indicators of sex-typical behavior and sex preference, the DZSSf's do not appear particularly less feminine. The latter had, if anything, more girl playmates (Table 43) and voiced more preference for their own sex kind (Table 44), as well as differed insignificantly on the femininity complex score itself.

It is of significance, relevant to the view that differences in combativeness influence judgments of masculinity or femininity, that the

MZm's, who were thought less combative and aggressive than matched singleton males, were judged by their teachers as somewhat sissyish when compared with nontwin controls. But one can readily see here, just as in girl twins, that when contrasted with DZSSm's, the MZm's listed more male playmates (Table 43), professed more preference for their own sex, and did not average lower on the masculinity complex score (Table 44).

That the MZf's averaged higher in cheerfulness than did singletons may result from the considerations that (1) the former children tend to be showered with much favorable attention; (2) they are temperamentally so highly similar and so close they have relatively little conflict; and (3) people lean over backward to treat them alike, thus virtually eliminating a common source of stress in children.

A comparison of the responses of the same-sex groups, the MZ's and DZSS's, in the interview with those given by nontwins emphasizes again the greater amount of sib association among twins and their freer sharing of friends and possessions, less quarreling, and the tendency to interpret more charitably the role of the sib in initiating their altercations (Table 47). Since a belief prevails that twins are very jealous, it is particularly interesting that the parents were reported more frequently by the children as treating both pair members similarly and impartially than was the case for singleton sibs (Table 47). The twins, moreover, very rarely expressed a desire to change places with the sib. The MZ's, it is true, try hard to keep abreast of each other, but this effort, according to von Bracken (1934), is less hostile than is usually implied in jealousy. Jealousy is somewhat more in evidence in fraternal pairs.

Fraternal Twins from Like-sex Pairs vs. Matched Singletons

The basic data are not presented since trends can be inferred on the basis of data offered in the previous section, but the general tone of the complex of attitudes of the DZSS group, the group in which the degree of sib likeness in genes is presumably not different from singletons, was found to be, in relation to that for non-twins, not unlike that obtaining among the MZ's. But the contrast between singletons and MZ's was not usually sufficiently marked to attain significance (Tables 38 and 47). The twins from both same-sex pair types, in comparison with matched nontwin sibs, tended to think less critically of the sib (Table 47). The former stated more frequently that they associated much with the sib and gave descriptions in the interview that suggested they had a better relation with him—i.e., the twins took more responsibility for initiating quarrels, and stated they shared friends more often (Table 47). The twins also more often asserted they were treated similarly by the parents, and less often affirmed a desire to change places with the sib than did matched singletons. Like identicals, too, the DZSSf's with greater frequency than nontwin sibs listed more same-age playmates and fewer younger ones (Table 48). The DZSS girls more often expressed a liking for school than comparable singleton sibs.

The DZSSm's' differences in general traits from matched singletons are actually few (Table 42). The DZSSm's were smaller, on the average, scored lower in PMA V-test, were less talkative, less cheerful, and less given to alibis. The DZSSf's, in contrast to males, exhibited better speech form than control singletons, but, like the males, scored lower on the PMA V-test (Table 42). Also in contrast to the males, the fraternal girls were thought to be more involved with children and less apprehensive socially, better leaders, and more popular (Table 42). Contrary to the trend among the MZf's, the DZSSf's were not judged more feminine than singleton girls nor more cheerful. A possible interpretation for the MZf's higher status in these two traits has already been suggested. It is of some interest that the DZSSf's described more unpleasant mother-child interactions and more pleasant father-child ones than did comparable singletons (Table 49)—i.e., the DZSSf's seemed more father-affiliated.

Sex-group Differences Relative to Comparable Singletons

As has been repeatedly stated, the two sex groups in the twins from like-sex pairs differed considerably in the pattern of their deviation from matched singletons. To throw this pattern into relief, although its parts had been revealed by other procedures, a two-way analysis of variance of twin-singleton differences was carried through. The mean of the male pairs' means was either significantly below that for singleton matches or was the same, whereas the direction of the deviation of the mean difference for the females was divergent from that for the males or less marked in the following traits: speech form, PMA V-test score, involvement with children, gregariousness, leadership, popularity, social nonapprehensiveness, confidence, friendliness to adults, friendliness to children, insistence on rights, finality, intensity, cheerfulness, originality, and number of interests. The greater relative femininity and lesser masculinity of especially MZ girls also shows clearly in Table 50. There was no significant disparity between twin and singleton boys in sex-typical behavior. Apparently, if one judges the total picture, being a twin is harder on boys than on girls. Since our hypotheses for the major sex differences have already been set forth, they will not be repeated here.

FRATERNAL, OPPOSITE-SEX TWIN PAIRS

DZOS vs. DZSS Twins

In studying co-twins who are unlike in sex, it will be well to look into their differences, if any, from fraternal pairs whose members are of the same sex. This comparison should illuminate, in addition to other things, the role of the sibling factor in the sex-role learning of the children. The contrasting, on the other hand, of the DZOS twins with matched singletons whose sib is also opposite in sex, will highlight the effect of a sib age-difference variable. One may ask, for instance, whether similarity in age intensifies sex rivalry or reduces it. That there may be biological forces as well as social ones that differentiate the two fraternal groups was explained in chapter 1.

The effect of sib difference in age was explored in an earlier piece of research dealing with singletons whose only sib differed from them by varying numbers of years from under two up to six. The twin groups furnish the condition of no disparity in sibling age. The fact that the degree of disparity in age of nontwin siblings proved in the singleton study an important determinant of the relations between them has made it seem well to try to plot the pattern of sib interaction when there was no age incongruity. The instances of singletons well matched with twin subjects were unfortunately not always sufficiently numerous to permit a plot of the detail of the age-difference curve. Hence the twin-singleton comparison offered here is of an all-or-none type. Although cases are few, the DZOSm's of all social classes were judged as more sissyish, on the average, than the DZSSm's, whereas the DZOS girls' ratings on tomboyishness did not exhibit a similar consistency.

Sibs of the same age, for instance, are victimized by more comparisons than are singleton sibs. The effect of this could be very damaging. It is also important to know whether the educational value of growing up with a member of the opposite sex at a very close range may compensate for all of the ego wounds resulting from the comparative set that society and finally the self creates.

To bring to the fore the question of the children's attitudes toward the sexes and the degree to which progress had been made by our young twin subjects in acquiring sex-typical behavior, a number of dragnets were thrown out. These have already been described, but let us enumerate the major ones again: (1) The teachers rated the appropriate sexes on sissiness and tomboyishness. (2) A masculinity and femininity attitude measure was developed that reflected status in a number of behavior areas in which the sexes typically differ considerably. (3) The children were questioned directly in relation to their sex preferences, and their playmate choices were scanned to reveal sex preference. (4) An effort was made to gauge the extent to which the child in his CAT stories dealt with parent figures of the two sexes. (5) The interview and ratings were also structured to revealed sex differences in attitude or effects tangential to, or more remote from, those involving a direct sex focus—e.g., we noted whether opposite-sex twins had more or more varied friends or fewer friends than did same-sex twins.

Some of the instruments employed were obviously crude but, judging from many of their intercorrelations, one could conclude that, whatever they measure, they do not overlap much. (The reader may wish to inspect Table 51.) What correlations are significant are meaningful.

Our subjects, it should be recalled, were at the age when, at least in the American culture, the sexes tend to begin to withdraw very noticeably from each other. The early school years have been dubbed, hence, the "homosexual" period. The intersex distance is known to increase as children first become more firmly enmeshed in the culture outside of the home, which is typically more patriarchal in tone than that of the home. Young males tend to come into their own, as they have occasion to associate with more and older boys and to learn to appreciate the great achievements and important social states of their own sex kind.

It is striking that the appropriately compared DZOS and DZSS groups did not differ significantly, on the average, according to the teachers' judgments of tomboyishness and sissiness (Table 52), nor was there a conspicuous difference in frequency of expressed preference for their own sex, nor in the masculinity or femininity complex score averages (Table 52), nor in the proportion of children of the two sexes proclaimed as friends (Tables 52 and 60). The fraternal twins as a group did not seem to differ from singletons in sex choice. There is only a very slight hint that DZOS girls were more prone to masculinity than the DZSSf's (Table 52), and the DZOS boys to greater femininity than the DZSSm's. If one scans the trait ratings made by the teachers, it is possible to see a similar apparent tempering of the sex-typical forms of behavior as a result of association with a twin opposite in sex, but the group disparities are so small as not to be significant. To illustrate the former point, the mean rating of the DZOSf's fell above the mean for the DZSSf's in uncooperativeness with peers, a trait usually more conspicuous in males, while a parallel comparison for the DZOS males shows them to score as less uncooperative than the DZSSm's (Table 53). Other traits exhibiting a similar trend are: tendency to project blame, selfishness (Table 53), ambition, originality, number of interests (Table 55), and obedience (Table 54). Although the gestalt just described cannot be taken very seriously because the group differences are so small, it does seem plausible. All that can be asserted, however, is that the influence of the DZOS pair members on each other's sex-correlated types of behavior and attitude is not very pronounced.

If, in contrast to the ratings, the responses to questions in the interview are compared, many intertwin group differences are uncovered (Table 39). The DZOS co-twins, especially the girls, appear less close to each other than do the fraternals from pairs with members of the same sex (Table 27). The DZOS's, for example, affirmed little desire to be like the sib or to have him in their class at school (Table 39). They stated that they played less with him and his friends, that they had more friends of their own, and that they felt less well accepted by the sib's friends. The DZOS's also more often expressed the view they would be happier without the sib. In fact, with less rarity than did the DZSS's, the members of the brother-sister pairs said they preferred to play alone over play with the sib, or to play with other children compared to play with the twin. They affirmed with lesser frequency that the sib was rarely bossy. It was, congruently, more usual for the DZOSf's than the DZSSf's to state that they objected much when the sib used their possessions without first getting permission. The opposite-sex pairs even confessed more often to initiating sibling quarrels than did the same-sex fraternals. The DZOSf's less frequently than the DZSSf's said they saw the father as neutral, and all DZOS's stated less often that they believed privileges and responsibilities were distributed with impartiality. Given a choice of sex for a new infant for the family, the DZOS's, compared with the DZSS's, more frequently chose their own sex. The questioning revealed that such an addition to the family was usually viewed by the twins as an opportunity to strengthen the phalanx of their own sex.

If it should now be asked whether there are any reverberations of the above attitudes in behaviors that are not particularly sex-oriented, it should be answered that in only a few instances do the two groups of fraternal twins exhibit much divergence. The DZOSf's were, however, judged less active and sensitive (Table 53), on the average, and less emotional (Table 54). The DZOSm's were rated, relative to the DZSSm's, as more cheerful (Table 54), possessed of better health (Table 53), and more planful (Table 55). The DZOSm's, compared with the DZSSm's, also told CAT stories that contained more catastrophe, negative themes, and unpleasant mother-child episodes (Table 56).

The picture just sketched of the DZOS's is that of somewhat subdued, rather unexpressive children. It is significant in this connection that the children played more on the hostility, catastrophe, and generally unpleasant themes in their stories, and resolved more of their tales in a way unfavorable to the little or identification character (Table 56). All of these observations may be signs of tension rooted in co-twin sex differences. It is impressive, too, that the DZOSm's liked school less than did the DZSSm's. Perhaps in their early days at school the DZOSm's rivalry and desperate efforts to keep abreast of the sib, not only for themselves but for the honor of their sex, resulted in the constriction in these children which the rating gestalt implies. Doubtless, also, each expected that his deviations or failures would be promptly reported at home.

It was not anticipated that the DZOS girls, since they were in most pairs the second-born and the lighter in birth weight, would be usually the dominant co-twin. This finding of ours is congruent with the mothers' opinions. (See discussion of this fact and its implications in chapter 7.) It is relevant that the DZOSm's more often thought the sib very bossy than did the DZOSf's (Table 57). Moreover, the DZOSf's chose others over the sib for a companion on a visit more frequently than did the DZOSm's—i.e., the girls seemed to reject the sib more. The girls, consistent with this view, expressed a preference for female playmates slightly more frequently than the boys did for male playmates (Table 57), more often stated they had friends of their own, and that they were favored by both parents. The interview revealed that in the area of school activities the DZOSm's tended to feel their sisters were superior and more approved. And the girls, in contrast, seemed somewhat ashamed of their brother's lesser "competence" and nonconformity. They struggled to keep their brothers in line. Notwithstanding this, the members of the two sexes were about equally often inclined to state that they wanted the sib in their class at school (Table 39). Although these trends are not strong enough to be judged very significant, they do suggest that the DZOS boys, relative to their sisters, respected their role less.

DZOS TWINS vs. MATCHED SINGLETONS

As mentioned earlier, although the social distance between the co-twins from unlike-sex pairs was considerable (Tables 27 and 39), this gap was less than that between singleton sibs who also were unlike in sex. It is worthy of attention that the DZOS's of both sexes listed not significantly more playmates of their own sex than did parallel singletons (Table 58), and neither more nor fewer playmates. In other words, being a twin did not seem to facilitate nor interfere with the acquisition of playmates. More of the OS fraternals' playmates, as for twins generally, tended to be their own age (Table 58) and, in the instance of the DZOSm's, the number and per cent of younger friends tended to be fewer.

When compared with singleton controls in general behavior, the DZOS's were assessed as less emotional and intense (Table 59), less exhibitionistic, less given to alibiing, and less incoherent in their story telling. In addition, the DZOSm's were rated less confident, active, selfish, and strong of voice, whereas the DZOSf's were gauged as less jealous, gregarious, moody, and sensitive. It was impressive that the latter group wove into their CAT stories more catastrophic episodes and negative themes than did singleton controls (Table 59).

The boys and girls from twin pairs whose members were dissimilar in sex held their own with matched singletons in speech form, in the coherence of their CAT stories (chapter 4), and in the more distinctly problem-solving tasks of the PMA (chapter 3). In the light of the high incidence of prematurity among the OS twins, this evidence of intellectual competence was unexpected.

On the whole, the picture the DZOS's present is that of competent, rather subdued, non-acting-out children, considerably occupied with a sex-role struggle, but not to a greater degree than are matched singleton sibs who differ in sex and little in age. The teachers' description of the DZOSm's as relatively low in intensity and sensitiveness (Table 59) is cause for wonder, although the children sketched no extreme picture of their attitudes. More frequently than did matched singletons these twins expressed the view that the parents were impartial. Compared with nontwin sibs, they stated more often that they played with the sib a moderate amount and that their quarreling was typically of only medium severity and frequency. In the main, the twins described themselves as quarreling more than did singletons and more often thought the sib bossy (Table 57). They were inclined to see their relations with the sib's friends as indifferent, instead of good or bad. The children's reports, in other words, seemed realistic and temperate in tone.

It is noteworthy that, in spite of the evidence of considerable anxiety rooted in sex difference, the DZOSf's, in comparison with the DZSSf's, were judged as less active, intense, emotional, and sensitive (Tables 53 and 54) and that, as assessed by their teachers with reference to their singleton counterparts, the DZOSf's were classed, in addition, as less exhibitionistic, jealous, and gregarious (Table 59). At a slightly lower than significance level of 5 per cent, the DZOS's, both male and female, were rated relative to same-sex fraternal twins as less active, sensitive, exhibitionistic, emotional, intense, moody, and given to tattling—all differences that suggest less anxiety (Tables 53 and 54). Or is it reserve, since among other things many of the OS twins were adjusting to being separated at school?

It seems not impossible, despite the struggle over unlikeness in sex which the children revealed clearly in the interview, that, in the last analysis, the DZOS's had fewer intrapersonal conflicts than did the DZSS's. The point has been made repeatedly, for instance, that twins tend to be compared excessively and that, whereas the identicals are usually scanned for likeness, the fraternal co-twins are compared more from the point of view of difference, which usually includes an overtone of a less favorable evaluation for one of the twins. Disparities in attitude and behavior between the DZOS pair members, however, as contrasted with those between the DZSS co-twins, are more likely to be accepted and even encouraged because the culture approves certain divergent behavioral and attitudinal emphases in the two sexes. Whereas even basic differences in temperament in DZSS co-twins may not be recognized, tolerated, or provided for adequately, parallel degrees of disparity in DZOS co-twins may be well accepted, the divergence being considered merely typical of the sexes. The children of the two sexes are rewarded for different behaviors. Now these dissimilarities in treatment, it is true, are often sources of much conflict for the DZOS twins, but they may also often be satisfying because they are congruent with inclination divergences rooted in the basic physiology of the two sexes. Boys, for instance, typically prefer more active pursuits and attacks on matters than do girls.

Since, then, this sex difference in temperament and training may result in less demand in the DZOS co-twins than in the DZSS's for similar rewards at the same time from the same agent, with its necessary frustration and increased drive, the DZOS may have less anxiety. What may not fit the picture is that their CAT stories dealt with more unpleasant mother-child interactions and unpleasant episodes generally.

The evidence we uncovered that supports the interpretation of greater conflict in the DZOSm's than DZOSf's was anticipated, too, because, no matter what the family holds for the DZOSm's in the way of expectations, in his early days and even in the early years of his life, his rewards and behavior model come more from the nurturing mother. The feminine pattern is, doubtless, in subtle ways reinforced by her and also by his sister. The father, whom the DZOSm is encouraged to imitate, is typically, in the United States and most Western cultures, absent from home territory for much of the day and may even take, when he is at home, a somewhat more disciplinary set toward his son than daughter (Sears, Maccoby, and Levin 1957, pp. 406, 409). The DZOSm's sister and her girl friends, moreover, may seem to him more comfortable companions because he has spent most of his early years in a female-dominated environment and because the former children have been trained in more nurturant ways than boy playmates, who have been encouraged rather more in the ways of independence and aggression. All of these considerations probably make the DZOSm less sure of his satisfaction with his own sex than the DZOSf is with hers.

The reader may wish to read the very interesting study of Rosenberg and Sutton-Smith (1964), which lends support of a sort to the present findings. These authors noted that first-borns from two-child same-sex sibships tended to report more anxiety symptoms (Children's Manifest Anxiety Scale) than did first-borns from opposite-sex sibships and that for second-borns the relations in degree of expressed anxiety seemed reversed. Rosenberg and Sutton-Smith interpret their results in terms of Hill's system of types of conditioning based on dependency drive and their situational determiners. In terms of the tenets described one could predict what was observed by us, namely, that the DZOS, especially the girls, would be somewhat less impulsive and anxious than the DZSS's. The parental and social attitudes of others outlined a few paragraphs earlier, which are encountered by the children from same-sex pairs, together with the great magnitude of their competing interests provide the possibility for frustrations and concerns that could raise the anxiety level of the same-sex fraternals above that of the DZOS's.

If the comparison is shifted to one between twins and singletons and it is asked whether twins tend to have a more stressful early existence than singleton sibs, one might, if he uses the Rosenberg and Sutton-Smith tenets, have to argue that there is more conflict in the life of the twin, since co-twin similarity should intensify the effect of competing interests. Twins seem provided with compensations, however, they suffer no dethronement, as is typical for first-born singletons. There is generally more effort made to treat twins impartially than is the case for singletons. There is much prestige in being a twin, especially an identical one. Twins are conditioned from the first to child and adult associates. The twin sib, then, although a competitor, may even very early satisfy curiosity or novelty interests—among other things the twin furnishes entertainment for the sib and finally support. In the face of these considerations, the MZ's could probably be expected to be under less early stress because of the sib than a child with a singleton sib close in age. A basic concern of identicals, according to von Bracken's (1934) evidence, is just keeping abreast of the twin, i.e., not outstripping him. This, since it is usually easy to do, may not raise the identicals' anxiety load above that of singleton sibs generally, in spite of extensively overlapping needs and desires. In the main, the identical twins at school support each other and the social rewards are greatest when the children are together and recognized as twins. This our subjects were even able to verbalize. In the light of all of the considerations sketched, few signs of stress levels in identical twins above those for singletons would be expected. This expectation was confirmed. Since girls tend typically to socialize earlier than boys and the factors that combine to bring this about may be greater especially in identical twin girls (these children are objects of much social interest), twin girls can be expected to be more sociable, on the bility of the group of young identical boys, it is suspected, stems in average, than singleton girls. In contrast, the rather low general socia- part from whatever it is that makes young boys less sociable than girls and in part from the presence in the identical male twin group of a number of slow learners. These slow-learning children would have less to offer others, in addition to building an accretion of social interests more slowly than would more talented children, and would doubtless feel more comfortable operating in familiar and less taxing surroundings.

DZSS fraternals can be expected to, and the subjects of the present study did, show more stress than identicals. These co-twins may be quite different from each other temperamentally, are probably treated less impartially, and tend to be compared unmercifully. The favorable factors that commonly obtain for twins probably scarcely compensate, when the DZSS's are compared with singletons, for the complications just recited. The anticipations for the DZSS's were realized. They did exhibit fewer differences from matched singletons than did the MZ's. The male fraternals did manifest some slight signs of more stress. They were judged, for instance, to be less talkative and less cheerful (Table 42), and dwelt more in their CAT stories on unpleasant mother-child interactions. It must be remembered, however, a considerable number of these boys were adjusting to being separated from their twin at school. These boys hence may have been unduly shy and insecure. The DZOS girls, in contrast to the boys, deviated from singletons, on the average, much as identical girls did, only less markedly perhaps. The DZSSf's, as explained earlier, tended to be more sociable than singleton controls but showed no difference in the way of competitiveness and emotionality. The adjustment of the DZOS's, relative to that of singletons, has already been discussed (Tables 57, 58, and 59).

In summary, let it be said that the lot of the twin does not appear to be a particularly difficult one, although the stress experienced does seem to vary with the type of twin and, no doubt, with the type of singleton with whom he is compared. Difference in age has been demonstrated to influence materially the stresses between siblings for example (Koch 1956a, 1960).

TWIN PREMATURITY AND PERSONALITY TRAITS

Since prematurity has been included in the twinning gestalt, we have not tried to deal with this variable systematically in this monograph. A paper dealing with prematurity in twins has already been published (Koch 1964). In one set of nine personality traits, however, known on the basis of an earlier analysis to be little influenced by the social-class variable, we have ignored social class and have conducted a two- or three-way analysis of variance in which one variable explored was maturity level at birth. The other variables are the usual ones of zygosity, sex, and sex of sib (see Tables 60 and 61).

It seems, as was apparent in the prematurity study (Koch 1964), than the slightly premature group (weight 4½ to 5½ pounds) tended in the early elementary school years to be most aggressive, gregarious, involved with adults, talkative, and exhibitionistic. These results agree with those yielded by the prematurity study, but this is perhaps to be expected, since the subjects for the former investigation were selected from among the twin subjects.

At any rate, the above constellation makes one wonder whether slightly early birth may not usually be the safest for twins. If the children are very premature, they are likely to be victims of both inadequate development and of complications that, in themselves, lie back of precocious arrival. On the other hand, two large term-size infants may produce physiological problems for the mother who carries them, as well as obstetrical hazards when they are being born. Congruent with this hypothesis is the observation that a number of term MZ's, especially the males, appear to have been presented with difficulties at birth. (See also Table 6 for evidence of a high incidence of defects among the term MZ's.) One may note that among males, the largest proportion were born at term and among females, the largest proportion were premature according to a weight criterion, and thus conclude that what is being witnessed in the trait gestalt described is a sex difference rather than the effects of pre- and perinatal complications. But in the prematurity study, in which a matched group procedure was followed and sex was one of the bases of the matching, the findings conform to those described in Tables 60 and 61. Also, of course, the analysis of variance procedure that resulted in the data set forth in these tables enables us to look into the matter of sex and birth weight interactions. It is striking that in 18 out of 24 series (six traits, four groups) presented in the first six traits in Table 60, the only slightly premature twins from same-sex pairs scored highest in the qualities analyzed—i.e., the latter children were, of the three birth-maturity-level groups, the most aggressive, gregarious, exhibitionistic, talkative, and involved with adults. Degree of precocity of advent seems related most consistently to the first four characteristics. Interestingly, involvement with children was, according to the teachers' ratings, not related to developmental level at birth. In the SSf's, femininity increased with degree of maturity at birth— i.e., the girls were more true to type when their early development was most normal. Earlier birth seemed to result in more male-typical or hostile behavior. Perhaps all this means is that prematures are more likely to be "spoiled." On the other hand, it could be that exposure to much stimulation at an early age, when responses tend to be diffuse and emotional in character, results in the generalization or fixing of these patterns of response.

The striking finding that those of moderately early birth tend to be more involved with adults and more socially aggressive could be interpreted as an effect of more contacts by the baby with his mother in the very early weeks of life and perhaps of more stimulation (see Koch 1964). This interpretation seems plausible because, in relation to the term group, the mildly premature infants would probably, because of their handicap, be the recipients of more ministration, concern, and stimulation, in addition perhaps to experiencing an easier birth (see Meier 1964). The slightly premature, on the other hand, it is thought might also have more contacts with the parents in the early weeks of postnatal life, as well as be exposed to a more stimulating world, in contrast to the extremely premature who may need to be retained in the hospital and under incubator monotony, because of likely complications, longer than their simple developmental age deficiency would lead one to expect. Those twins delivered somewhat before or near term may also have more opportunity to form those very early attachments that seem (according to research with animals) to be particularly potent and durable (see Hess 1959; Denenberg 1960, on imprinting). Also, because of generalization, it could be anticipated that they would become more demanding or expecting of attention. Of course, the reader must realize that our interpretation of the observed trait gestalt of these slightly prematurely born children is largely hunch. We know, for example, very little about the effects of very early social contacts upon human beings, i.e., the information we have is based largely on studies of the behavior of simple animal forms. The chief point of this section, at any rate, is to stress the view that there is probably a network of interlocking physical and social forces that produce the observation described.

SUMMARY

1. All of the twin groups gave evidence of the pair members being closer to each other generally (playing more together, sharing friends and possessions more and with less friction, etc.) than were matched singleton sibs. The mean degree of closeness in the various groups was in the order MZ, DZSS, and DZOS.

2. Twins from like-sex dyads seemed more often to believe that their parents were impartial than did parallel singleton brothers and sisters. The DZOS twins deviated significantly from the other twins in the lesser relative frequency with which they maintained this view. Nevertheless the DZOS's were less inclined than singletons to the opinion that their parents showed favoritism. Our data, in fact, do not support a current belief that twins tend to be unduly jealous.

3. Twin rivalry seemed greater among fraternals than identicals. The MZm's, for example, were rated significantly less competitive and insistent on their rights than were the DZSSm's. But there was no evidence in the data that the DZSSf's differed significantly in rivalry and competitiveness from the MZf's.

4. All of the groups of twins were judged to alibi less, on the average, than matched singletons. Could this mean that when interact-

ing with their chief youthful companion, the twins had found defenses of a semirational sort relatively ineffectual? Or did the twins merely feel less need to be on the defensive?

5. The girl twins from same-sex pairs were assessed as more mature and effective socially than parallel singletons, but the males from like-sex dyads, especially the MZm's, seemed more withdrawn, shy, subdued, and socially apprehensive, as well as less adequate in speech, less original and possessed of fewer interests than parallel nontwin sibs. How much of the relative lack of aggressiveness and sociability of the MZm's stemmed from mechanisms inherent in the twins, resemblances in temperament, greater similarity of treatment, and so forth, and how much from a lower IQ is a question. It is notable in this connection that intraclass r's for female pair-member closeness for the two zygosity groups differed (being larger for MZ's than DZSS's, and thus at least consistent with, but not very convincing evidence for a genetic interpretation). But the males showed no significant zygosity group disparity. This suggests the operation of some nongenetic variables.

6. Twin girls, especially the MZ's, tended to be judged more feminine than matched singletons, whereas the twin boys and singletons generally showed no significant disparity in masculinity.

7. No marked zygosity group differences in strength of directly expressed sex preferences were observed among SS pairs, although there was some indication that the MZm's were more effeminate in behavior than DZSSm's, and the MZf's more feminine than singleton controls. Surprisingly, the DZOS's did not differ significantly from matched singletons, on the average, in any of the measures of sex-typical behavior or sex preference.

8. The fraternal twins whose sib was not similar in sex seemed, however, to have had a slight and consistent (but not statistically significant) tempering effect on each others' sex role learning and attitudes. Each sex group among the DZOS's tended to show slightly less strongly, on the average, the sex-typical behavior that those fraternal twins exhibited whose sib was of their own sex.

9. Among the DZOS's the girl, although she usually was the second-born and had the smaller birth weight, tended at school age to be the dominant member of the pair in social matters. The boys appeared to struggle valiantly against this dominance but apparently felt less self-assured than did the girls.

10. Both sexes from unlike-sex twin pairs appeared more controlled emotionally, less expressive and more constricted in behavior at school than did parallel singletons. Compared with the DZSS twins, however, the former group had a higher average rating in cheerfulness. In their CAT stories, on the other hand, the DZOS's dealt more than did the DZSS's with hostility, catastrophe, negative themes, and with unpleasant mother-child interactions. This finding may well reflect greater anxiety in the DZOS group centering around parent, sib, and school relations, although other measures suggest otherwise.

11. The DZOS boys less often asserted that they liked school than did the DZSSm's, a fact which, it is suspected, stems from the feeling of the DZOSf's that their sisters were more approved in the school setting. The OS twin girls tended to be both more critical and protective of their brothers than vice versa. The girls less frequently expressed the wish to have their brothers in their class at school.

12. The DZOS's constantly tried not to let their twins outstrip them. This was particularly noticeable in the boys who, accordingly, we believe, were rated as slightly more ambitious and possessed of wider interests than the DZSS males.

13. None of the twin groups appeared deficient, as compared with singletons, in the number of playmates they listed, nor in indicated child contacts, but the MZm's were believed by their teachers to be less gregarious and less good leaders than the DZSSm's or comparable male singletons. In contrast, girls of both zygosities, although differing little from each other, were assessed as more sociable and socially effective than were matched singletons—being a twin seemed to facilitate the girls' socialization. The DZSSf's, it may be significant, were judged to be slightly more aggressive, original, and planful than the MZf's.

14. All the twins listed proportionally more same-age playmates than did singleton sibs, a condition that, coupled with the fact the pair members tended to play with the same children, could restrict the experience range.

15. The twins, in the main, did not seem less involved with adults than did singletons, as some have alleged them to be. The MZf's averaged slightly higher than DZSSf's on involvement with adults.

16. It is suspected that there were more individuals with signs of mild brain impairment in the MZ group than among other twins and more among males than females. Possibly, then, neurological lack

rather than special social stimulation deficiences lies back of the less able and less dynamic character the MZm's were described as possessing. This is not to be taken to imply that the intertwin reactions of this group were not also less stressful because of co-twin similarity in temperament and ability. Since the identical co-twins of both sexes appear to give each other good support, society's attitude toward the girls, and possibly the nature of the creatures, may result in their readier socialization. At any rate, being a twin seemed to present boys with more difficulties than it did girls.

17. The slightly prematurely born children seemed to be more gregarious, aggressive, exhibitionistic, talkative, and involved with adults than were those of very precocious birth. Involvement with children was not correlated with level of maturity at birth.

CHAPTER VII

The Effect of Closeness and Dominance in Twins and Twin Separation at School

CLOSENESS IN TWINS AND TWIN ATTITUDES

PROBLEMS

The problem of the influence on the development of a young individual of a very close constant relationship with one person of his own age is a general sociological one and not of interest merely to the student of twins. It has been singled out for some attention because concern is frequently expressed about twins lest their devotion to each other be damaging to their social development. These are a few of the fears that have been voiced: (1) If the twins are very close, this will isolate them from other children and possibly even from adults. Since they will prefer each other's company, they will be less responsive to other individuals. (2) If the twins are very close, they will be speech- and hand-preference models to each other and the result may be to retard proper learning in the named areas or to produce deviate learning. (3) If the twins are very comfortable, this may restrict the range of their contacts and interests, thus making them less experienced, original, curious, intelligent, and possessed of less adequate vocabulary. (4) If very close to each other, the twins may be less influenced by their parents or other adult models and guides in the matter of social and moral attitudes, and of social skills. (5) Partly emphasizing the positive side of the relationship is the view that if the twins are very close, this should make them less selfish when dealing with each other, less hostile, and less competitive—attitudes that

124

may be generalized to their relations with others. The lesser competitiveness may, on the other hand, result also in less striving, in less emotionality, in less activeness, and in greater security. (6) If the twins are of the same sex and very devoted, this may strengthen their identification with their own sex.

Both the premises and conclusions in the above propositions need careful examination, because they refer to conditions that may or may not obtain or do not follow. Basic questions are whether having a twin actually does tend to weaken the relationship to the parents or weakens it at the most crucial points—i.e., reduces the admiration for the parents, the feeling of trust in them when difficulty arises, the desire to be like the parents, the need to conform to get parent approval or to please a loved one. On the other hand, it is possible that the twin sib strengthens the child's ties with the parent, since the sib becomes essentially a part of the self and reinforces the typical reactions to the parents. But twins may support each other in resistance to authority as well as reinforce conformity attitudes. The demonstration of the usual trend of the effects of closeness and the discovery of the conditions under which the trend varies is, then, much needed.

To obtain an answer to the most fundamental question—namely, that of the nature of differences between the influence of closeness with an adult in early life and closeness with a child—it probably would be desirable, in order to maximize forces, to separate the two experiences. The potency and bias of an undiluted relation with a warm, accepting adult is often revealed in the only child. The power and molding force of a very close child relationship have, on the other hand, seldom been explored intensively, and they are usually blurred by a close adult relationship that the child has at the same time. A very rare study by Anna Freud and Sophie Dann (1951) of a small group of children who lost their parents during the war and were shifted about together from one detention camp to another comes near being what we believe will be the most illuminating approach. A study of twin relationships represents a sort of intermediate design but, unfortunately, provides data that are, accordingly, difficult to interpret. At any rate, the values involved in the issues described are significant ones and overlap with those that should be considered when deciding on child-spacing in the family.

On the parents' side, there is the matter of whether those who have twins can be as giving and assuring, when two children instead of one clamor for attention and love. Are parents more involved with their twins than parents tend to be with their singleton children, and are they given more opportunity to learn to practice justice and basic impartiality, as well as to become very sensitive to child needs by seeing them mirrored twice in most situations.

It will, in addition to clarifying the issues listed above, be important to determine through a study of properly selected families with twins the effect on the latter of various forms and contents of family teaching and parental attitudes. What are the ramifications of constant urging or pressuring of the twins to be different, to be themselves, or, conversely, to be alike and devoted? Of course, this teaching can not be divorced from a consideration of the motivations of the parents who do the pressuring. If they feel that the production of twins reflects to their glory, they may, among other things, try to make the twins conspicuous, dress them alike, give them alliterative names, keep them together, and remind them they are similar. Some parents, in contrast, may, simply in their effort to be just, try to treat the pair members as nearly similarly as possible, even in the face of fundamental differences in the children. Furthermore, the question of the sequelae of different attitudes and expectations relative to twins obtaining in the general culture surrounding them must not be ignored.

Not only, then, is it important for us to realize the complexity of the problem of intertwin and twin-adult relations, but also to meditate about what is revealed by our present measure of closeness, as well as by the indicators for other conditions or traits involved in the various relations explored. Our measure of so-called closeness is, as will be recalled (see chapter 6), a count of the number of questions out of twelve in which a preference for the co-twin over others was expressed by the child. Now such a measure may be suspect because the children interviewed, being very young, may not have known their feelings or they may have said what they believed the examiner wanted to hear or what they thought they should tell. The presence of these attitudes in massive degrees we doubt. The twins were obviously trained some in family loyalty. As the children's confidence was gained, however, we had the impression their remarks were, in the main, spontaneous and did reflect their feelings, at least at the time of response. How abiding their feelings were is a question. When the children were able to give reasons for their attitudes, the reasons usually had point and seemed to a substantial degree convincing. Whatever the measure of so-called closeness reflects (see chapter 6), it does seem rather reliable (corrected split-half $r = .93$).

We do wonder, too, to what extent a given closeness score always represents the same feeling or motivation dimension. It appears to us that closeness, as measured, may have a range of casts. It may be rooted in enjoyment of sib companionship, in fear, in dependence on the sib for leadership and defense, in need for a satellite, in the desire to keep abreast of the sib, or in the striving to maximize the prestige that being a twin tends to give. These attitudes, if they exist, may have diverse relationships with the variables studied, relationships that may even be opposed. Our observations on closeness, then, may be viewed at best as a sort of first probe into an important but shadowy sociological area.

The following is an enumeration of the specific questions to which the present analyses will be addressed. Since many of these were not problems we had in mind when the twin study was planned, the analyses can not be so sharply focused as might be desirable. Ours has been chiefly a correlational approach, although the attempted extensive comparison of twins and singletons has relevance. Hundreds of r's were computed but only those large enough to be significant are included in Table 65. The insignificant ones, however, must not be completely ignored. It is well to know where the relations are significant and where not, i.e., these differences may be lawful.

Are the twins who are gene-identical closer than fraternals who are not? Are MZ's more similar to each other in degree of closeness—i.e., more reciprocating of this feeling for any one of a number of reasons —than are fraternals? Does a difference in sex affect the closeness and quality of relation between the co-twins? In other words, are the girl twins closer to each other than the boys? Are twins who have been separated at school and encouraged to go their own ways less close than those who have been kept together and whose twinness has been emphasized? Do twins who are most devoted show signs of being less involved with adults? Is the level of closeness exhibited by the twins related positively or negatively to their interest in and extent of involvement with other children? Do twins who are most compatible tend to be more generous, sociable, noncombative, nonrivalrous, and more understanding, not only with the sib but generally? Do twins who are closest tend to have less skill in leadership, less drive, ambition, and competitive spirit? Does the speech form of the closest twins tend to be less adequate than that of the pairs who are not so close? Are more left-handed children to be noted among the closer? Do the more devoted tend to be less able, less informed, less original, less broadly interested, and possessed of a more limited vocabulary?

RESULTS

It is clear from Tables 26, 27, and 38 that zygosity, sex, and sex of sib all are related to closeness. The MZ's, who are the most similar in physique and physiology and probably in temperament (see chapter 6), are closer than fraternals, even the ones from same-sex pairs. We are not implying that the greater gene similarity of the MZ's is alone responsible for their greater closeness, although this hypothesis may well be entertained. It may be, on the other hand, that the MZ's are expected to be closer than are fraternals and are treated as if they were, or in such a way as to make them closer—e.g., they are given a larger area of common experience.

If we compute the intraclass r's for the closeness scores of co-twins in the various same-sex subgroups of twins, we find no zygosity group differences in the r's in the male (r for both identicals and same-sex fraternals $= .41$ [Table 62]). This finding would not be expected if genetic likeness were a very important determinant of closeness. The identical female co-twins reciprocated, however, or resembled each other somewhat more in closeness than did the DZSSf's. What this sex difference means we do not know. It is notable that in the DZOS's, the r between the brother's and sister's closeness score is not only insignificant but even slightly negative ($-.035$).

If we study the correlation between closeness and sex preference scores, we observe no significant r between the former variables nor between scores describing closeness and masculinity or femininity of behavior in the male and female subgroups (Table 63), except that the degree of femininity of behavior of DZOS males, as mentioned above, correlated nearly significantly with the measure of closeness to their sister. We did obtain also a significant correlation in the SS male groups between degree of difference in closeness and degree of difference in sex preference (Table 64), i.e., those children reciprocating in closeness seemed more like each other in degree of sex preference.

It is true, moreover, that the MZm's, who were very close, expressed a stronger male preference than did the DZSSm's (see chapter 6 and Table 49). That in the DZOS group the degree of closeness to the sib and degree of feminine behavior were correlated to a near significant degree is in line with the trend hinted at in the data reported on pages 109–16, which suggest that the boys in the DZOS group were more bent in their behavior toward their sister's pattern than vice versa. The traits with which the closeness score of the DZOSm's were correlated tended to be those in which girls seem to excel. The sex alignment of the girl in the OS group appears to be unrelated, on the other hand, with the closeness she alleged she felt toward her brother (Table 63). Since the girls at the age of school entrance tend to be the dominant members of the OS pairs, it is probably not surprising they were less, or little, swayed by the male-oriented values of their brothers.

It is noteworthy that among the females from same-sex pairs, quite contrary to males, there was very little relation between closeness and sex preference (Table 63). The girl twins from same-sex groups tended to be closer than the male twins (Tables 26 and 27), a finding in line with the typically feminine characteristic of emphasis on interpersonal relationships and concerns. Perhaps it is the smaller range in their closeness scores that resulted in the lower r's that obtained in this group between the former measures and various behavior indexes including that for sex preference. Although the variability in closeness score for DZOSf's was greater than that for the female twins in same-sex pairs, the fact, as mentioned earlier, that the DZOSf girls were, as a rule, the dominant member of the pair probably kept them from being particularly responsive to their brothers as a model.

Now if it is asked whether the devotion of co-twins facilitates or interferes with sociability and leadership generally, the following are relevant findings. It has already been noted that the MZm's, who were as a group very close, did exhibit less sociability and leadership than did the other SS twins (Table 40). This trend was opposite to that observed for the girls and mixed-sex groups. No relation was evident in any of the groups between twin intimacy and number of playmates listed, and only just barely significant positive r's were to be noted between the twin intimacy score and ratings on gregariousness or extent of involvement with children. A not quite significant r of $-.14$ was obtained in the instance of the total group between closeness and social apprehensiveness—i.e., the closer tend to be more confident in social situations. Although most of the correlations in Table 65 are very low, they tend to intimate that the closer children were judged generally more affectionate, responsible, and jealous. In addition, the DZOS boys who were closest to their sisters tended to be judged more poised and effective socially. What significant correlations there are in Table 65 seem, then, to indicate a positive, rather than negative, direction in the relation between closeness and sociability variables, thus suggesting that closeness did not tend to restrict social experiences. That the MZm group seemed to present an exception to the trend may stem from the lower mean intelligence of this group.

The appropriate correlations, too, give us little evidence of a strong relation between closeness and speech behavior (Table 65), except in the MZf's where there is a hint that the more devoted tended to have the poorer speech form. There is an intimation, also, that the closer the children were to each other the less likely they were to stutter. It would not be too difficult to rationalize this result.

Not only, then, does the closeness score seem to be virtually uncorrelated with measures of sociability, but the data in Table 65 do not, in the main, suggest that the closer twins tend to be less able. The r between closeness and PMA IQ, ratings of originality, and of number of interests were, with one exception, insignificant. In the case of the DZSSm's, a barely significant positive r was observed between some of the PMA subtest scores and closeness, thus indicating a trend, if anything, in the opposite direction to the one feared. And among the DZOSf's, there seemed to be a borderline positive relationship between closeness and number of interests.

If our attention is now shifted to outside forces that might encourage closeness between co-twins, it is to be noted that, when the mothers were older at the birth of the twins, the closer their co-twin daughters tended to be to each other (Table 65). These older mothers had typically struggled long and hard to have children and were, in the main, warm and devoted. They, doubtless, tended to encourage closeness in their daughters either through direct teaching or through the model they presented.

That those twins who were placed in the same class at school tended to be closer to each other is also of some interest. In this instance we suspect strongly that the schools may have had a policy of not separating the co-twins of the closest pairs. In the MZm's a reverse relation seemed to obtain. The problem will be discussed further in a later section.

In the face of all of the above findings there seems little cause for alarm over the effects of twin closeness, and we wonder whether the few significant *r*'s (usually just barely significant at that) are more than would be obtained by chance. About 500 *r*'s were computed and only 42 (not much above the 25 expected by chance) were found significant at the 5 per cent level or better. Probably these few, small, barely significant *r*'s based on the total twin population are the most worthy of attention. The somewhat sketchy picture for the DZOSm's seemed, however, particularly meaningful to us because of the internal consistency of the gestalt. The males in this group who professed to be closest to their sisters tended to be judged less submissive, more confident socially, more popular, more involved with children, more affectionate, and somewhat effeminate in attitude (all characteristics in which the females tended to excel). More of these boys, furthermore, tended to be right-handed, a trait females also tend typically to exhibit somewhat more frequently than do males.

The closer DZOS girls, on the other hand, seemed not much distinguished by qualities with a male cast. All we observed was that the closer among them appeared to have more interests and to talk more and more correctly, as well as to portray mother-child relationships less favorably in their stories. Since girls tend to be less strong and active than boys, these girls may have had to step up their verbal efforts to compensate for their strength and agility lacks.

Twin compatibility we could not relate consistently to any measure of involvement with parents (it had been opined that the closer the twins were to each other the less involved they might be with the parents) except that the DZOSf's who were closest to their brothers described in their CAT stories fewer pleasant mother-child interactions. It is well to remember, however, that, with the exception of the MZf's, the twins did not show themselves to be more or less involved with adults than were singleton controls.

The more devoted DZSSm's seemed to include in their CAT stories more father figures, and the DZOSf's, as just mentioned, to describe fewer pleasant interactions between child and mother. Whether the latter *r*'s reflect anxiety over relationship with parents in the groups mentioned, or more pleasure in them, or greater concern with them, or not any of these, is not clear. We wonder whether in the second observation these DZOS girls thought their mother was siding with their brother and consequently felt less friendly toward her. Girls typically use more mother figures in their stories and these usually in pleasant activities with children.

When the gestalts in our data, then, are surveyed, we see little need for concern over possible restricting effects of twin devotion. If anything, co-twin compatibility appeared to be positively associated with positive social and cognitive attitudes, instead of with intellectual and social lack, as has been alleged. Of course, our subjects were young. Whether a lifetime of great intimacy with the twin would result in the same conformation is a question. It should be pointed out in this connection that Shields (1962) discovered that separated and nonseparated identicals did not differ in marriage rate. Kallmann and Bondy (1952), too, found no excess of single individuals among twins, a fact that does not support the view that twin compatibility results in such social crippling that it tends to prevent marriage. The degree of success of the marriages studied was, unfortunately, not estimated by the aforementioned authors. Shields (1962) did, however, note that the childhood leader in a twin pair tended to marry first and that the identical co-twins who were reared apart tended to differ more from each other in marriage age and family size than did the nonseparated identical controls. There was no significant difference in mean family size, however, between Shields' separated a nonseparated groups.

The quality of the relationship between co-twins along lines other than closeness, and the educational implications deserves some thought. Two of the issues receive attention in the following sections.

SUMMARY

1. Identical co-twins tended to be closer to each other than fraternals from like-sex pairs, and fraternals from like-sex pairs closer than fraternal co-twins who were unlike in sex.
2. Girl co-twins tended to be more compatible than did boys.
3. There was no evidence in the data of a strong negative relation

between pair-member closeness and degree of involvement with adults. If anything, there was a positive relation between these two variables.

4. Support is lacking for the view that the more compatible co-twins tend to have fewer playmates and lesser social skills. Indeed a slight, barely significant, positive relation between these latter qualities and closeness seemed to obtain. Among the DZOSm's, co-twin compatibility was positively associated with popularity, involvement with children, and social confidence.

5. Reciprocity in the closeness level of the pair members in the DZOS group was negligibly related to co-twin preference for their own sex, but in same-sex male pairs those reciprocating most in feeling of closeness tended to resemble each other most in sex preference. Significantly, degree of sib closeness of the males in the DZOS pairs was correlated with a small degree of shading of behavior toward the feminine. No parallel relationship was observable in the DZOSf's.

6. Only in the MZf's was a low negative correlation noted between co-twin closeness and speech form, as judged by the teacher. The more devoted the DZSSm co-twins, the higher was the number of syntax errors they tended to display in their cat stories, but the relation was reversed in the DZSSf's.

7. Among the DZOSm's, closeness and right-hand preference were positively associated, but in all other groups no relation between the hand preference and twin devotion variables was apparent.

8. No positive association between IQ or rated originality and twin closeness was glimpsed.

9. Devotion between pair members from like-sex girl pairs tended to be positively associated with mother's age at the birth of the twins.

10. Lack of stuttering showed a low relation to co-twin closeness; i.e., the closer the twins the less likely they were to stutter.

11. In most of the traits scrutinized and most of the twin groups examined, the correlation between co-twin compatibility and social attitudes and skills was insignificant; but, when twins and singletons are compared, more of significance is revealed (see chapter 6). These twin-singleton differences may, however, not be functions of closeness.

12. We have seen few grounds for alarm over the relation between intertwin closeness attitudes generally and the social development of the children.

TWIN SEPARATION AT SCHOOL

VIEWS RELATIVE TO SEPARATION

In the previous section the common practice of separating twins at school was mentioned as a course of action for combating possible undesirable effects of twin closeness. It seems well to comment on and summarize here thoughts and data bearing on this procedure. There have been endless assertions about the hazards of not keeping twin-pair members apart at school, and the time for disjoining is usually affirmed to be when the children enter school. It is a common belief that twins on entrance to school have, because of their youth, fabulous powers of adjustment and that dissociation from the sib for a few hours each day will be no more serious than separation of the child from the home situation during school hours. It is maintained that, while in any case, the twin pair members will tend to be rivalrous, be concerned about favoritism and being cheated, be given to indulging in self comparisons, and so forth, all this is intensified by the twins being enrolled in the same class and subjected to the constant contrasting that goes on at the hands of their teachers, classmates, and school associates. Even small failures suffered by only one member of the pair will tend to produce a double wound. Other educators, in contrast, defend the view that although disjoining avoids some of the ills just described, it does not eliminate the child's concern about his status relative to his sib. The separated child tends to wonder whether the sib does not have the better teacher, the more interesting and effective program, the more fascinating classmates, and so on. The child has no way of checking on matters of this sort in the firsthand, direct fashion he is privileged to use when he is in the same class as the sib. Then the differences he senses are at least not ballooned by fantasy rooted in vague, nebulous fears. On the positive side of the argument for keeping the twins together is the contention that the twins' rivalrous attitudes serve as stimulants to achievement. This is thought especially valuable for males in the OS pairs, who tend to take less gracefully to school than do their sisters. It is, in addition, maintained that the comfort, support, and companionship sibs can give each other when associating at close range is, in large measure, lost if the sibs are kept apart. Team play then is impossible. True, the antagonists argue, but while sibs can support each other in good works, they can also support each other in mischief. And this in some cases can prove devastating and demoralizing. In rebuttal, however, it is emphasized that, since it is not improbable that the mischief is motivated by attitudes learned chiefly before entering school, it is questionable whether these attitudes would escape expression fully if the children were separated—an argument countered by the assertion that the copying of the bad example would not be unmotivated by the conditions promoting rivalry and jealousy that are intensified when the children are face to face. There are further ramifications to the argument with the emphasis placed not so much on goals as on means. One group of thinkers, for instance, defends the policy of separating the twin-pair members when they seem to be different personalities (e.g., twins of unlike sex), and the other group of educators, when they feel the twins are most alike. Both positions aim to preserve individuality and comfort with the self. There is little doubt but that all contentions contain a measure of truth. But what the trend of the balance of forces is likely to be is not known and, of course, this trend would not indicate the balance for each pair of twins, in any case, and routine handling of the matter would not seem justified. Unfortunately, there are few studies available to help us discover even the usual short-term effects in the two educational plans. Actually, longitudinal long-term studies are needed most. And it is particularly important to try to proceed in such a way that one is helped to decide what is cause and what is effect, as the variables whose relationships are explored are usually interacting. For example, if ability differences are observed, one might discover that children who differ in school skills have been enrolled in different classes by the school because of their ability differences, rather than, as it was hoped, because the segregation would deprive the twins of the motivations that would tend to result in fruitless efforts on their part toward equalization of skills. The employment of identical twins in an investigation of separation effects may be helpful. Some will want to assume, if disjoining is correlated with difference, that it is responsible for the disparity, because the genes of the pair are identical and thus furnish control of one large area of forces. But it is possible for the twins to be very uneven in capacity because of differential, unfavorable prenatal conditions and birth trauma. The control of genetic variables does not touch the problem of control of those pre- and postnatal environmental forces that result, for example, in abiding neurophysiological differences.

Our hope that we might be able to gather some interpretable data bearing on the question of the consequences of separating or not separating the twins at school was blasted by the lack of consistency in their experience—i.e., some pairs were kept apart in the kindergarten but placed together in the first grade, and the reverse was true for others. Very few children had the same type of placement during even their total half, or year-and-a-half period in school. It seemed that the status of some was shifted every few months. The grounds for shifting were various, some quite independent of any characteristics of the children. One school, for instance, had two kindergartens, thus permitting twin separation, but only one first grade into which the children could be fitted on the basis of their academic achievement or ability. In another school this situation was reversed. In some instances the children were segregated in the public school kindergarten, but on entering first grade in a parochial school to which they transferred, they were as a matter of school policy placed in the same class. Either before or after watching their twins' adjustment at school, some parents insisted on the children being separated, whereas other parents were adamant that the twins be kept together. In several instances, when the children were separated, they behaved so autistically for so long that the schools capitulated and returned them to the same class. Sometimes when the twin-pair members in the same class proved very difficult to control, the result was a prompt decision by the school to place them in different classes.

FINDINGS

A 2 by 3 X^2 between separation and social class was insignificant, thus suggesting that the practice of keeping or not keeping the twins apart was not rooted in the educational philosophies that distinguished schools in which upper, middle, and lower class children were enrolled. In 63 per cent of the cases, the identical pair members were permitted to be classmates, as were 69 per cent of the fraternal pairs of the same sex, and 53 per cent of those of opposite sex (Table 66); —in other words, the trend in school policy apparently was favorable to nonseparation. There was no significant zygosity group difference between the girls, but for males the practice of separating did vary slightly with ovularity. In the males, 61 per cent of the MZ's were placed in different classes, but only 39 per cent of the DZSSm's were (Table 66). This is a surprising reversal of the trend noted for females, in which 12 per cent of the identicals and 24 per cent of the fraternals were placed in different classes. In both zygosity groups, sex seemed to be grounds for keeping the co-twins apart ($X^2 = 7.03$; $p = .01$), that is, the boy twins were more frequently enrolled in different classes than were girls. More of the females, as stated, escaped separation and, in the main, they thoroughly approved being classmates. It was unanticipated that more DZSSf's than MZf's would indicate, as they did, that they wanted the sib in their class, but this difference proved statistically insignificant (Table 67). Although the MZ's of both sexes wished for nonseparation with about the same frequency, there was a clear-cut difference in the fraternals. Thirty-three per cent of the DZSSm's said they liked to be in a different class from the sib, whereas only 6 per cent of the DZSSf's did (Table 67). Parallel per cents for the DZOS's were 42 and 53. In other words, the wish to be separated at school was much higher among the opposite-sex fraternal pairs than among the same-sex, and among the fraternals, the OS girls seemed more rejecting of their brothers than vice versa. This is congruent with evidence presented in chapter 6.

The total picture sketched above is a bit difficult to interpret. It may be that the sex difference is due merely to a cultural attitude which assumes boys are tougher than girls and can be treated accordingly. The fact, however, that somewhat more of the MZm's were separated than DZSSm's may have resulted from the schools' appreciation of the MZm's specific tendencies to withdrawal and dependence rather than of general co-twin similarity. In other words, the separation of the MZm co-twins may have represented an effort to break up their great dependence on each other. It is possible, too, since the MZm group contained a number of near retardates, that some of the SS were not alert enough to reach out to others than the sib or to offer each other much socially. The school might, hence, have thought it well to provide the slow-learning MZm's with companions who might be more stimulating than the sib. In addition, in a few cases a suspicion is justified that the boy twins were separated because of the support in mischief they tended to give each other. Their jealousy of each other in the school situation apparently provoked in some cases much unconstructive attention seeking. Also, since their activities had been controlled in great detail at home some of the boys seemed to let loose in school the hostility that the home restraints had generated. Hence it seemed advisable to separate them.

It is problematical, however, whether the MZ's, who tend to be so similar, ought, as some insist, routinely to be separated on entering school. Enrollment as a pupil in the kindergarten or first grade alone requires major adjustments, and when this is coupled with learning suddenly to get along without the companionship of an individual who has played a role in the experiences of almost every waking minute, the practice seems to be requiring much. It is probably true, as some remind us, that the longer the children remain together the greater may become the association complex that has to be sundered if the twins are ever going to be able to go their own ways. On the other hand, the adjustment demanded of the separated MZ twins at school entrance, since they are, among other things, basically or genetically similar, seems more severe than that which devoted wives have to learn to master when they lose their husbands. A more appropriate parallel perhaps for the sudden separation of twins at school, since the identicals typically have never been separated from birth, would be the loss of an arm or leg, because, as here, every experience must seem incomplete and strange without the sib a part of it. Now if before they enter school, the identicals have been kept apart much, encouraged to be independent and to make their own friends, then probably being placed in different classes or even being sent to different educational institutions would not be traumatic. But a history of the aforementioned type of experience was unfortunately seldom uncovered by us. Among the cases revealing severe adjustment difficulty were two instances of extreme and persistent autistic-like behavior. This condition cleared up when the children were placed in the same class. When one of the little boys was asked what he was thinking of when, for months, he had spent most of the school day gazing out of the window, he answered promptly, "I am always worrying about where my brother is." In contrast is another pair of slow-learning MZ boys who when separated were, because of the relatively low ability, completely out of step with the children with whom each was placed. Thus they were getting neither stimulation nor support. They might have risked more social participation had they been kept together. At any rate, they would have felt more comfortable at school.

Apparently there is considerable inclination to place the DZOS twin-pair members in different classes. About half of the pairs were so treated (Table 66). Since many of the boys from the OS pairs appeared to be severely henpecked, it may have been desirable to get some of them out from under their sister's domination. It is interesting that, in spite of this dominance situation, eleven males wanted to be classmates of their sisters and only eight did not, whereas nine females gave an affirmative answer to the question concerning their desire to have the sib in their class and ten gave a negative one (Table 67). In only five pairs were feelings reciprocated. The boys' attitude is surprising in the light of their forceful professions of devotion to males.

About two-thirds of the OS twins' alleged desires were in agreement with the placement they experienced (Table 68). This is not much above chance. The expressed preferences of the children, however, were not always the real ones, as it was discovered, for some of the children had obviously been told it was best for them to be separated and they were trying to accept this. They tended to give us detailed explanations of their desires in words that sounded as if their mothers were speaking but, after more intimate conversations, a number of children confessed to us they really wanted to be with the sib. Their reasons were various. It is significant that more boys were separated when they did not want to be than was the case for girls (Table 68). It is noteworthy, too, that the boys in our three subgroups stated with about equal frequency (about two-thirds) that they desired the sib as a classmate, but the group differences for the females were large (Table 67). Whereas 94 per cent of the DZSSf's, for example, wanted the sib as classmate, only 47 per cent of the DZOSf's did (Table 67). The latter girls were not infrequently ashamed of their brother's mischievousness, lesser obedience, and poorer school performance, and found it painful to witness this. These girls were, accordingly, more likely to want separation. Some of the girls were almost too conforming at school, were very dominating toward and critical of their brothers, and were tale-bearers. The boys, nevertheless, often expressed a desire for their sister's protection and help, or they indicated they wanted to make sure, since the sister was considered the abler in school usually, that they kept up with her or that she not be given advantages. Since separation was sometimes taken as evidence of disapproval for the males or of inferior status, they often did not like being placed in a class different from that in which their sisters were enrolled. The twins generally tended to be sensitive about being separated. When asked about their placement, the children who were not in the same class with their sib usually hastened to explain that they were in different classes because their teachers and their parents believed this would be good for them, that it helped them to be more independent.

Although for reasons outlined earlier we do not feel confident of being able to interpret the findings, we could not resist looking at a few data summaries that might reveal significant relations between separation and twin attitudes. Since we know of no adequate studies on the short-term effects of separation, much less any on long-time effects of consistent separation, our data, with all their lacks, are as good as are available. Most of what we find in the literature is dogma and opinion, only a few clinical studies of individual cases providing some relevant observations. We have asked whether, in accordance with the thinking of the protagonists of separation, twins who are not kept together are (in accordance with one theory), more original, better informed, possessed of more interests and better speech habits, are more communicative, better workers, more ambitious, more aggressive, competitive, insistent on their rights, exhibitionistic, hostile, and more involved with their peers and less with attracting adult attention (Table 69). As has been said, little actually is expected from our efforts because the period of separation of our subject pair members was short and their treatment inconsistent. Probably as disturbing was the realization that without a detailed history of each case, it would be impossible to determine which characteristics were likely causes and which effects of separation. In fact, it is our belief that we are dealing chiefly with the causes. For instance, among the subjects found to be segregated from their sib, there were more often the large, healthy, older, moody, disobedient, hostile, socially involved with peers, and widely interested (Table 69). Since a few months of separation would probably not have produced so impressive a gestalt, we strongly suspect the separated children proved more difficult to deal with both at home and at school and, hence, were placed in different classes. Nonseparation seemed to be correlated with twin closeness, obedience, responsibleness, ambition, apprehensiveness, involvement with adults, femininity, and babyish speech. Of course, most of the r's in Table 69 are low and barely significant and are for any given trait not typically found in more than one or two groups. These correlations can usually be interpreted in opposite ways, but, as explained, we find more cogency in the view that the schools tend to separate the troublemakers, or those who seem vigorous enough to make it on their own, or are so energetic both intellectually and physically that they are difficult to keep constructively employed. This view also seems more congruent with the finding that more boy twins are kept apart than girl twins.

Believing the schools might have placed twins in different classes if there seemed to be a rather large difference in learning ability between them, we computed a X^2 between the fact of separation and an IQ difference between pair members of ten points or more. The relation was significant at near the 5 per cent level. Thus it does look as if the schools were paying some attention to ability differences in arriving at a decision about twin separation. Separation in this case seemed to be used as a protective device, e. g., a protection against too advanced placement or from feelings of failure that might be generated by witnessing only the more competent performance of one's abler sib. Relevant to this interpretation, it is noteworthy that such correlations as were significant between separation and IQ, instead of IQ difference, indicated usually (MZf's were the exception) that the abler co-twins were least likely to be segregated (Table 69).

It is of some interest that the co-twins who dealt more with parent figures in their CAT stories tended to be found in the same class in school, whereas those who dwelt on episodes representing conflict between parents and children tended to be separated. This suggests, like some of the findings described above, a relation between hostility or conflict and separation. The observation that the number of listed playmates seems to show a positive association with separation, whereas popularity tends to be negatively correlated also points in the same direction (Table 69).

We likewise found food for thought in the discovery that the pairs in which dominance was described as shifting from one co-twin to the other were more likely to be separated ones. It was reported by the mothers of several of these pairs that the dominance status between the co-twins altered when the children entered school and were placed in different classes. Here it does seem as if the separation may have been the cause of the change in dominance status. We were also intrigued by the findings that in one or more groups greater talkativeness, less baby talk, fewer syntax errors, incoherence in storytelling and absence of stuttering were associated with twin separation.

What is cause and what is effect is again not clear but, if we are witnessing effects, the removal of the twin model for part of the day would seem beneficial to speech. On the other hand, if we are witnessing cause, then it looks as if self assurance and not only ability to, but also tendency to communicate freely may result in separate placement for twins.

It was of some significance that the older the mother was at the birth of her identical twins, the less was the likelihood the twins would be separated, but the trend for fraternal twins was the reverse. We had expected that the older mothers who had struggled a long time to have children would want a warm relation to exist between the children and, hence, would desire to keep them together. This is what may have occurred in identical twins. Also monozygotic twins have much prestige value and contribute to the status of the mother. If the twins are separated, their identicalness is less conspicuous. This the mothers may not appreciate, especially if they see their offspring as a great achievement for themselves. But why, contrary to the case of identical twins, did the fraternal twins who were separated tend to be the offspring of older mothers? Perhaps the older mothers of fraternal twins find the greater rivalry of their children difficult to deal with and see in their separation at school something of an antidote for the twins' competitiveness. The MZm's from the lower social class were more often separated but, in the main, social class, as explained earlier, did not seem to be related to the policy of keeping the twins apart at school.

SUMMARY

1. The separation of same-sex co-twins at school occurred about half as frequently as keeping them in the same class, but about half of the time the twins from opposite-sex pairs received different placement.

2. Boys were more likely to be separated at school than girls.

3. Although the MZm's were more frequently enrolled in different classes than not, only about one-eighth of the identical females were kept apart. Of all of our twin groups, it was the identical females who were most frequently placed in the same class.

4. Children from various social classes seemed to be found with the same relative frequency among the separated and nonseparated.

5. More males wished to be separated than did females. There was less disagreement between fact and desire in the matter of placement in the case of the girls than boys, but whether twins' desire or the cultural tendency to deal more gently with girls is responsible for the fact is a question.

6. The more vigorous, older, and aggressive of the twin pairs tended more frequently to be separated, and the closer, more conforming, and scholastically able co-twins tended to be kept together. Although it is not clear whether we are witnessing in this trend the cause or the effect of the procedure, we feel that it is usually the child's traits that are the causes.

7. The greater the difference of the co-twins in IQ the greater was the likelihood of their separation at school.

8. Better speech form and more freedom from stuttering seemed to be associated with the placement of twins in different classes at school.

9. There was some association between shifting dominance in the twin pair and their being kept apart at school. This was more conspicuous among identical twins.

10. When both twins were enrolled in the same class, they tended to be rated more popular. Perhaps when the twins are in the same class they can capitalize more on the distinction of being twins, as well as on support from the sib in their social activities. Since, however, conformity in school in the early years tends to be related to popularity (Koch 1933), we may find in this fact the explanation for the observed relation between popularity and nonseparation.

DOMINANCE IN TWIN PAIRS

THE PROBLEM

One of the frequently expressed concerns relative to the adjustment of twins is the alleged fact that in each pair one member is always dominant and the other has little opportunity to develop his individuality. One may question, first, whether such a relationship always exists and what the distribution of degrees of the relationship is in any case, and secondly whether, if a super-subordinate intrageminal status exists, (1) it tends to be stable over the years; (2) to be general, both as to activity and persons, or limited—e.g., is one twin likely to win more frequently in matters requiring brawn; the other, in matters requiring problem solving or social manipulation. One might fractionate further. It will be important, moreover, to raise the issue of whether a dominant-subordinate status is necessarily a bad one or whether its merit or lack thereof is a function of many variables. Can not a strong—even dependent—relationship with one person be enriching and stimulating, instead of devastating or destroying individuality? One may wonder whether a struggle for exact equality in power might not destroy the peace of twins just as it does that of nations.

It has been asserted that dominance tends to be broadly generalized and is characterized by power, confidence, and independence, whereas submissiveness is sometimes viewed as a state of fearful, resentful dependence. One may inquire, however, whether a sib's ascendance is usually feared or resented. It seems not unlikely that the sib's leadership and protection may be appreciated rather than unwanted. Indeed it is not out of the realm of the possible that the ascendant member of a twin pair may be the more dependent—e.g., need his satellite more than the latter needs him.

The literature dealing with the concept of the structure of dominance is voluminous (see Schjelderup-Ebbe 1922; Jack 1934; Anderson 1939; Ginsburg and Allee 1943; Cattell 1946; Thurstone 1951; Eysenck 1951, 1956; Cattell, Blewett, and Beloff 1955; Guilford and Zimmerman 1956; Gellert 1961; Kagan and Moss 1962). Some of the studies are based on factor-analyzed scores of pencil and paper tests. Not a great amount of detailed study of behavior such as Schjelderup-Ebbe (1922) and his followers (e.g., Ginsburg and Allee 1943) put into their work on the peck-order in animals is available for human beings, and developmental data are scarce indeed. (See, as an example of one type of study that is needed, Kagan and Moss [1962] who give an account of stability in dependence and passivity from childhood to adulthood.)

It is needless to say that those who fear an ascendant-subordinate relationship in twins favor separating the children as much as possible, for the sake of developing their individuality. Some of the intricacies of this issue were discussed in the previous section and will not be repeated. Let it be said here that if mere individuality, judged by difference between the pair members, is sought, the pattern into which the individual is edged by society's machinations may differ from the one in which he, if left to his own devices, would feel most comfortable. May not an identical twin be best expressing his individuality when he is most like his co-twin, since the two have identical genes? In fact, Shields (1962) believes, on the basis of his study of separated identicals, that the influence of the genes is so powerful that the twins tend to become more similar with the passing years, even though reared apart. Whether "individuality" is maximized by interference is, then, a question. Need one, moreover, assume, if he finds, as Eysenck (1956) did, that the submissive twin showed more neuroticism, or as Slater (1953) did, that the submissive twin tended to have the less good mental health, that it is the twin relationship which is the total cause of the difference? Could it not be that it is the verities in the situation—genes and the developments stemming from prenatal or postnatal contingencies, for example (see Dencker 1958; and Dencker *et. al.* 1961)—that lie back of the relationship in the first place that are critical? Shields' work may be more convincing than most, even though it is not flawless, because it analyzes more the effects of parallel happenings and attitudes than is usual in investigations of twins. There is a serious dearth of detailed longitudinal studies, but the situation is improving.

From among the many problems the subject presents, only a few will be focused upon here. It is of central interest whether the attitudes of ascendance and submission tend to generalize beyond the twin relationship; whether dominance gravitates toward stability over the years; and whether the stability varies with type of twin, the areas of ascendance, and the cultural processes that impinge on the individual. For instance, although data to answer the question are not available at this stage, we wonder whether the dominance in the OS pairs shifts as the children age, and the boy harnesses better his drives and becomes increasingly aware of the rather aggressive sex-role behavior his culture approves (see Kagan and Moss, 1962). It is of importance, too, to discover how the group that surrounds the twins values the more and less ascendant individual. Is the individual who is nondominant in the twins' relationship less effective or less appealing socially?

DETERMINATION OF INTRAPAIR DOMINANCE

Dominance within each twin pair at the time of the study was judged by three or four people—the mother of the twins, the teacher, and the experimenters. The experimenters' contacts with the children were limited, but careful attention was given, during the brief time the children were studied, to such behaviors or relations as the following: which twin spoke for the pair when questions were posed; which twin decided first to come with the E to the experimental room and egged the other on to do the same; which seemed to lay the plans for the pair, particularly when the youngsters were at play; which instructed and directed; which walked ahead of the other and led the way; which talked the more when the pair were together, and represented the two; which initiated mischief in which both were involved, if any was perpetrated; which seemed to look after the sib; which won in altercations; which, if either, expressed a desire to change places with the sib? (As an aside relative to this last point, let it be said the dominant twin not infrequently asserted he coveted his sib's status, believing sometimes the latter was the more beloved [see Carpenter and Eisenberg 1938 for a parallel finding].)

The mothers of the fraternal twins seldom hesitated in their responses when they were asked who was the leader of the pair, or who usually or the more frequently got his way; but arriving at similar answers for the MZ pairs was sometimes difficult. In several instances, the mother's reply to us was, "If you had asked me that question a month or so ago, I would have said Twin 1, but at the present time Twin 2 seems to be riding high." An illness, according to the mothers, seemed sometimes to cause such a shift, or entrance into school, or differences in the twins' teachers' ability to inspire confidence in the child, or the partiality of a visiting relative. In other instances, the mothers affirmed one twin was, and had always been, the stronger and more assertive, winning usually when matters were decided by force, whereas the other could cut circles about his sib in intellectual concerns, having then, as a rule, the prestige of doing better work at school. Some twins appeared to get their way by a nagging persistence and by attacking the Achilles heel of the sib; others, by superior skills. In several instances it was reported a twin might yield to much nagging but, once aroused, carry through the fight to success. If this were the case, this twin was classified as the ascendant, even though he seemed to yield often to avoid the distraction of a "fuss."

In making their assessments, the judges were requested to base them on the twins' interactions with each other and not on behavior unrelated to the sib. The evaluations of three judges tended to agree surprisingly well. If there was some disagreement, the matter was discussed and clarification was attempted. In one or two instances, the discussion produced no resolution, chiefly because the judges' range of contacts with the children varied enormously. If a mother held a particular view that the investigators questioned and defended her position well, the child was classified on the basis of the mother's opinion.

In connection with the problem of gauging dominance among identicals, it is interesting that Shields (1962) felt reasonably confident of his estimates in thirty-five adult pairs out of forty and Gedda and Bérard-Magistretti (see Shields 1962, p. 84), in fifty-seven out of sixty-nine. Had these authors had more extended direct contact with the twins while the latter were interacting, it is probable that the number of estimates made with confidence would have increased. On the other hand, it seems clear that among the MZ's the report of an all-encompassing dominance was rather rare. It not infrequently had a spotty, or areal, or changing character and, of course, it varied in degree from pair to pair.

If the twins' status relative to each other was unstable or changed from time to time, each was classified for this part of the study on the basis of what seemed to obtain at the time the children were seen by us. In fifty-five of the pairs it appeared that ascendance had been rather uniform through the years and not infrequently broad in range, but in thirty-five cases its stability was either unknown by us, because no contact with the mother was possible, or had not been consistent. It was frequently reported deep-rooted and firm in the OS pairs but, even here, the dominance seemed limited to areas of activities. The boys could often "throw" their sisters in a physical tussle, but in social situations such as the school presented the girls usually took the lead and showed more confidence. This was the dominance the teachers and the examiner saw chiefly, and this should be kept in mind by the reader. Dominance seemed more stable in the same-sex girl pairs ($N = 25$) than in the parallel boy pairs ($N = 16$), if the mothers' reports are accepted as evidence. (See for a similar trend Kagan and Moss 1962 on the question of the stability of dependency and passivity in the two sexes.) Although these authors studied different relations from those upon which the present study concentrated—on dominance concerning people in general rather than merely in relation to sibs—the sex differences noted present a parallel pattern.

Some of the data on consistency of dominance through time will be analyzed in a later unit of this section. It was our hunch that a fast, firm relationship might be more molding, but the constant struggle to maintain or achieve a favored status might be highly disturbing, as well as determining of the twins' attitudes on many points.

An attempt was made, then, to arrive at a classification of the children in relation to their twin on the basis of behavior at the time of the study and of the duration of the dominance. Weight was also given leadership in school situations, although we are aware that the peckorder might have been established by physical force when the children were very young. It is also possible for one twin to dominate at home (Von Bracken's [1934] "Innenminister") and the other at school ("*Aussenminister*"). Although there were a few cases like this, the mother's report and the teacher's impression usually agreed. If the mother insisted one twin quite uniformly dominated at home, however, this was the classification we accepted.

RESULTS—COMPARISON OF DOMINANT AND NONDOMINANT TWIN-PAIR MEMBERS

First, let it be asked whether those dominant and nondominant in relation to the twin tended to be quite different types of people. Secondly, is the submissive one inclined to be submissive generally both relative to the sib and to others? Does the testimony bearing on these issues seem to vary with the zygosity group, the sex group, and the same- and opposite-sex fraternal pairs?

In most traits in which the ascendant and nonascendant pair members were compared there was no significant difference between them generally, on the average (see Table 74). Even if a significant general intrapair disparity were shown in one type of twin, it usually was not exhibited by the other subgroups. (See Tables 70 and 71.) The dominant-nondominant twin differences were, among others, analyzed with a two-way analysis of variance procedure, involving all same-sex pairs as subjects and dealing with zygosity and sex group differences. A simple t-test comparison of the dominant-nondominant co-twin differences in each of the subgroups was first made, however. Table 74, which is not selective as are most of the tables, presents all of the data and permits a survey of trends in traits showing no significant differences as well as those that do. So few disparities were exhibited by the ascendant and nonascendant identicals that one can argue that the so-called significant findings may be chance results. Among the MZm's, the intrapair dominant group was judged to have less good health, on the average, than did the nondominant, a surprising result, but one that we think could be mediated by family support for the weaker individual. In the MZf's the ascendant co-twins were assessed as more disobedient, on the average, less indirect, and given more to projecting blame. These findings would suggest some slight generalization of ascendant attitude or response tendencies. Both sex groups of identical nonascendants tended to exhibit slightly more right-handedness (Table 71), a finding related perhaps to one we mentioned earlier of an association between resistance and left-handedness.

The picture presented gives no basis for worry about the general social behavior of the submissive co-twins in either of the MZ groups. These were socially effective and appealing children and did not seem to differ much from children generally.

As might be expected, there were a few more significant ascendant-nonascendant group disparities among the fraternals. The pair members judged dominant among the DZSSm's had had the heavier weight at birth, were more frequently reported to have stammered, averaged higher in ratings on aggressiveness, quarrelsomeness, tendency to alibi, uncooperativeness with peers, moodiness, exhibitionism, friendliness to children, and stood relatively lower in ratings on social and physical apprehensiveness and obedience. The dominant boys also listed proportionally fewer younger playmates. The trait gestalt described above is congruent with one usually given of ascendant children. Whether the behavior trends had their origins in the twin relationship we do not know. Genes and other verities such as superior size and intelligence may have been determining (see Ginsburg and Allee 1943; Cattell 1946; Eysenck 1956; Shields 1962). The DZSSf ascendant co-twins were judged, on the average, to be the heavier members of their pairs, the less affectionate, and the less given to dawdling.

It is striking that in not one of the groups was there a suggestion that intelligence distinguished the dominant from the nondominant. This might have been the result of the highly selected nature of the population used in the investigation—only children competent enough to be in school were studied. Nor was there evidence in any group that general hostility, popularity, leadership, number of playmates, gregariousness, involvement with adults and children, competitiveness, emotionality, cheerfulness and enthusiasm, activeness, speech skills, originality, number of interests distinguished the dominant from the nondominant co-twins.

If we look at Table 70, which summarizes the data for the total population of same-sex pairs, few dominant-nondominant group differences are to be noted. The ascendant MZ's seemed to exhibit a tendency to make more syntax errors than did the nonascendant, but the reverse, if anything, obtained for the fraternals. The dominant MZ's were judged to have less good health, on the average, and to be less curious; the dominant DZSS's, the reverse. The ascendant DZSS's seemed to use the alibi more, to tease more, to have fewer younger playmates; the MZ's revealed no differences. The dominant boys were judged to be less obedient, to dawdle more, and to be friendlier to children. They indicated in the interview that they had fewer younger and more same-age playmates than the less ascendant. Among the females no such relations were observed. The playmate lists of the dominant MZ females disclose that they had more younger playmates, of the DZSSf's, that they had fewer younger associates.

Table 70 reveals a number of significant interactions. Since reporting all of these verbally would be tedious, the reader is referred to the table. Most of the specific differences are probably chance effects and the clear demonstration of significant basic group disparities is rare indeed.

Such significant group disparities as were noted seemed, in the main, to make good sense, if one thinks in terms of behavior generalization and genetic diversity and genetically conditioned status. It is of some interest that the dominant children of the two sexes seemed to exhibit somewhat different traits—i.e., the two sexes apparently tend to express their ascendance in diverse fashions (see Kagan [1964], pp. 137–45 for a similar view.) The dominant boys were inclined to a pattern of aggressiveness, exhibitionism, combativeness, lack of physical apprehensiveness, and friendliness to adults and children; whereas among the DZSS girls, on the other hand, the ascendant ones were characterized by less inclination to dawdle, tendency to project blame, lesser affectionateness, and greater distance from adults (Table 70). Although there is a slight hint the girls tend to be ascendant in typically feminine ways and the boys in typically masculine ones, it should be emphasized that marked sex differences in pattern of dominance were few.

If the attitude trends the children expressed toward the sib in the interview are now examined (Table 71), it can be noted that the children who tended to play a subordinate role with respect to the sib were more likely to think the sib bossy, to feel they were less effective than the sib in their quarrels, to seek out more younger playmates, and to prefer to have the sib accompany them when they sallied forth on a visit into somewhat unfamiliar territory. And they seemingly envied the sib's lot, that is, more of the former expressed a desire to change places with the latter.

The MZ co-twins revealed few differences in attitude in the interview. The subordinate more frequently than the ascendant identicals asserted they preferred to play with the sib than to play with others, and more often stated they were unable to do what the sib could do, an unusual confession for a six-year-old (Table 71).

The submissive DZSSm's confessed with greater frequency that they preferred to play alone than with the sib, and that they liked to play alone (this seems like an escape tendency). They also reported more quarreling with the sib. Apparently the same quarreling situations impressed and worried the nonascendants more (Table 71).

The DZOSm's, who usually in social situations played a role subordinate to their sisters, showed most signs of stress. These boys affirmed less often a wish to have the family increased by an infant (no doubt fearing more competition), reported they played less with the sib than vice versa, expressed more often the belief the sib was bossy, affirmed that they would rather have the sib accompany them on a visit than go alone, were less inclined to think the sib initiated their quarrels, and more often stated a wish to become the sib (Table 71). The foregoing pattern, however, probably reflects largely a sex difference rather than that the DZOSm's were markedly different from other boys—the sisters of the former probably cannot be held entirely responsible.

If the data for the total group of twins are assembled and summarized, one notes, in addition to the trends just described, that the nonascendants were reported to have had more difficulty in acquiring good speech form. They also professed less enjoyment of school.

That the nonascendants thought the sib bossy, that the ascendants more frequently were the victors in their quarrels, and that the lot of the ascendants was preferable to theirs can be taken as evidence of conflict. Also the fact that these subjects revealed they more frequently played with younger children probably indicates some effort to escape from the underdog role. Possibly the hint of their lesser liking for school, too, stems from fear of exposure of their lacks in this situation. The DZOSm's seemed to suffer most from having to play a subordinate role, realizing perhaps, even at the early age of five or six years, that in our culture this is no role for a male to play in relation to females.

That there were so few signs of gross distress in the total twin picture, however, should be emphasized. Both ascendant and nonascendant children usually stated that they liked being twins, thought the parents were impartial, and did not feel there was often undue difficulty with the sib over possessions. The submissives did not state significantly more frequently that they would be happier without the sib and that they did not want him in their class in school, nor did they indicate they preferred an older or younger sib to a twin. The same-sex twins, both ascendant and nonascendant, usually stated that they wanted to dress like the sib. In the main, there were no significant group disparities in expressed liking for the teacher. Most twins, whether dominant or not, indicated that being a twin was a happy state and a distinction to be valued.

We have the impression that generally the signs of conflict and stress were very much less than those noted in our study of singleton sibs (Koch 1956a, 1960). Since rearing without conflict is unthinkable and a mild dominance-subordination relation exists in almost any sort of interacting pair, we are of the opinion that our data furnish no cause for general alarm over the ascendance-nonascendance relationship, especially in same-sex pairs of twins. That there will be individual cases, probably more among the fraternals, showing undue dependence or concern over their status is to be anticipated, and these can be dealt with in terms appropriate for the promoting conditions. It simply does not seem to us that it is wise to follow routinely any policy, such as separation, to deal with the problems of twins.

STABILITY OF DOMINANCE THROUGH THE YEARS

The stability of the dominance role did not appear to be related to the zygosity of the pairs, as had been predicted by us. This might have been due to difficulty in judging accurately significant change—

e.g., to the mothers having included too many trends of insufficient range to be classed as real shifts. Sex group differences in constancy among fraternals, however, were exhibited, the girls showing the greater consistency in status over time. The co-twins from the opposite-sex and same-sex fraternal pairs in the narrow and early age range we covered did not appear to differ in amount of shifting in relative ascendance.

Although the relations between pair stability in dominance status and status in thirty-six variables was investigated, only four proved significant. These we shall merely enumerate here. The more stable pairs tended to be characterized by the least developmental defect, as well as by greater willingness to have an infant added to the family, and by preference for having the sib as companion on visits over going alone. The fact that those who did not want an infant sib were members of unstable pairs may have indicated fear of competition and suggests that an active struggle for dominance status was afoot in these pairs. It was surprising that the members of the more stable dyads felt they were required to do what the sib was not, a state of affairs that may be attributable to more interference by the parents in behalf of the nondominant child because he was so clearly this. In the main, it was impressive that there was so little evidence that degree of stability of the dominance-submission relationship was related significantly to the intersib attitudes explored. Had we had enough cases to justify a four-way analysis of variance we might have been able to uncover more relations between personality traits and the relative constancy in the ascendance roles the pair members played.

SUMMARY

1. The dominance-submission relationship was sometimes limited to areas of activity and sometimes it was shifting. In 61 per cent of the pairs, however, the relationship was reported by the twins' mothers to have obtained rather stably through the years.

2. A relative dominance-submission status tended to be less clear-cut among identicals than fraternals. Whether among fraternal pairs the twin was of the same or opposite sex seemed little related to the variableness of the status in the age range covered.

3. There were many ways of being ascendant. They ranged from nagging persistently until what was desired was obtained up to offer-

ing superior, appealing ideas with enthusiasm. A peckorder might have been achieved early by force or physical combat, but at school age at least, it was apparently maintained more by social skills or by the effects—probably largely unconscious—of an earlier established status.

4. Although there was some generalization of the ascendant and submissive attitudes prevailing in the twin relation, the two groups of children in their general behavior among others, especially at school, did not seem to differ much.

5. There was more evidence of generalization of the ascendant attitude beyond the twin interactions in fraternals, particularly among the members of same-sex boy pairs, than in identicals. Whether the traits or generalized ascendance resulted from what was learned in intertwin interactions or lay embedded in, for instance, gene-determined differences between the fraternal twins is a question. This view, on the basis of studies on the genetic components of differences in ascendance and extraversion, seems a tenable one.

6. Only in the DZSSm's was birth weight significantly associated with ascendance in the selected twin population studied. Whether this represents a bona fide or chance group difference is a question.

7. Size difference at school age seemed consistently associated with ascendance only for the DZSSf pairs.

8. Disparity in IQ did not seem to differentiate consistently the dominant from the subordinate members of twin pairs in the groups investigated.

9. In the same-sex pairs, the first-born of the co-twins tended to be very slightly more often the dominant (58 per cent for MZ's and 55 per cent for DZSS's), whereas in the opposite-sex pairs, the first-borns were dominant only 27 per cent of the time. The fact that the girls in the OS pairs tended to be both leaders in social matters and second-borns seems related to the association of these two variables here in a direction the reverse of that noted among the pairs whose members were of the same sex.

10. According to the teachers' assessments, the ascendant MZm's tended to have less good health, on the average, than did the nonascendant. Perhaps these boys received more attention and help because of their ill-fortune and developed thereby the expectation of getting their way. Again there is a question about whether the group differ-

ence is a dependable one.

11. The dominant children exhibited some tendency to be generally more disobedient, aggressive, and inclined to project blame.

12. The submissive member of the twin pairs was more likely to think the sib was bossy than vice versa, to describe him as victor in their altercations more often, to give a higher estimate of the amount of quarreling that was done by the pair, to state more frequently he liked to play alone, or was more indifferent in the matter of play with others over play with the sib, to list proportionally more younger playmates, to wish to change places with the sib, and to feel more threatened by the thought of acquiring an infant sib. When going on a visit, the submissive ones tended to prefer more often, however, to have the sib accompany them than to go visiting alone. Some of the above seem to be devices for escaping from under the domination of the twin—e.g., to seek companions who could, in turn, be dominated; but the inclination last described seems to indicate that the protection of the sib was appreciated when the situation was somewhat exposing. The interview responses yielded a bit of evidence about the twins' awareness of, and ability to verbalize on the pair members' dominance-submission relation.

13. The less dominant child did not more frequently than the ascendant express an objection to having the twin in his class, nor a belief he would be happier without the sib, nor an objection to dressing alike, nor to sharing a bedroom with the sib. The two ascendancy groups were not significantly disparate in frequency of stated preference for the twin over others as playmate, nor for an older or younger sib over a twin sib, nor for a sib of a different sex. Nor was evidence acquired that degree of closeness was related to ascendance-submission differences.

14. Those from DZOS pairs, especially the boys, indicated considerable conflict over playing a subordinate role.

15. When the dominance had been shifting, the children seemed less inclined to want an additional sib, and if the parents were thought somewhat partial, more shifting in ascendancy status seems to have occurred.

16. There was little indication to justify the fear that a dominance-submission relationship between the co-twins would render either one of them consistently less effective or appealing socially or less accom-

plished. Nor did we discover more cause for concern over the relationships among twins than among siblings generally, although it is not impossible that the twins and singletons used different standards for making the judgments they expressed to us in the interview. Perhaps the latter described as moderate or little quarreling what the former characterized as much.

CHAPTER VIII

General Summary and Discussion

TWIN-TYPE CHARACTERIZATIONS

A brief summary in the form of a characterization of twins of various types may prove useful to those who have a particular pair of twins in tow, even though at this point little interpretation of trends will be offered. The reader should remember that the subjects used in this investigation are a highly selected group. Moreover, even the same sort of complication, if there is any—e.g. mild brain damage—may result in behavior ranging from the hyperpassive to the hyperkinetic, depending on the location and extent of nervous system impairment. Hence, because of the very wide variation possible and the smallness of our groups, apparent trends cannot be taken too seriously.

MZm's

The MZm subjects in this study, compared with nontwin controls, were at five to six years of age relatively short but well enough padded, slightly slower mentally on the average, relatively low in gregariousness, and rather nonaggressive. Their passivity and their comparatively low social initiative, low rivalrousness, and low aggressiveness may have caused them to be rated, among other ways, as veering toward the feminine. In relation to the single-born controls, they averaged rather low in speech, and in their performance on all sections of the Primary Mental Abilities Test, except the perceptual

157

and motor. Such playmates as they said they had seemed more often of their own age than those of nontwins. The pair members were very dependent on each other and very close, closer, in fact, than were the co-twins of the other male twin types. This may, in part, lie back of the MZm's apparent serenity or passivity.

DZSSm's

The DZSSm's, relative to the MZm's, were rated, on the average, less healthy at five to six years, and lighter in weight; they were the smallest of the three male groups. The DZSSm's had a very slightly higher mean score on the Primary Mental Abilities Test than did the identical males and were appraised as possessed of a small advantage in speech form. Congruently, their syntax-error score mean was lower. They were rated higher in originality, too, than were the identicals. In short, the dizygotic males seemed a bit more able than the monozygotic.

The former, according to their responses in the interview, indicated they tended to feel less close to the sib than did the latter; the DZSSm's stated they played less with their brothers and the latter's friends, saw themselves and their brothers as unlike in more ways, and dressed alike less frequently because they disliked this practice. Their lesser closeness to the sib may have generated tensions that had ramifications such as the following: the DZSSm's, in contrast to the MZm's, were gauged as not only more gregarious but also as more aggressive —higher in leadership, more insistent on their rights, more involved with children, and more selfish, indirect, and exhibitionistic. Strangely, the DZSSm's listed more female and fewer male playmates. It is difficult to tell whether this represents preference or rather what the neighborhood offered. It seems not unlikely, however, that it reflects a bona fide choice because these DZSS boys were both small and relatively frail.

With reference to singleton controls, too, the DZSSm's were shorter and lighter on the average and were judged as having less good health. Also with respect to nontwins, the DZSSm's were rated lower in articulatory form; and they exhibited more syntax errors in the Children's Apperception Test stories, were thought less talkative at school at least, and averaged lower on the Verbal Section of the PMA. In our measures of other aspects of speech and language, no significant differences between the performance of these twins and the single-born controls were apparent. As is generally true of gemini, the DZSSm's listed more playmates of their own age than did the nontwins. The formers' CAT stories were characterized by fewer episodes involving unpleasant types of mother-child interactions, as well as more episodes portraying pleasant father-child exchanges. These two scores suggest that these twins tend to be less at odds with their parents than do parallel singletons.

In summary, then, the fraternal males from same-sex pairs seem more aggressive, rivalrous, and to a small degree more competent, on the average, than the identical males. With respect to single-borns, however, the DZSSm's appeared somewhat less skilled in speech and language and were less talkative. The CAT stories with their more frequent references to pleasant parent-child interactions hint that these boys may have less discordant relations with their parents than do appropriately matched nontwins.

DZOSm's

The DZOSm's, in contrast to male twins from same-sex pairs, exhibited speech form at a merit level on a par with that of singletons. The former held their own quite well, too, with non-twin controls in their performance on the Primary Mental Abilities Test. These DZOS males were described as rather sober and subdued when compared with nontwins—they were rated lower in activeness, loudness, confidence, intensity, selfishness, and inclination to project blame. There was an intimation of a tendency on their part to play more with girls. At first it was thought these DZOSm's showed their sisters' influence in being relatively feminine in behavior pattern—less selfish. more responsible, more obedient, less exhibitionistic, less moody, and less active than parallel singletons. The DZOSm's did not, however, differ significantly from the DZSSm's in these traits. Hence it looks as if the former were, at least in part, conforming to generally approved behavior patterns rather than merely copying the sister's behavior. If this is the case, then the fact that they were subject to much comparison with the twin may be responsible for their rather mild behavior relative to the singleton standard. Although the DZOSm's differed insignificantly from the DZSSm's, the small differences between them were in the direction of the feminine. The mean ratings for activeness were slightly lower for the DZOSm's than for the DZSSm's. The former were also thought more cheerful, possessed of more interests, more planful and more obedient. Relative to the identical male twins, the DZOSm's performed more competently on the PMA and were judged more gregarious. Although the DZOSm's listed comparatively fewer playmates, their average rating was about on a par with those for matched singletons in the scores for involvement with children and with adults and for popularity.

In the interview, the responses of the boys from opposite-sex twin pairs suggest they felt less close to the sib than did the pair members in other male twin groups. The tension underlying this relationship, with its family ramifications, may have revealed itself in the stories the DZOSm's told about the pictures in the Children's Apperception Test. There was much catastrophe and stress described in the stories and much comment on family activities. Episodes involving unpleasant mother-child interactions were rather numerous, although they were actually fewer than were descriptions of pleasant interactions. This emphasis on family themes makes one suspect that these children, compared with other twins, had more conflict with respect to their families and their own general status, especially their sex role. In relation to the stories of comparable singletons, however, those of the DZOSm's were not deviant in the directions mentioned; that is, the DZOSm's did not seem more anxious than did parallel nontwins who had sibs opposite to them in sex.

Within limits, the DZOSm's gave evidence in the interview of appreciation of their sister's guidance and protection, but at the same time, revealed they felt threatened by her greater social maturity and the approval this begot for her. It is significant that the DZOSm's seemed less critical of their sisters than vice versa. These boys appeared to have relatively few friends, a state of affairs which may have stemmed from the frequent rejection of their company by their sisters and the latters' friends. Rejecting attitudes on the part of the sisters were revealed often in the interview.

MZF's

The MZf's were still relatively short in stature at school age compared with singletons, which seems to be usual with twins. But the MZf's were judged in good health. On the average, the identical girl twins did not, as did the parallel males, score significantly lower than the controls on the PMA, except on the Verbal section. Even here, the negative deviation was not large. The MZf's did, however, average lower than the DZSSf's, as they did also in judged originality and speech form. The articulation performance level of the MZf's was not estimated to be significantly deviant from the merit level of control nontwins, however, although their small divergence in most measures was in a negative direction. It is noteworthy that the MZf's were judged to have more interests than singleton controls. Although their intellectual performance was at least not outstanding, these identical girls were rated, on the average, as socially more involved (both with adults and children) and confident than were single-born controls. They were also appraised above the singletons in popularity, leadership, and cheerfulness. In their strong social interests and effectiveness the MZf's stood in contrast also to the MZm's. Relative to the DZSSf's, the identical girls were gauged as more adult centered. The members of the identical pairs were very close, probably closer than were any of the other twins, except the MZm's. In terms of the feminine complex score, the identical girl twins ranked significantly high and correspondingly low on the masculine complex gestalt— these were distinctly feminine girls.

DZSSf's

The DZSSf's, although like the MZf's in their strong social interests and confidence, were, in contrast, assessed on the average as significantly more skilled in speech and language than were the latter. In fact, the formers' performance in the speech area was even above that of singleton controls, a trend not usually expected in twins. Among the twin groups the DZSSf's ranked highest in speech and language performance.

Compared with the MZf's, the dizygotic females from same-sex pairs were thought less strongly feminine, although, relative to singleton controls, not deficient in this respect. The DZSSf's were probably our most vivacious, outgoing subjects, although their differences from the MZf's in these respects were often not large. The former, with reference to the latter, were appraised as less adult centered, less resistant, and less given to fault finding.

The CAT stories of the fraternal girls from same-sex pairs, with their many references to parent-child interactions, may indicate more concern with family relationships than characterized the identicals. The monozygotic twins in the interview indicated they were more wrapped up in each other, felt the same about many things, and believed they were treated the same by their parents, whereas the DZSSf's gave evidence of not being quite so sure about these points.

Scanning the responses given in the interview, one notes that DZSSf's expressed more often no desire to be like the sib, stated more frequently a preference for play alone over play with the sib, revealed more stress over sharing possessions, and confessed they felt less accepted by the sib's friends. These trends reflect the greater distance just referred to between the DZSSf co-twins, as contrasted with the MZf's, but the difference does not seem large. One should rather be impressed, perhaps, with how few of the interrogations the MZf's and DZSSf's responded to very differently. For instance, with about equal frequency these two female groups stated they thought their parents impartial and that responsibilities and privileges were meted out fairly. The two groups also took responsibility equally as often for initiating their quarrels with the sib and admitted a generous number of sib victories in their intertwin fracases.

DZOSf's

The DZOSf's, like their brothers, when judged in relation to control singletons, were assessed as rather subdued, e.g., relatively low in expressions of jealousy, in tendency to project blame or tattle, in exhibitionism, sociability, and aggressiveness. The DZOSf's were also thought less involved with adults but, surprisingly, in view of the probably lesser contact with adult models, they made fewer syntax errors and told more coherent stories. The latter trend may result from the DZOSf's having more varied social contacts generally.

The trait differences between twin and singleton in the language areas described above seem more a function of twinness than of having a sib opposite in sex, since the DZOSf's and DZSSf's were not judged significantly discrepant in social behavior or language skills.

The DZOSf's were apparently, however, less close to the sib than were the DZSSf's. The disparity was not marked but the direction of the response frequency divergences was very consistent. Fewer DZOSf's than DZSSf's stated they were like the sib in any way, or wished to be like him in some respect, or desired to have him in their class in school. More of the former affirmed the sib to be bossy and complained about his cavalier use of their possessions. The DZOSf's with lesser frequency asserted they played much with the sib and more often claimed they had their own friends. The DZOSf's affirmed more often the father favored them; that is, there was evidence of belief on the part of a substantial number of the DZOSf's that their parents were not strictly impartial. Very few of the DZOSf's expressed a desire for a male sib, if they had a choice, and this, even if the male sib were an infant. Indeed the DZOSf's seemed more rejecting of their brothers than vice versa.

The DZOSf's did not seem to be "masculinized" by their brothers' influence as much as the brothers were "femininized" by theirs. The striking divergence noted between the sexes when two groups, uniform in sex, are compared is not apparent in the two sex groups derived from opposite-sex pairs. It would be difficult to say whether the genetic and family similarity of the opposite-sex pairs or their social influence on each other is responsible for the relation observed. In the main, the girls in the DZOS group were judged the more dominant members of the pairs in social matters, a trend that might account for their attitudes being less colored by their brothers'. The DZOSf's did not seem to show as much rivalry toward their brothers as did singleton girl controls who had a male sib near in age.

In summary, although we have qualms in stating the hunch because of the limited nature of our data, it appears to us that twins with identical genes tend to be closer to each other and seem to be milder individuals than fraternals. As genetic similarity and experience overlap decrease, sib closeness appears to decrease and conflict to augment, along with an apparent growth in competence.

BIOLOGICAL PROBLEMS RELATED TO TWINNING AND TWINS

The organization of data presentation up to this point, with the exception of that for twin-group characterization, has been largely on a trait or instrument basis. It seems in order that an effort now be made to summarize major questions on which twin research and the investigator's thinking have impinged. Although the chapter may seem repetitious, it may prove helpful to those wishing merely an overview of the research issues and to those who have been bogged down by the detail of the data analysis.

LISTING OF BIOLOGICAL QUESTIONS

What are the biological factors that initiate twinning? Is twinning hazardous for human beings and, if so, why? Does the mortality rate vary with the type of twin or the period, ante- or postnatal, in the developmental cycle? Are girls in opposite-sex pairs possessed of lesser size, more defect, and poorer health than the girls in the fraternal same-sex pairs—i.e., is a male womb companion a more strenuous competitor than a female? Are the boys in opposite-sex pairs correspondingly favorably or unfavorably located with respect to DZSSm's? What are some of the negative effects of twin prematurity and how persistent are these? Is mild prematurity advantageous for twins? Is the bearing of twins correlated with the age of the mother? If this is the case, what are the mechanisms that determine the relationship? Does the larger twin tend to be born first? Do twins tend to average persistently smaller in size than singletons? If so, what are the biological mechanisms responsible?

INITIATION OF TWINNING

As explained in chapter 1, the concern of this investigator is chiefly with the psychological effects, direct and indirect, that twins have on each other. These questions are, however, embedded in the most basic problems of biology or perhaps even physics. Although the present study has made virtually no contributions to these questions, it is hoped the reader can be given some appreciation of the broad biological setting of the twin problem. For example, why do human beings typically bear one offspring at a time? Why do most investigators believe only one ovarian follicle tends to "ripen" at a time or at least, only one ovum tends to survive? What lies back of the reduction division? Why cannot or does not the second polar body participate, as a rule, in the generation of a person? What are the controls or processes involved in the above phenomena that are violated when multiple offspring occur?

Unfortunately many facets of the problem of what initiates twinning of either of the two recognized sorts are still not well understood. The questions posed above that need to be answered before fraternal twinning, for instance, can be fully understood, although certainly not neglected heretofore by research workers, seem to be receiving increasing attention. Witness the feverish study, motivated in part by a desire to achieve birth control, to understand the modus operandi of drugs and hormones that inhibit ovulation or stimulate it, or the factors that control fertilization, or zygote survival.

Since it involves double ovulation, fraternal twinning has been attributed chiefly to mechanisms in the mother. The twins conceived by older mothers tend more frequently to be of the dizygotic type (probably less because of aging as such than because of the mother's specific difficulties in conceiving).

For identical twins, the underlying biological trend that is violated appears to be organismic integration or unity. On this problem biologists have labored long, providing us with much information on conditioning variables. Present interest in the forces, organic and inorganic, that bind and separate is tremendous. Mere alteration of the blastoderm's metabolism by cooling at a critical stage may, for instance, be enough to cause a separation of the blastomeres. Newman (1917, 1923) believed delay in implantation to be related to twinning. When organismic integration is well enough understood, then we shall be on the way to comprehending such breakdowns as are represented in twinning (see Mintz 1958). That "normal" twinning can be successfully achieved only in the blastocyst stage or earlier is a problem that throws into relief the intricacies of the processes of differentiation and their effects, the irreversibility of development, and the criticalness of process timing.

Is There a Third Type of Twin?

A third problem pertinent to twin type is, as expounded in chapter 1, that of the number of different kinds. Current dogma specifies only two varieties. But there is still persistent questioning as to whether there may be a third type, with the pair members identical in their complement of maternal genes and different in the paternal. It seems well merely to point out here the bearing of the question on that of the mysteries of the polar bodies, thought by some to be responsible for a third type of twin. What do these latter cells normally tend to lack and why does the reduction division result in unequal cells in the first place? There are a few *in vitro* studies dealing with human material in which there has been direct observation of fertilization of the second polar body and the initiation of its development. Of course, what is necessary for the continuation of development may be the key question, instead of merely what initiates development.

HAZARDS OF TWIN DEVELOPMENT, OPEN QUESTIONS AND THEIR THEORETICAL SIGNIFICANCE

It has, of course, long been known that twinning tends to be hazardous for human beings. Why multiple births are not perilous for some animal forms and are for others, such as human beings, is an intriguing issue. Indeed "uncomplicated" human twinning itself, since the process is a deviation from the usual, may be viewed as anomalous. It may even be a consequence of biological conditions that obtain only very briefly but at a critical period, and that later in development would have no observable negative effects (see Mintz 1958). Since a great variety of conditions may result in the same developmental anomalies, it is possible that the phenomenon of some multiple births should be included in this series of deviations, and its causes then sought among perhaps many not too unusual forces but influences operating out of phase or in the wrong degree at some critical period (see Anon 1965; Gemzell 1965).

The fetal and neonatal death rate among even "reportable" twins tends to be relatively high. Potter (1963) noted in about 52,000 births that the death rate of twins during and shortly after birth was about eight times that of singletons and later fetal mortality was about three times. Very early abortions (these would not be included in Potter's population of newborns) some believe are frequent, but the cases are difficult to detect, to collect, and to classify. In a population like Potter's, serious developmental defects in surviving twins seem to be about twice that observed in singletons.

When the great array of data bearing on gemini is surveyed, it is not immediately apparent whether the difficulties observed stem chiefly from intertwin interference in the prenatal period, or from the inadequate support the mother is able to provide because of her double burden, or because of more uniquely disturbing conditions within her or the fetus. No doubt these sets of forces interact. Potter and others present evidence, since major pathology is often not apparent in the fetuses, to support the view that a common cause, or probably the commonest cause, of twin mortality is simple premature delivery. Potter's (1963) estimate is 42.5 per cent. Prematurity may occur in about three-fifths of the twins even in populations in which maternal gynecological and general medical care are good. Within limits, the smaller the size of the infant at birth, the greater is the likelihood of death since size can be taken as a rough indicator of the general level of the child's physiological competence. At any rate, it seems possible the "uncomplicated" early birth of twins can probably be interpreted largely in terms of mother inadequacy. Potter, however, did observe that the more cramped the housing and the closer the implantation of the germ—e.g., in monoamniotic or monochorionic forms or in forms with fused chorions and placentas—the greater the frequency of fetal and perinatal death tends to be. This suggests that intertwin interference may often be bedevilling.

Growth Retardation

Question, it is true, has been raised in connection with the observation of the persistence of smaller size among those twins who had been born prematurely. It cannot be assumed that the very early borns, although they survive and function "normally," are necessarily unblighted in all respects. There have been queries, however, in relation to the question of the cause of the small size of twins, as to whether there may be some genetic association between smallness in parents and smallness of offspring, which then causes the latter to be classified as premature when a birth-weight criterion is used. Apropos of the matter of the criteria of prematurity, it is of significance Drillien (1964) presents some evidence indicating that prematurely born offspring of tall parents, in contrast to those of short ones, are more likely to correct to some degree the size lag by two years, but at four years the prematures still lagged; i.e., the increment of height and weight increase per year was less than that of babies weighing over 5½ pounds at birth. Whether the prematures ultimately reached the size their parents' stature and weight would dictate is another question. And possibly the twins whose birth weight is under 5½ pounds might not be judged premature, if a more functional criterion than weight is employed—e.g., bone ossification and connective tissue development. It is relevant to this issue that survival rate among twin "prematures" tends to be higher than among singletons of the same birth weight (see Potter 1963). This observation also makes one wonder whether the prematurity in twins is typically related to simple mechanical factors—the weight of the twin pair in the later stages of her pregnancy may be more than the mother can carry or the pair be more than she can nourish—whereas in singletons more basic or unique physiological disturbances in mother and child may more often determine the latters' early arrival.

Although the prematurity picture may not be discouraging, one still cannot jump to the conclusion that prematurity or the conditions which produce it have not left some sort of slight negative impress. Alm (1953), Wiener (1962), and Drillien (1964) have reported that the premature singletons they studied tended to remain smaller, on the average, than term-borns (see chapter 2); and Douglas (1956) and Drillien (1964) have presented evidence that the school performance of premature subjects tends to average slightly below that of control nonprematures. The deficiencies of the early borns, hence, appear often to be durable and may stem from some still not understood brief complication at a critical period for which there is no adequate compensation.

Twin Type, Mortality, and Health

The fact of greater mortality in male twins than in female in the fetal or perinatal period, as well as the greater frequency of developmental anomalies in males, are probably related to the well-known greater vulnerability of males virtually all through life. The problem is not limited just to twins.

Like, and contingent in part on, the relation described for maleness is that between zygotic types and twin survival. Fetal and perinatal mortality, according to the findings of Potter (1963) and others, tends to be higher for monozygotics than for dizygotics. Potter also informs us that the fetal and perinatal mortality rate of DZOS pairs was the lowest in her rather extensive twin population (567 cases). The death rate of the DZOS pairs among her subjects was about a half to a third of that for twins from same-sex pairs, a trend that can be accounted for, partly at least, in terms of what is known about the influence of zygosity and sex variables, as explained earlier. But why not then the lowest mortality rate for the DZSSf's? It is difficult to learn whether proportionally more of the DZOS pairs abort early (before the "reportable" period), those surviving to somewhere near term being the relatively hardy. It is possible even that proportionally more of the female embryos with a male competitor succumb earlier than the female with a female competitor, thus leaving as DZOS survivors those who were the hardier or were the more favorably placed in the uterus. The above are rank hunches.

Postnatal Death Rate of Older Fraternal Twins

Data presented by Osborne and DeGeorge (1959), which have been described earlier at some length, suggest, quite in contrast to Potter's (1963) observations on newborns, that the incidence of dizygotic twins in older populations tends to be relatively low—the incidence of this type of twin seems to decrease with the age of the subject population. In contrast, once identicals are launched in their extra-uterine environment, they seem to grow and fare reasonably well. The dizygotics, on the other hand, appear to be beset, as they age, by relatively more complications. The conspicuous waning incidence of fraternal twins that Osborne and DeGeorge noted they believe may be related to pair-member differences in blood type (on the ABO dimension, especially). Potter, studying Ss in the fetal and perinatal periods, did not observe any association between mortality and the concordance of her fraternal co-twins in three blood characteristics (ABO, MN, and CDEce), when she controlled for "biological intimacy" or crowding. It may be, however, that this very physical closeness of the twin fetuses which was controlled produces the conditions (mutual circulation or small exchanges of blood with attendant sensitization effects) which Osborne and DeGeorge suspect may initiate effects that may be damaging. These authors, in addition, observed a drop in availability of dizygotics in older twin populations. This decrease, it is true, could be due, in some degree at least, to motivation lacks on the part of possible subjects, but there is reason to question whether this is the whole story. The factor of twin-pair members' discordance in blood type (ABO dimension) probably cannot be ignored, since Osborne and DeGeorge ascertained that intertwin concordance in blood type in fraternal twins was higher than that between nontwin sibs or between twin and nontwin sibs. In other words, the former authors favor the view that pairs differing in the blood-type area named above tend to die off more readily than do those with similar blood. If this assumption is correct, the older the population the higher should be the incidence of fraternal twins who are concordant in blood assessed with respect to the ABO factor. The loss of discordant pairs may be due to persistent sensitization effects, or early damage of other sorts resulting from these effects. It would be interesting to know whether fraternal twins with discordant blood types tend to suffer from anemia or other likely immunological difficulties. What gives Osborne and DeGeorge's hypothesis additional plausibility is, as explained earlier in the monograph, the recent discovery of blood chimerism in several pairs of twins (see Booth *et al.* 1957; Nicholas, Jenkins, and Marsh 1957; Chown Lewis, and Bowman 1963). It is true the known cases of human chimerism are rare, but the discovery of a method appropriate for revealing it, as well as systematic search by many agencies, is relatively recent. Also death may early weed out the severely afflicted or sensitized, as Osborne and DeGeorge maintain.

In chapter 1 it was explained that our data were not such as illuminate clearly the thesis that Osborne and DeGeorge present. It is not out of line, however, with their hypothesis that our DZSSm subjects, who averaged no less in birth weight than did our other parallel twin subjects, were significantly lighter and smaller in size at five to six years of age and were rated poorer in health than were the MZm's. (Pair members among the latter are, of course, always of the same blood type.) The DZSSm twins, moreover, were, in the first place, particularly difficult to locate. But this is impressive only if one makes some assumptions relative to the composition of the germ population such as Weinberg (1901, 1902) makes. One can infer differential mortality only by contrasting strictly comparable samples of an older and younger population and not simply by ease of locating subjects of a given age. Indeed, since obtaining strictly comparable samples may be impossible, a longitudinal study approach may be necessary. Even this, with its possibility of differential loss owing to non-health factors may not be helpful.

Potter (1963) reported erythroblastosis as a cause of about five per cent of the deaths in her twin population. This incidence, possibly significantly for the Osborne and DeGeorge thesis, was highest in the group which was composed of same-sex pairs who were probably chiefly fraternals. The most convincing interpretation of Potter's data is not readily apparent, however, since among other things, we were not told how many of the twins, or singleton controls in the research population, were saved from death by skillful immunological corrective procedures.

Would that hospitals could be persuaded to make blood analyses on all mothers and their newborn twins! There is need also of longitudinal data that would give the specific causes of death through the years of not only twins but of their mothers as well. Such information might clarify the blood-type problem and the possibility of sensitization effects.

Our DZOSm's, although merely on a par with other male twins in birth weight, were at five to six years significantly heavier and taller than the DZSSm's. The DZOSf's, too, although they were most frequently premature and below par in size at birth, were not at school entrance significantly deviant in height and weight, on the average, from same-sex twin pairs, whether MZf's or DZSSf's. The DZOSf's, perhaps pertinently, however, were judged lower in health, on the average, at five and six years. Also the defect rate in this group was relatively high. But many of the defects noted among these DZOS girls were ocular and some of the ocular complications, it is known, were the result of early postnatal care of a damaging character. The frequency of premature births among the DZOSf's being high, more retrolental fibroplasia could be expected, since the treatment that prevailed at the time these twins were born involved what proved to be undue exposure of the infants to oxygen or oxygen under too much pressure. It is worth noting, apropos of this interpretation, that a very high proportion of the DZOS twins, compared to singleton controls, wore glasses at school entrance. Indeed, glasses were more common in all twin groups, the DZOS's merely having the highest rate.

Since the DZOSm's seemed, at least at birth, to hold their own physically with other male twins, whereas the DZOSf's appeared somewhat more handicapped relative to other female twins, this makes one wonder whether a male womb companion might not be biologically more demanding than a female competitor. Per contra, one would anticipate that the male with a female companion would fare reasonably well—i.e., better than the DZSSm's. Our data are congruent with this expectation.

It is of some interest that the freemartin phenomenon is believed not to occur in humans. Hence the DZOSf's cannot be expected to be sterile, as bovines are, where mutual circulation between litter mates occurs. We are not however, ready to believe that the possibility of other types of effects, direct or indirect, between DZOS pair members are necessarily nonexistent or that the two sexes fare equally well in health.

MATERNAL AGE AND TWINNING

Our own data, as well as those of many other investigators (see Yerushalmy and Sheerar 1940; Waterhouse 1953), indicate that fraternal twins tend to be born relatively more frequently to older mothers than would be expected by chance. The question is whether some processes related to aging are responsible for this or whether the mothers of some fraternals have difficulty conceiving. Such mothers may by persistent effort or, aided by some treatment, achieve success late, and hence their age when offspring arrive would be higher, on the average, than would that of any group that had no particular difficulty in begetting children. Our data reveal a larger mean interval between marriage and arrival of twins among the mothers of the dizygotic subjects than among the mothers of identicals, but at the same time there were no group differences in age at marriage. We are not implying that the mothers of identical twins had no problems. In the main, there seemed merely to be less delay in achieving successful conception and fewer disturbed pregnancies in this group than among the mothers of the DZSS's and DZOS's.

It is noteworthy in connection with the thesis posed above that the Gemzell (1965) treatment (Anon, 1965) with gonadotrophins of women with a particular type of sterility sometimes resulted in multiple births. These fetuses were all from separate ovulations. Also several sets of quintuplets and even a set of septuplets have been reported being born recently to women receiving treatment of the general sort described by Donini, Puzzuoli, and Montezemolo (1964) and Gemzell (1965). Possibly the regimen injects into the women quantities of hormone too large to be kept under the control of that marvelous network of body processes, which, with its checks and counterchecks, typically results in limiting human offspring to one at any one pregnancy.

First- vs. Second-born Twins

It is probably an obstetrical problem that the twin born first tends to be larger and in better condition than does the second. That the lead of the first-born and the fetal and maternal conditions that result in this lead cannot be taken lightly is attested by the fact first-born twins tend to retain their advantage. Our first-born subjects, even at school age, tended to be larger, on the average, than did the second-born and to be judged as having the better health.

Schatz (see Newman 1923) to be sure, held an opposing view relative to the larger twin, when there had been mutual circulation in the prenatal period. He believed the larger twin was often not the more efficient physiologically after birth or the one who survived the longer. Schatz was of the opinion, for instance, that the heart of the larger twin, when there had been mutual circulation, bore a greater burden in the prenatal period, a state of affairs that was sometimes weakening. The data we have cannot be brought to bear in a critical way on the problem Schatz described because we had no adequate information on whether or not there had been mutual circulation in the prenatal period. We did not note, however, among the monozygotic group, the group in which there might have been substantial blood vessel anastamoses in the placenta in some pairs, any significant negative association of the variables of birth weight and health later in life. Indeed a slight positive correlation of the two variables was observed. Unfortunately, our measure of health was crude and may not have been disassociated in the teachers' minds from a body-size criterion of health. At any rate, only about half as many mothers reported they thought that the smaller twin had the better health of the pair. This percentage did not vary with zygosity. It is worthy of attention that in our data the correlation of health measures seemed to be slightly higher, but not significantly so, with birth order than with birth size.

Birth Order in DZOS Pairs

In bi-sex fraternal pairs the boy was in most cases first-born (80%). Even in the five instances in which he was the lighter, he was born second only once. This finding concerning the relation of sex to birth order is contrary to Potter's (1963) observation. Her data indicate that birth order does not vary with sex; if anything, a few more males in her population of 177 opposite-sex pairs were born second (96) than first (81). The males who were born second had a higher prenatal death rate (12.3%) than those born first (4.9%). The reverse obtained for females (3.7% *vs.* 7.2%). Of course, the instances of death were few and, hence, the measures of incidence were rather unreliable. We have no thoroughly convincing basis for accounting for difference between Potter's findings and ours relative to birth order and sex. The difference in the size and age of the populations could, however, be responsible variables. Potter's population was composed of newborns; ours, of children of five or six years—i.e., our subjects were children who had survived the preschool years. Perhaps the DZOS males who are born second tend to be weak males and have a relatively low survival rate. Our DZOSm's, then, who did survive, might have been particularly large and hardy ones who by their size and vigor managed to lead the exodus from the womb.

Sinistrality in Twins

Some theorists have sought the cause for sinistrality, among other ways, in disturbances of metabolic gradients resulting from early fission, as in identical twins. It is to be expected, if the theory is correct, that there would be more sinistrality among identicals than fraternals. Our data do not support this alleged zygosity difference. Even if it is assumed the major determinants of sinistrality are biological, however, it is not necessary to seek them in the processes of fission or early cell separation, for there can be other critical biological operations. Some (Wilson and Jones 1932) for instance, hold the view that the way the fetuses are placed in the womb can alter growth-rate patterns and change laterality thereby. The third possibility is that laterality is developed largely after birth as a result chiefly of social pressures or mechanical pressures mediated by the cultural environment. Apropos of this hypothesis, it is significant that although 28 per cent of our twins showed some consistent left preference for a time in the years before five or six, by this age only about two per cent of the twins exhibited this trait. The reader should be reminded that although the above observation suggests the potency of environmental pressures in determining laterality, it does not, of course, eliminate the possibility of some biological determinants also. There may well be biosocial multiple causality. We have no convincing evidence of more sinistrality among twins than singletons because we had no adequate control group for comparative purposes, as we had for many other traits; but such rough control data as were located do not indicate more left preference among twins.

In the preschool years more males than females in our twin population were reported to have exhibited sinistrality of some duration, but the sex difference was slight by the end of the first grade. There were a few L-L pairs, very slightly more among identical than fraternal twins. In the pairs with one right- and one left-handed member the mothers tended to report the child with the left preference to be the dominant co-twin and the teachers' ratings support this trend essentially. The R and L members in these mixed-laterality pairs were compared on many traits such as competitiveness, dominance, birth weight, birth order, height and weight at five to six years, IQ, speech disorders, involvement with children, and sex. Only in competitiveness, dominance, and sex did the two groups differ significantly, the left member of the pairs being more aggressive and slightly more frequently the male.

Our data, then, do not indicate that twins are a major source of sinistrals. The fact that the sinistral member in the mixed laterality pairs tended to be dominant and less cooperative suggests that these children may have resisted social pressure generally and hence, took a longer time to acquire the approved dextrality. Such a mechanism would probably not be unique to twins. But we can even see why there might be a few more sinistrals among twins, to wit, two infants often have to be dealt with at the same time and a fair amount of consistency in handling (location of the child's bed, his place at the table, and in the perambulator, etc., always on a given side) tends to be the rule. Hence, one twin might be stimulated or pressured more from the left than the other is. This, of course, is a simple hunch. We have no impressive body of direct evidence.

STUTTERING

It is a common belief that sinistrality and stuttering tend to be in some way associated. If one also holds the opinion that left preference occurs with slightly more frequency in twins, then it is in order, although not necessary, to anticipate more stuttering in the latter population. Although our search through the literature did not locate nontwin groups strictly comparable to our subjects, we feel fairly sure more of our subjects stuttered than would occur in a strictly parallel group of nontwins.

Since the findings of this study did not demonstrate twins as a major source of sinistrals, it was not surprising to uncover no significant relationship between left preference and stuttering among our subjects at school age. It was noted, nevertheless, consistent with the current hypothesis, that the subjects who exhibited a stable left preference, even after entering school, had in greater numbers in their preschool years experienced a substantial period of stuttering. Notwithstanding this association of handedness and stuttering, since others have noted it in nontwin groups, there is no reason to believe it is unique to twin populations.

The data of the present study give a weak confirmation to the usual observation that more males tend to stutter than females. That stuttering was not significantly correlated with maturity at birth or degree of prematurity was a bit surprising, but it supports an earlier analysis of ours (1964) (based, however, on an overlapping population).

PSYCHOSOCIAL PROBLEMS RELATED TO TWINS

LISTING OF PROBLEMS

Below is a summary list of some of the largely open questions or freely made allegations that need resolution or confirmation, if we are to understand the major aspects of the psychosocial development and behavior of twins. Most have already been discussed at some point in the monograph. It is evident that our data have illuminated only some of the issues and these often only partially. Some of the questions have been left in limbo, since we have been able to offer only a description of the consequent behavior and not of the antecedent major biological and social conditions that may prompt the former. A Barker-type (1954) of study of twins' relevant environments and treatments would be desirable.

1. What are some of the effects on ability, behavior, and attitudes of the early birth that characterizes about three-fifths of the twins? Is mild prematurity—$4\frac{1}{2}$ to $5\frac{1}{2}$ pound birth weight—even favorable

for twins? Does the infant's being in an incubator for a considerable time cut down on his opportunity to develop a close relationship with his mother? Are the parents of prematures more anxious about their infants and, correspondingly, more indulgent—attitudes they might continue even after the child is well developed? Is there any evidence of competence level in children at school age being correlated with degree of prematurity at birth? Does general competence at five and six years tend to be less in the children with the largest number of prenatally acquired developmental defects? Could an early birth, which results in the infant's being catapulted into a highly variable world at a time when he is largely incapable of responding except in a diffuse, relatively general, nonspecific, nondiscriminating way, leave him, through a process of conditioning, with a stronger tendency to respond in this fashion later in his life than a child more mature on arrival? Is the mildly premature, who is typically not kept in the hospital more than a few days longer than term-borns, likely to develop a more intense dependent relation with the mother than is an infant who must be retained for a long time and, hence, comes to his mother's care only after he matures to term level or overcomes the major threats to his existence caused by some defect? Is there a tendency for the intensity of an infant's early relationship to his mother to be watered down as a result of a longer hospitalization after birth? Do twins tend to be as adult-oriented as singletons, since the former may well be left more to entertain each other, or they receive less satisfying stimulation of various sorts from the mother because she is so busy caring for two infants? Are twin babies, for example, talked to as much as are singletons, or played with, or read to?

2. Are twins inclined to be understimulated because of being so much alike biologically (in age, sex, genes, etc.) and being treated so similarly? Is their preschool social and physical environment as varied as is that of nontwins? Is constant association with someone who mirrors the self as educating and challenging as is association with individuals who differ much from him? Are twins less rivalrous than singletons, also because of being so similar and treated so much alike? Or is it similarity of this very sort, involving extensive overlap in interests and values, that intensifies competition? Are dependence and closeness between the twins then apt to serve as curbs on intellectual advance? Is there evidence that identical twins, who among twin pairs are inclined to be the most alike, are usually stimulated less than are

fraternals? Are the members of opposite-sex pairs challenged the most by each other? Do twins tend to have lower IQ's than singletons because of lesser variety in the stimulation to which they are subjected (see Koch [1954] on the effect of having a brother)? Are twins likely to have as varied playmates as do singleton sibs? Is there evidence twins are inclined to be retarded in their learning of articulation and the elements of sentence structure because they are each other's chief models, particularly in the years when the critical speech skills are being mastered? Is language learning difficulty related to closeness in twin-pair members, or to IQ, or both? Is imaginativeness and skill in story construction related to the extent of the child's involvement with adults or children, especially older ones, to IQ, and to range of experiences? Do speech form deficiencies tend to be readily corrected when the children are exposed to a wider social environment, such as the school furnishes? Is any of the retardation in early speech learning due to the physical complications of twinning? Do twins who are members of a large family tend to have as much difficulty in mastering articulation and syntax as do twins who are "only" children?

3. Do twins tend to be as sociable with adults and children as single-borns? Or do the former find each other's companionship so satisfying they are less likely to reach out to others? Do twin relations with others tend to be as intimate as those of singletons, or is intimacy saved for the sib?

4. Does being a "biological specimen," a unique human form, tend to win a superficial type of attention for twins and generate a prima donna-like attitude or an appetite for attention in them? Are identical girls, who would be most prone to this sort of attention because of being most conspicuous, inclined to show more of a prima donna set or attention hunger than are other twins?

5. What are some of the behavior and attitude effects of being compared as twins tend to be? Or does such attention come to be ignored and discounted?

6. Does a dominance-submission relationship between co-twins tend to develop? As set forth in chapter 7, some of the major questions, apropos of this issue, are as follows. If such a relationship is acquired, how early does it appear, how stable is it, and what traits and conditions predispose one pair member to learning the dominant role and the other, the submissive? Is the intertwin D-S relationship,

general, or specific, or areal? Does separation of the twins at school tend to dissipate the D-S relationship? Do twins by school age at least recognize the D-S relationship, if one exists, and accept it, or are they likely to be resentful? Which co-twin tends to be the more dependent for general satisfaction on the other, the dominant or nondominant?

7. Are twins from opposite-sex pairs inclined to be retarded in sex-role learning or are they accelerated? Do they have much conflict over their sex status? Do the boys tend to be sissyish and the girls, boyish in behavior, values, and attitudes? Does the girl or does the boy tend to be the dominant member in mixed-sex pairs? Does this dominance vary with the age of the twins? Are the girls inclined to be dominant in the early years because of the typically more rapid progress in socialization in females? Are the boys prone to dominate later because of the cultural emphases on dominance in the male?

8. Do twins tend to marry at about the same age as singletons and with the same frequency? Are the formers' marriages likely to be stable or do they tend to be marred by the twins' dependence on the sib? How intimate and warm is the marriage relationship likely to be between twin and spouse? Does this relationship vary with the type of twin, e.g., are twins from opposite-sex pairs particularly satisfying or successful as spouses or vice versa? Are females from OS pairs inclined to be rivalrous wives and the DZOSm's submissive, or jealous husbands? Does a twin's dominance role influence substantially his success in marriage? Of course, the answers to some of the questions depend, in part, on the kind of person sought in the marriage partner.

9. What is the effect of separating twins in school? Does this practice dissipate or alter the dominance-submission relationship between pair members? Does twin scholarship tend to improve with separation because of the increase in variety of experience, as well as less ready sib support? What is the role of the family in determining the effect of the separation? Do most twins who are separated come to prefer it? Which is more upset initially by the separation at school, the dominant or submissive pair member?

PREMATURITY

Since most twins are born prematurely, the influence of early birth on behavior and attitudes needs exploring here. In the previous section a discussion was given of some of the physical precursors of, and/or correlates of, prematurity as well as the relation of these to survival, physical size, and defect in twins. At this point the focus of the discussion is behavior, instead.

A consistent, although not always significant difference, is apparent in the PMA Test performance of the severely premature children (birth weight under 4½ pounds) and those mildly so (birth weight 4½ to 5½ pounds). (See Koch 1964.) The children who were severely premature averaged consistently, but not significantly, below the latter, not only in total score but also on performance on the V, Q, M, and S subsections. This finding is in line with the trend Drillien (1964) observed. Findings such as these make one wonder whether there has been more pre- or perinatal damage to the nervous system in the extremely premature. This issue was treated earlier and will not be discussed further, other than to remind the reader that the lacks reflected in the PMA performance may be those that influence a wide range of behaviors.

It is noteworthy that our term-borns and mildly premature twins did not differ significantly in PMA score average but, surprisingly, there is a hint of less good speech form in the term group. This, in turn, becomes impressive in that, at school age at least, the term group were also judged less involved with adults. Moreover, although only one of the birth-weight group score differences is significant, all measures based on the CAT and involving parent figures were lower in the term-born children than in the mildly premature. Indeed, if one looks at the total gestalt, and ignores for the moment attention to significance level, the data suggest a different relationship between parent and child in the term group as opposed to the slightly premature group. The term group exhibited fewer signs of adult involvement, dependence, and adult instruction (see Koch, 1964). It seems not impossible that greater emotionality on the part of the slightly early born infants, relative to the term-borns, might have attracted more adult ministrations to the former. What is really antecedent in the relation, however, or what was originally, and what is consequent is a question. Since greater emotionality in prematures has been mentioned by many investigators, we are inclined to suspect this is antecedent. (Could it be that the general, diffuse, emotional behavior pattern of the immature fetus may be persisting as a result of early conditioning.) If, moreover, the baby's emotionality attracts adult attention, then one would expect the response pattern observed—i.e., seeking more contact with adults, better speech because of the better model which the adult furnishes, greater range of information of the type adults tend to give, and more stories about parents or parents and children in the CAT. This last is probably a rough indicator of involvement with adults and family.

But the perplexing question that remains is that the pattern described is not intensified in the extreme prematures. Following is our hunch as to the reason, for whatever it is worth. In the first place, more of the severely prematures probably are damaged and more, hence, may have to spend a long time in an incubator, or at least in the hospital nursery, where ministrations may not be very readily or immediately forthcoming. In other words, perhaps it is learned by even very tiny infants that expressing emotions does not pay particularly. Also, even if a response is elicited from the nursing staff, it may come from one of a bevy of different individuals, each with her unique approach. If, in addition, the extremely premature babies tend to be slower learners and the responses they elicit early from their social world by their behaviors are of the more impersonal, variable, and less clearly or immediately comforting sort, one might expect the relation that the child develops with adults (and possibly ultimately the parents) to be less dependent and intimate than that which the mildly premature develop. Let it be emphasized again that the above is merely an interesting hypothesis.

Since our subjects included all levels of prematurity, and data are at hand that indicate that maturity level at birth may have different sorts of physical and psychological ramifications of considerable duration, it might be well to try to discount prematurity when analyzing behavior trends in twins (see Tables 60 and 61). Although early birth practically inheres in twinning and probably should not be controlled if practical considerations dictate the analysis, it is still important to inquire how many so-called twin-singleton or even twin-group differences may possibly be traced to prematurity rather than to other effects or correlates to twinning.

If maturity level at birth is controlled, significant zygosity group differences are noted only in the following trait ratings: gregariousness, talkativeness, finality, and femininity. This is about the number one would expect by chance and since there are many group differences when maturity level is not controlled, this is a very significant finding, as it suggests that prematurity and its antecedents and sequelae may be the major determinant of the unique qualities of twin types. Whether the birth weight variable also plays a major role in determining twin-singleton differences our data did not permit us to estimate because no information on birth weight and birth condition of singletons was available to us. Since it is well known that prematurity is much less common among singletons than twins, there are grounds for the suspicion that the prematurity variable may be responsible for much of twin-singleton disparity.

STIMULATION AND DRIVE IN TWINS

Some hold the view that twins contribute fewer highly competent persons to the population than their incidence would lead one to expect and interpret their belief in terms of twin "understimulation," or early biological impairment. Let us ask first whether there is any direct evidence for twins' experiencing a lesser number of, or less varied, social stimulations than single-borns. If one judges by what the twin subjects of our study reported, the pair members tended to spend much of their time together—more, typically, than did the singleton controls (Table 47). This could mean that, at least early in their lives, twins receive less varied stimulation from their sib than do singletons, since the pair members, for instance, are of the same age, rather similar usually in ability, and more than half of the time are of the same sex. This state of affairs could create a flow of happenings of lesser variety than that to which single-borns are normally exposed. Moreover, the children listed by our twins as their playmates were more likely to be of the twins' age than were the playfellows named by singletons. Hence the variety of child associates with whom the twins spend time may be somewhat restricted. This might be especially true when the twins are compared with singleton controls who have an older sib. It seems reasonable to expect, too, although we can offer no precise, direct evidence, that the twins might receive fewer play and tutorial contacts from their parents than would single-borns because the physical care of the former might occupy so much of the parents' time. Lastly, people go to great lengths to treat twins alike—give them the same sorts of toys, clothe them similarly, place them often in the same class in school, and send them abroad together to play. This could result in the twins having fewer diverse experiences to share and in being less competitive than singleton sibs would be.

Of course, one might argue conversely that a closely knit team of two should increase the range of stimulations of an interesting and assimilable type. Co-twins may, because they are conspicuous and viewed as persons of distinction, attract children to them. The gemini, moreover, may support each other well in gathering playmates about them. The playmates, unfortunately, lured by co-twins apparently tend to include fewer different children than those listed by singleton pairs.

It is noteworthy in connection with the plausibility of the hypothesis just outlined—namely that twins would be less experienced—that the PMA scores were not significantly related to scores for adult involvement ($r = .14$), but they were positively correlated with the rating complex score designated, "involvement with children" ($r = .34$). Indeed, the correlation between involvement with children and talkativeness was .48; number of interests, .36; competitiveness, .33; and intensity, .42.

There were few significant r's, on the other hand, between twin closeness, or the number of playmates listed, or measures of the twins' drive. The number of playmates was correlated only with the rating on number of interests and then only slightly ($r = .21$). Competitiveness, which is a better measure of drive than most of our items, was correlated with measures of excellence in articulation ($r = .25$); involvement with adults ($r = .33$); involvement with children ($r = .70$); originality ($r = .44$); number of interests ($r = .44$); and curiosity ($r = .46$).

The above correlations, then, suggest that our beliefs relative to certain sources as determinants of stimulation and achievement in twins are at least plausible; but the correlations do not, of course, indicate what is cause and what is effect among the variables. Indeed, they do not have a direct bearing on the question of twin-singleton differences in drive and stimulation. We still need to make twin-singleton group comparisons on the basis of both achievement of various sorts and of possible sources of stimulation such as were sketched in the previous paragraph. The knowledge of a lesser variety in the child contacts of twins might, in view of the correlations cited above, cause one to look for twin-singleton differences in range of information and skills, such as language, originality, number of interests, competitiveness, and ambition (see Getzels and Jackson 1962).

The gemini in the present study, it is true, did tend to score slightly lower on the PMA Test, even though favored by the testing conditions (Table 18), than did singleton controls. But usually they scored significantly lower on the Verbal secion. The V section, as explained earlier, appears to tap verbal information, a type of acquisition one might expect to be influenced by range of social contacts and experiences. We are not implying, of course, that only a lesser involvement with children or adults on the part of twins could be responsible for the PMA picture. The tendency for twins to score a bit low on the PMA could, among other things, be due to slower learning, resulting from mild physical impairment, which, in turn, is contingent on prematurity or prenatal complications. Our twin subjects, other than the MZf's were apparently not more nor less involved with adults at school than were singletons. And contrary to the stimulation theory, the MZf's, despite being more concerned with adults than singletons, tended to score *below* the latter on the PMA V-quotient. What the relation would have been had home contacts been observed is another question. At any rate, it does not seem as if the twin-singleton difference in IQ can be attributed at least to what our rating of adult involvement measures. (Practically all *r*'s with this measure are insignificant.)

The picture for involvement with children is different. This measure is significantly correlated with most of the PMA quotient scores. Although the twin girls from same-sex pairs tended to be more involved with children than were singleton controls, this trend was not associated with superior performance on the PMA on the part of the former. Fraternal males, whether DZSS or DZOS, did not differ significantly from nontwins in involvement with children. Only the MZm's fell below singletons markedly on the PMA and were lacking in child contacts as well. All in all, then, it does not seem that twin-singleton differences on the PMA Test, even that on the V score, can be accounted for simply by differences in degree of involvement with children or adults. Nor is it clear from the little relationship observed what the dynamics of the MZm pairs was. My supposition is that the low status of the MZm's stemmed from mild brain impairment in a few pairs. Twin and singleton group means, moreover, did not differ significantly in disparity in the ratings on originality or curiosity. In only one group—the MZm's again—was the twin-singleton divergence in even competitiveness significant. The MZm's were less competitive.

If one considers achievement in articulation and syntax, as it relates to child involvement, there is a hint of a relation in only one group; the DZSSf's rated above singletons both in articulation and involvement with peers. Since no other twin group exhibited a relevant association, one can scarcely be impressed with the theory that twin understimulation by peers at school age contributes to difficulty in mastering language in our group of twins. If it were known what the stimulation situation was in the early preschool years, the conclusion might be different.

The data of this study yield no evidence of a significant twin-singleton disparity in ambition except in one group, the MZm's. Once again, these twins, as previously stated, were judged the less competitive.

In the light of the findings described in the last few paragraphs, the conclusion does not seem to be warranted that twins are less stimulated and motivated than singletons. Thus it seems desirable that the belief that twins do not contribute to the population their share of very distinguished persons should be carefully checked. If the belief is verified, prenatal and perinatal impairment could be the more likely sources of the differences observed rather than mere understimulation of one kind or another, directly or indirectly caused by the degree of likeness of the typical experiences co-twins tend to have.

Adult Involvement of Twins

Some believe that the mothers of twins have less time to spend with each child than do the mothers of singletons with each member of their broods and, hence, this leaves the twins more to their own company. It is maintained, then, that as a consequence of less extensive and satisfying association with the mother, twins become, first, less parent-dependent and, finally, by transfer of learning, less adult-dependent or oriented. If this should be true, association with adults should provide less security and stimulation for twins than it would for singletons. Of those theorists preferring the deprivation-drive theory, some will probably come to the opposite conclusion; namely, that twins will have an insatiable appetite for attention from adults.

Some theorists, thinking in terms of possible imprinting, are of the opinion that the several weeks or months that prematures may have to spend in an incubator or hospital nursery weakens the infant's opportunity to develop a strong, dependent relationship on his mother. The truth of this belief has never been adequately demonstrated, unfortunately. Since ours is not a longitudinal study, we are in no position to determine whether there is any relationship between the length of the infant's stay in the hospital and the quality of his ultimate relationship to his mother. It is being asked, hence, whether twins, who tend to become much involved with each other, are inclined to be less concerned with adults.

The chief indicator of interest in adults employed in this study is the complex score labeled "involvement with adults." This, the reader will remember, is the mean of the standard scores of the ratings given for the following behavior patterns or traits: friendliness to adults, tendency to ask help from adults, tendency to seek attention from adults, inclination to respond well to adults' praise and sympathy, affectionateness, and tendency to tattle to adults. Attention was also paid to concentration of the children's CAT stories on episodes involving parent figures in some way or other. The CAT scores, presumably descriptive of the above trends, are simple counts of the stories containing appropriate episodes or parent-mentions.

First, an effort was made to determine whether twins or singletons scored higher on appropriate ratings and CAT measures. We have also looked to see if there was a negative correlation between twin closeness (this based on what the children told us about their attitudes toward each other) and the ratings on involvement with adults.

There was only one small, but significant, correlation between the measures describing twin closeness to each other and their interaction with adults but, in this instance, the r was positive; that is, the closer the twins were to each other, the more involved with adults they tended to be. This is the reverse of what would have been predicted on the basis of the simple conditioning hypothesis described above, but it is at least not at odds with the deprivation-drive theory.

The MZm's were judged to interact more with adults than did either single-born controls or the DZSSm's. The first relation is contrary to what would be expected on the basis of a simple conditioning theory. The rating complex, presumably reflecting to a degree extent of contact with adults at school, did not correlate significantly with any of the CAT story scores. The DZSSm's, however, described fewer (but barely significantly so) unpleasant episodes between a mother and child than did single-borns. In the main, then, the above findings give little support for the notion that twins generally tend to be less dependent on, or less involved with, adults than are singletons.

It has occurred to us that the involvement of MZf's with adults may result from the mother's pride in her twins. Identical twin girls beget much attention for the mother, and the former are viewed as a great achievement for the latter. This fact may come to involve the mother and identical twin girls in a relationship that transfers to other adult women. It is also possible adult women tend to take more initiative in approach to identical girls because they find the latter "cute."

There was in all of the various analyses only one major instance of a strong significant relation between child involvement with adults and some characteristic of the former at birth. The term-born children, as mentioned in chapter 6, when discussing another of our studies (Koch 1964), seemed at school age to be less concerned with adults, both on the basis of the complex ratings and the CAT data, than were the children mildly premature at birth. Apropos of this, it may be relevant that the former tended to have less good speech form than the latter. As will be recalled from the aforementioned discussion in chapter 6, the children with a birth poundage between 4½ and 5½ were generally not only the most adult-centered of the three birth-weight groups studied but apparently the most aggressive and probably the most alert. It may be worthy of mention that, with birth weight controlled, the MZf's, who were cited as much involved with adults, were not more so than were fraternal girls from same-sex pairs. This is additional evidence, then, that prematurity level may influence relations with adults.

It seems possible that the mildly premature may have had their first extensive contacts with their mothers at an earlier age than did the term or severely premature infants. The greater involvement of the mildly premature with the mother would then be an observation roughly congruent with, but not a necessary sequel of, imprinting theory. The possibility of imprinting in human beings and the conditions under which it might occur, if indeed it does, still needs much study.

In summary, let it be repeated, there does not seem to be much evidence that twins generally are low in the extent of involvement with adults. Indeed, the MZf's even scored relatively high, instead of the expected low. It is also relevant to note that the twin closeness scores correlated slightly, but still significantly and positively, with concern with adults, a relationship the opposite of what would be expected on the basis of the belief that twins' devotion to others would tend to be negatively related to the strength of their involvement with the mother. The observation is not incongruent with what would be predicted on the basis of a deprivation-drive hypothesis. The finding is also rather consistent with the view that family atmosphere is likely to be so loving and helpful as to encourage devotion to both sib and parents.

EFFECTS OF COMPARISON AND EQUALITY OF TREATMENT OF TWINS

Some contend that the constant comparison to which twins are subjected makes them rivalrous, competitive, and self-conscious. Although few would doubt that twins are compared much, it may well be found that twins of various types are subjected to quite different kinds of comparisons, as mentioned earlier in the monograph. Comparison for likeness may have a different influence than comparison for difference. Identical twins, it is suspected, may be subjected more to the former kind; fraternals, relatively more to the latter. It was interesting to observe that some of our identical subjects, when questioned about their likeness to or difference from the sib found it impossible to mention a difference, saying over and over, "We are alike." Although the task of specifying likeness and difference is typically not an easy one for children of five and six years, the fraternals had more success than did the identicals in specifying disparities. Of course, there were more differences to be discriminated in the former case! It is true that the differences mentioned usually seemed trivial to the examiner but they may not have been so assessed by her subjects. Specific questioning relative to specific traits might have resulted in a better gauge of the twins' awareness of likeness and difference and the ways in which they are evaluated.

At any rate, the data at hand have little bearing on the nature of the antecedent condition of, or even awareness of, relative status. But in spite of this lack in our instrument, an effort was made to discover whether, for whatever reason, twins might tend to be more rivalrous and competitive than singletons and whether such attitudes might vary with twin type (Table 42).

When the data dealing with twin attitudes and behavior were scanned, there were few grounds discovered for believing that the twins generally were excessively rivalrous with each other and competitive, or that these attitudes had extended their scope to include others than the sib. If anything, the general trend among our subjects was in a direction the opposite of that which was expected. The teachers' ratings of the children in one or another group on jealousy, insistence on rights, exhibitionism, tendency to project blame, selfishness, and ambition are not uniformly higher than those for control singletons who had one sib (Tables 42 and 59). The twins' responses in the interview, moreover, which expressed directly some of their attitudes relative to the sib and their parents, lend support to the teachers' judgment that the twins studied were not particularly rivalrous. These children, even more frequently than singleton controls, stated they thought their parents impartial. Also, as mentioned earlier, when the twins were asked about their quarrels (which, by the way, they usually freely admitted), they shared responsibility for initiating them more often than nontwins and credited the sib with a goodly share of the victories (Table 57). The twins also less frequently than singletons expressed a desire to change places with the sib, and more often admitted the sib could do things they could not do.

Von Bracken (1934) believed his data indicated that identicals tend not to be particularly rivalrous, beyond wanting to keep abreast of the sib. Von Bracken even witnessed efforts on the part of some of his monozygotic subjects in a competitive situation to help bring the sib's performance up to their own level. The state of affairs in fraternals, on the other hand, was very different. Here it was noted an effort to outstrip the sib was the usual reaction in a competitive situation.

The teachers' ratings in the present study indicate on the part of the DZSSm's, compared with the MZm's, better leadership, greater decisiveness, insistence on rights, and indirectness. These trends are at least congruent with von Bracken's belief that fraternal twins tend to be the more competitive than control singletons and the MZm's tend clearly to be less.

If one asks why twins may be less rivalrous and competitive, in spite of the comparisons to which they are subjected, the answer may be found in the prevailing tendency to try to treat twins as nearly alike as possible. It is assumed that equality in need and interest, in twins with inadequate means for satisfying these within the situation, results in great rivalry. In co-twins, however, both typically are given the same sorts of possessions and general treatment, with the consequence that the occasions for rivalry may be much reduced. Distinct favoritism on the part of friends or relatives, it is true, may create much stress but instances of extreme situations seem to be few, compared to what was noticed among singleton sibs.

It probably can be assumed that if twins differ in sex, their interests and needs will differ more than is the case for same-sex pairs. Hence, satisfying the different needs of these children may be more difficult than meeting those of co-twins who are the same in sex. Our MZ's seemed less rivalrous and competitive with each other than were their singleton controls. The same-sex fraternals were, again with respect to each other, more rivalrous than were the MZm's, and the DZOS's gave evidence of having considerable conflict (see Tables 38, 39, 41, and 42). The latter shared less readily, felt less favored, etc., than did the other twin groups. There is little to suggest, however, the generalization of these intersib attitudes among the twins into a comprehensive competitiveness and rivalry with others. It should probably be stressed that, with respect to singletons, the MZm's seemed less competitive, and the other groups did not differ significantly from parallel controls.

Twin Interest in and Involvement with Children

It has been suspected that the close relationship that develops between co-twins early in their lives might interfere with the building up of friendships and friendly relations with other children. This is a complementary issue to the one dealt with in the section on twin relations with adults, where it was revealed that closeness of association with the twin sib did not seem to weaken interest in, or intimacy with, those who were their elders. The assumption is made that twins come to react similarly to happenings and people. This is thought to be especially true for identicals. The twins' compatibility and similarity of response may cause other children to seem less predictable and less satisfying as companions. It is questionable, on the other hand, whether association with others might not be looked forward to, not only because of the variety of new experiences it offered, but also because the gratifying experiences with the sib create the expectation of a reasonably friendly response from other children—i.e., there may be a transfer from the learning achieved in interaction with the sib. In checking the theory, of course, the quality or intimacy of the twins' relations with children other than the sib should be gauged, but we are not sure our measures reflect the detail necessary to make an accurate assessment of quality of relationship. The reader should keep this in mind.

At any rate, it should be noted that girls from same-sex pairs, whether identical or fraternal, were rated by their teachers as more sociable and child-involved than were nontwin controls, whereas the fraternal males from same-sex pairs and children from opposite-sex twosomes differed insignificantly on our measures from singleton controls. It is also significant that twins did not list fewer playmates than did parallel single-borns. Support is, hence, lacking for the belief that the twins' relationship to each other interferes with effective interaction with peers. As a matter of fact, for girls from same-sex pairs, intimacy with the twin appeared even to strengthen involvement with peers. It may be, however, that other children take the initiative in involving twins because the latter seem to be persons of special importance. If this is so, it may not be twins predominantly who make the choice of association but rather their peers. This idea needs checking. The measure of closeness of relation with the twin did correlate positively, but just barely significantly, with the measures of involvement with children ($r = .16$) and affectionateness ($r = .17$). The r's are surprisingly low and the picture does not suggest that relations twins have with each other tend to influence uniquely interest in, or involvement with others, except perhaps in the case of same-sex girls. At any rate clearly the correlations are not negative.

ROLE OF PRIMA DONNA

Twins seem to fall heir to a sort of distinction through being biological deviates (deviates who, fortunately, are received with pleasure). Identicals are viewed as especially unique and studied as specimens by the layman. Both identical and fraternal twin girls are made particularly conspicuous by being given alliterative names, being dressed alike, and dressed more attractively than normal. This it has been thought may result in their being forced into the role of prima donnas. The reader may find it revealing in this connection to read the *Genain Quadruplets* (Rosenthal 1963). It became apparent to the investigators who conducted this most detailed study of four much disturbed children that the latter had their chief and most satisfying contacts with others in the role of entertainers; that is, they displayed themselves in ways people thought "cute."

Although the evidence is tangential only, it was impressive that our twin subjects who were not separated at school and could be readily recognized as twins were judged more popular than were those who were enrolled in different classes and could not so readily be recognized as twins. Of course, there are several ways of interpreting the above relationship; for example, the more aggressive twins and less agreeable children may have been separated and these, in turn, may have been correspondingly less enjoyed or been less popular with their peers. The former interpretation seemed to have some cogency, for many times our twin subjects told us they liked to dress alike because then they were recognized as twins and were the recipients of more attention. One of our pairs of identical twin girls who were visited when they were teen-agers regaled us with a long account of their effort to discontinue the practice of dressing alike. They finally gave up the effort and returned to dressing alike partly because they believed the quantity of favorable attention they received had fallen off markedly from what they were accustomed to.

One wonders whether this "unearned" attention twins receive would make for more superficial relations with others or serve, instead, to facilitate the development of relations with deeper roots. Since an answer to this question was not planned for when our investigation was designed, we have few observations that bear directly on it. Exhibitionism, less abiding friendships, less thoughtfulness and generosity, a tendency to withdraw when the stage is not held, and much time spent in self-beautification are traits one might expect in a prima donna. But few of these traits were included for assessment in our study. According to the teachers' ratings, however, twins were not found to differ from singletons in qualities such as responsibleness, tenacity in a difficult task, selfishness, affectionateness, or exhibitionism.

Since the MZ's are more unique and conspicuous, one might expect them to play the prima donna role more than the DZSS's. Hence a check on this hunch was attempted. It is worth noting that the MZf's, in relation to DZSSf's, were judged less responsive to adult sympathy and approval, less planful, less decisive, less good leaders, less original, and more resistant, critical, and selfish. This general picture is at least consistent with the prima donna hypothesis. But when the MZ girls are compared with control singletons, these twins seem characterized by greater social interest, affability, and sociability. The DZSSf's were a similarly friendly and sociable lot. The complex of twin-singleton differences here can then scarcely be characterized as revealing any marked or uniquely prima-donna-like tendencies. The data gestalt for the boys, congruently enough, since boy twins are less conspicuous than girls, was not parallel to that for the girls when identicals and fraternals were compared. In fact, our data provide no evidence of any prima-donna-like tendencies in male twins.

SPEECH LEARNING OF TWINS

It has long been maintained that some twins tend to have more than a normal amount of difficulty in learning the elements of speech, i.e., articulation and basic syntax. The difficulty has been interpreted largely as a result of the fact twins are poor speech models for each other.

It seems in order, then, although the issue has been skirted in previous sections, (1) to ask whether twins really do tend to have more difficulty than a well-selected and assessed control group of singletons; (2) to determine whether the closer the twins, the more time they spend together, and the more isolated from others they are, the more problems they have in mastering the elements of speech, and (3) to note the relation between IQ, sex, social interest, and speech variables, which our correlation data suggest are interrelated in the twin populations.

Unfortunately we did not have any opportunity to observe twins during the early stages of their speech learning, as our subjects were all five or six years old when studied. It is true the mothers were asked whether they were of the opinion that their twins exhibited a delay in beginning to speak or that baby talk by the twins persisted unduly, but this crude measure was the only one we had that dealt with behavior in the early preschool period. The teachers judged the children's speech skill during the time the latter were in the kindergarten or first grade. One examiner rated the speech form of the twins when telling their CAT stories, and a count was made of the syntax errors accumulated in 400 words of story and comment. Three of the measures represent somewhat different stages in speech learning. For only the last three measures were control group data available, since, as explained above, the mothers of singletons were not interviewed.

Two controls per twin were available for two of the speech measures, but less than one for the syntax score.

When studied as a total group, the twins did not fall much, if any, below nontwin subjects in speech, IQ, or sociability. The twin subgroups, however, showed quite different patterns. The order of merit of the groups based on mean score on closeness was not the reverse of the order in which the groups would have been ranked on the basis of speech performance, as the speech model theory would lead one to expect. Hence it has seemed well to characterize the groups on the basis of several variables that the correlation tables suggest may be related to speech skills.

The DZSSf's, who excelled even singletons in speech and performed somewhat better than did most twins, were rather close but below the MZf's. The DZSSf's were very sociable, and held their own with singletons in IQ. Although the differences usually were not significant, the MZf's, relative to the DZSSf's, performed less well in speech, and IQ, were closer, and a bit less dynamic socially. In articulation and basic syntax and IQ the MZf's tended, relative to singletons, to deviate slightly in a negative direction. As in nontwins, girls tended to excel the males in speech and sociability.

The DZOS's scored on a par with singletons in speech and IQ. The DZOSf's were somewhat less sociable than were the DZSSf's, whereas the DZOSm's performed very similarly to the DZSSm's and singleton controls. Of all the twins the DZOS co-twins were the least close. Apropos of this point, it is well to note their speech was not retarded but was quite normal.

The DZSSm's scored as less close than the MZm's but closer than the DZOSm's. The former spoke less well than the DZSSf's but about on a par with singleton males. Their IQ mean showed a slight negative, but not significant, deviation from the controls, as did also their speech. They were less sociable than DZOSf's but on a par with singleton males. It is conspicuous that the identical male co-twins who were very close to each other, were least successful in speech, relatively low in IQ, and rather withdrawn.

The PMA and Speech Performance

The correlations between four measures of speech (delay in speech and persistent baby talk, syntax error counts, teachers' rating of articulation, and examiner's rating of errors in speech form in the CAT) with the PMA total quotient score, as well as the V- and Q-subtest quotient scores, were significant for the total group, for the male identicals and, in most instances, for the MZf's and DZSSm's. It is surprising that in the SS groups the four measures of speech correlated significantly with Q quotients in 18 out of 20 instances. The Q quotient r's in 16 instances out of 20 were higher even than the V quotient r's. The correlations involving the DZOS's were generally not significant possibly because the two sex groups here had about half as many subjects as did the SS groups.

Since our highly selected group of twins showed a tendency to rank slightly lower on the PMA quotient scores than singletons, possibly because of complications associated with the former's prematurity, it seems reasonable to expect that, whatever is reflected in the PMA scores, especially the total and Q- and V-subtests, may be coloring the speech learning picture in twins. In closing it probably should be repeated that, had the twin language picture been sketched when the twins were younger, it might have been different and colored more by twin closeness. At school age there is only a slight intimation in our data of the speech form deficiency other workers have reported.

SEX-ROLE LEARNING IN TWINS

The major questions relative to the sex role learning of twins are the following: Do twins assimilate sex-role behavior more readily or less readily than do nontwins? Do the children from opposite-sex pairs have much conflict over their sex differences? If they do, does this increase their sensitivity to, or discrimination of, society's dictates for each sex, and arouse conflict with respect to their status? Even if this is so, does the twins' behavior provide a model that in subtle ways is followed without the subject being aware of its sex significance? Lastly, should one view learning by DZOS's as mediated chiefly by a desire to conform to the sex code as understood, or does the child tend to veer merely toward generally sanctioned or commended behavior? The girl in the DZOS pair, being less obstreperous, combative, active, and noisy than her brother, is likely to be more approved but not necessarily because she is knowingly conducting herself in a feminine fashion. The boy, merely noting what does receive approbation in his sister, may try to conform to this pattern. If this interpretation is essentially correct, the DZOSm's behavior should become somewhat feminine in cast—gentler and more controlled—and the DZOSf's behavior should not take on much of the coloring of the boisterous, vigorous behavior of the brother, which is likely to be less commended.

One might expect sex-role learning to be influenced some by the child's twin sib, but whether a twin sib has more influence in this matter than do nontwin sibs is the critical question. The MZf's, all of whose main models—sib, mother, teacher—were of the child's sex, were judged particularly feminine and lower correspondingly in masculine-type behavior than were nontwin controls. The DZSSf's, surprisingly, did not differ in femininity from single-born controls. Nor did the various male groups deviate significantly in masculine-type behavior (masculine complex score) from singletons whose sib differed from them in age. The MZm's, moreover, were judged rather sissyish by their teachers, instead of more than normally boyish. Suggesting the cues the teachers may have used in arriving at their judgment, the MZ boys were thought to be significantly less marked than singletons in their insistence on their rights and in competitiveness. At any rate, one obviously cannot make sweeping statements on the basis of the above findings about the extent of twins' influence on the sex typing of each other's behavior.

It seems not unlikely, if there does appear to be a slight tendency toward a more feminine type of behavior on the part of twin boys, that this may be due to the latter's efforts to do what is approved. Since the twins play so much together they may not experience so often the kind of correction which, for instance, an older sib or other children might provide. Indeed, being a twin in a same-sex pair and having no other sib may have a sort of neutralizing effect on sex-role learning. At least on the home scene there may be little opportunity for great conflict to develop over the sex type classification of any behavior of the child. When, however, the twin-pair members are different in sex, then there may be more concern on the part of a youngster if he discovers his conduct is not thought to conform to the sex-role code. This code, however, probably is not particularly well defined, especially when the child is under seven. One effect of this vagueness could be much protestation on the part of a twin and extolling of the merits of his sex, but with his actual behavior not impressively congruent with the sex code, as explained above. The vigorous, aggressive, male-type behavior, is likely to be punished, at school at least, but a milder, female-type may be approved. The DZOS males can then be expected to show more confusion than controls and more of the generally approved type of conduct that is normally more common in young female children than males.

Consistent with the above hypotheses, the DZOSm's were judged less than normally active for males, less emotional and explosive, less given to projecting blame, and less exhibitionistic, loud, and selfish. These are trends that would probably be generally rewarded rather than punished. Despite the brother's efforts to be conforming, the highly conforming DZOS girls seemed rather disapproving of his behavior, and it was the latter's roughness that was generally mentioned critically. The girls from the DZOS twosomes more often affirmed they did not want to be like their brother, did not desire to have the latter in their classes at school, and stated they disliked his roughness and cavalier use of their possessions. Again this may not have been so much a protest against males as an expression of disapprobation of rough and disturbing behavior, which tended to be frowned upon wherever it occurred.

There was considerable evidence of conflict expressed in the interview over their sex and even individual status on the part of the members of the OS pairs. This was, of course, also true of singleton sibs. The DZOS twins were more frequently inclined than other gemini to feel the parents were partial. The more frequent disapproval that the boys received may have resulted in their becoming, as we noted, actually relatively controlled, planful, and subdued, a posture in overt behavior that veers toward the feminine. Much of the DZOS boys' concern and conflict was over the disapproval they received. This they seemed to express more in their CAT stories than in their overt behavior at school. Their CAT stories contained more hostility and catastrophe themes and dealt with more unpleasant mother-child episodes than did the stories of the twins from same-sex pairs. The same trend was noted in the DZOS females but usually not to so significant a degree.

We have no data bearing on the long-time effects of being a twin from either a same- or opposite-sex pair. It has seemed important to us, however, to mention some of the open questions that ought to be explored that are relative to the behavior of the twins of various types in marriage and at different ages in their lives. Do boys, as they age, receive more approbation for conduct in accordance with the male-type code? The possibility of psychiatric trends in the more con-flicted children needs investigation, and this not in relation to the heredity-environment problem, as is the usual practice, but rather in relation to the effects of the play of likely social pressures on the twins. Actually the whole problem of adjustment in adult twins has scarcely been touched.

DOMINANCE-SUBMISSION RELATIONSHIP BETWEEN CO-TWINS

One of the fears parents and educators have is that one twin will come to dominate the other to such an extent that the latter's individ-uality will not come to full fruition. Since chapter 7 has been devoted to this question, all that will be attempted here is a brief summary of issues and a listing of our most relevant findings. Among the major considerations in the dominance-submission issue are the following: Is a D-S relationship necessarily bad? Should conclusions related to a D-S relationship be limited to twins or can the reasoning be carried over to people generally, especially marriage partners, or even nations? Must one's choice depend on how much he values peace, or, in contrast, striving? What happens if there is equality of power and determination on the part of each member of the pair to maintain his status? Can the roles be supporting? Can one child lead in one area and the other, in another, each dominating in the area in which he excels? Is a D-S relationship likely to be stable and long persisting? How early does the relationship develop and what determines it? Is a stable relationship associated with more conflict than a shifting one.

Below are some observations: (1) Evidence of a dominance-non-dominance relationship of a rather clear and stable sort was obtained in the case of about 61 per cent of our pairs. (2) The relationship tended to be less clear-cut and constant in identical twins; sometimes the role shifted, the dominant child becoming the nondominant. (3) Except perhaps in its underlying motivations, closeness between pair members did not seem to be related to the role the child played in the dominance-nondominance relationship area. (4) At the age at which our subjects were studied, dominance seemed to be maintained more by social skills than by physical force. The peck order may have been established earlier on the basis of force, but it is questionable that this follows. (5) Neither birth weight, size at school age, nor IQ was consistently correlated with dominance in most of the twin groups, although each of the first two variables was positively associated in one of the groups. Birth weight and dominance were positively related in the DZSSm's, and size at school age and dominance, in the DZSSf's. (6) In 81 per cent of the pairs in the DZOS group the girl, at school entrance, was the leader in social situations. The DZOS boys showed considerable conflict over playing the subordinate role. (7) The submissive member often seemed aware of the nature of his role —he, for instance, thought the sib more often bossy, stated more frequently he liked to play alone, wished with greater frequency to change places with the sib, and tended to seek out younger playmates. Thus it is clear that some of the twins were not only well aware of their status but did not always like it.

Separation of the Twins at School

As explained earlier, no carefully assembled body of evidence on the trend of effects of separating twins at school has as yet been gathered. Nor does this study add anything substantial, since the paucity of subjects who met the selection criteria prevented the location of an adequate number of subjects who had been submitted to a properly consistent educational regimen.

Since schools often arbitrarily separate or do not separate twins, it is disturbing not to have better factual support for the allegations relative to the psychological influence of the various policies advocated. Such data as were presented in chapter 7 we do not consider to illuminate the question of whether separation preserves individuality. It is believed the findings, at best, may cast some light on what lies back of the separation of any pair. Even this area needs much more extensive exploring. It is very important to state the problem and its ramifications with attention to values implied. For example, one should ask whether twins who, as adults, function in different vocational areas, are necessarily making a better use of their talents than a pair who, like the elder Piccards, explore the same area of science. Would the world of twins be better off if the D-S relationship, against which separation is supposed to protect twins, could be banished from it (which, of course, it cannot)? The question of the optimal time for separating twins at school, if such a policy seems desirable, deserves study, as does also the issue of whether sudden separation is a better procedure than a gradual divorcement.

Evidence has been accumulated during the course of this investigation about what motivates the policy of separating twins. Part of the motivation may be the convenience and comfort of the children's mentors. Vigorous and rivalrous boy pairs, for example, may be difficult to control. Whether this justifies keeping the cotwins apart is a question. Perhaps other ingenious controls could be worked out. At any rate, it is apparent in our data that boys, the more aggressive children, the older, and those possessed of better speech, tended to be found with greater frequency among the separated children, whereas girls, the closer, the more conforming, and the scholastically more able were found in greater numbers among the nonseparated. Separation was common when pair members differed considerably in IQ. When both twins were enrolled in the same class, they were judged more popular. This observation is consistent with a point made earlier that recognition of children as twins tends to beget for them special attention.

THE FIELD OF TWIN RESEARCH

No doubt the variables that condition twin development and attitudes, as is usual with phenomena, are fabulous in number. Sweeping generalizations regarding twins probably are not warranted. Since there are many basic biological and psychological questions that may be illuminated by probes involving twins, it is hoped that many individuals with inclinations for research will see the challenge of discovering what lies buried in the twin area and will direct their efforts into turning up its treasures.

Appendix

Even the casual reader is encouraged to refer to the tables often to achieve full appreciation of the details of the pattern of the results. In addition to the short tables, three large ones that summarize much of the data gathered, other than those yielded by the interviews, are offered at the end of the table list. Since the short tables deal chiefly with significant findings and the more refined statistical analyses, it seemed well to give the reader some opportunity to discover in how many respects the groups compared did *not* differ significantly. This information may be of great significance to those concerned with the adjustment and education of twins. It is of considerable importance, for instance, to know both when twins do and when they do not differ from matched singletons. If the significant differences are few, this may be a source of much relief to some parents. Also, since our data are crude, the reader may find something of interest in group differences below the arbitrary five per cent significance level. The tables make it possible to note readily consistencies in trend from group to group, even though some disparities do not meet the usual significance test.

Table 72 permits twin subgroup comparisons. The table also indicates by a *C* or *F* before an item involving teachers' ratings whether the trait judged was one included in the California Behavior Inventory for Nursery School Children (Conrad 1933) or was included in the Fels Child Behavior Scales (see Richards and Powell [1941] for an analysis of these scales). A *C* means that the rating scale used was taken from the California series; an *F*, from the Fels Scales. Table 73 presents data on twin-singleton differences. Table 74 contains information bearing on the difference between ascendant and nonascendant co-twins. It makes clear that there are very few differences and calls into question the common belief that the nonascendant co-twin tends to be an ineffective person.

Subgroups	Twin Subgroups						Matched Singleton Subgroups					
	N	Age M (Mo.)	σ (Dist.)	Relative frequency of social classes (per cent of group) Class I[a]	Class II	Class III	N	Age M (Mo.)	σ (Dist.)	Relative frequency of social classes (per cent of group) Class I	Class II	Class III
MZm	36	74.2	7.47	44	22	33	72	72.9	6.59	40	25	35
MZf	34	69.5	7.04	29	18	53	64	70.1	5.94	28	30	42
DZSSm	36	70.7	8.40	31	50	19	72	70.3	7.53	43	26	31
DZSSf	36	72.7	6.88	31	31	38	72	72.5	6.38	36	28	36
DZOSm	19	74.5	6.87	37	26	37	76	73.4	6.88	33	24	43
DZOSf	19	74.5	6.87	37	26	37	76	72.9	6.69	30	24	46
Total	180						432					

[a] Class I includes people in the professions, those in higher level executive positions, research workers, people whose training has had to be extensive—contractors, accountants, brokers, welfare workers, pilots, engineers, apothecaries. Class II includes skilled craftsmen, minor executives, owners of retail establishments of moderate size and status—e.g., clothing stores, stores for automobile accessories, florist shops. Trained nurses, typesetters, photographers, insurance agents, postmasters, real estate agents, salesmen selling semitechnical materials would be classified in Class II. Class III includes semi- and unskilled laborers, clerks, chauffeurs, conductors, linemen, brakemen, switchmen, miners, cooks, waiters, mail carriers, domestics, truckers, owners of small stores selling non-technical items— e.g., small butcher shops, and grocery stores, confectioners' shops and saloons. See Minnesota Scale of Occupations (Goodenough and Anderson 1931). Our Class I covers Classes I and II in the Minnesota Scale; our Class II, the Minnesota Class II; our Class III, the Minnesota Classes V, VI, and VII. For the classification of new occupations the census grouping was followed.

Table 2

Mean, Maximums, and Minimums of Pair-member Finger-ridge Count Score Differences

Variables	Slater-Shields-Allen-Nixon linear discriminant function scores					Newman score difference				
	Zygosity groups					Zygosity groups				
	MZ		DZSS		DZOS	MZ		DZSS		DZOS
	Male	Female	Male	Female		Male	Female	Male	Female	
No. of pairs	18	17	14	16	16	18	17	14	16	16
Mean	2.340	3.988	6.650	5.463	9.225	4.7	6.2	29.2	18.0	30.7
Maximum	5.466	6.857	17.479	8.353	13.063	12.0	17.0	82.0	43.0	68.0
Minimum	.618	.728	2.853	2.459	4.169	1.0	0.0	4.0	1.0	2.0

Table 3

Mean Number of Finger Pairs per Pair of Twins in which Fingerprint Patterns Were Similar

Variables	Zygosity groups				
	MZ		DZSS		DZOS
	Male	Female	Male	Female	
No. of pairs	18	17	14	16	16
Mean	8.3	7.4	5.0	4.0	3.8
Maximum	10	9	8	7	8
Minimum	6	6	1	3	0

Table 4

Per Cent of Concordance in Selected Traits between Twin Pair Members

Variable	Zygosity groups				
	MZ		DZSS		DZOS
	Male	Female	Male	Female	
No. of pairs	18	17	18	17	19
Mean per cent of concordance	95	93	45	41	27
Maximum	100	100	58	69	58
Minimum	83	75	25	25	17

Table 5

Mean Birth Weight, and Weight and Height at Five to Six Years of Subjects in Various Twin and Social Class Subgroups

(Three-way Analysis of Variance—Zygosity, Sex, Social Class)

Social class	Twin subgroups							
	MZ				DZSS			
	Male		Female		Male		Female	
	N	M	N	M	N	M	N	M
Birth Weight (Pounds)								
I	16	5.4	10	5.0	12	5.5	9	4.9
II	8	6.1	6	6.3	14	5.3	10	4.7
III	12	5.0	18	4.5	6	6.1	12	5.7
Total	36	16.5	34	15.8	32	16.9	30	15.3

Sex — F = 3.45; p = .10 — .05
Zygosity x class — F = 9.85; p = .01 — .001

Social class	MZ				DZSS			
	Male		Female		Male		Female	
Weight at Five to Six Years (Pounds)								
I	16	48.5	10	45.1	12	42.0	12	48.3
II	8	45.9	6	49.7	14	44.1	10	46.7
III	12	52.5	18	43.5	6	45.2	12	45.3
Total	36	146.9	34	138.3	32	131.3	34	140.3

Zygosity — F = 3.35; p = .10 — .05
Zygosity x sex — F = 8.93; p = .01 — .001

Social class	MZ				DZSS			
	Male		Female		Male		Female	
Height at Five to Six Years (Inches)								
I	16	46.3	10	45.9	12	44.1	12	46.5
II	8	46.0	6	47.5	14	45.7	10	46.0
III	12	43.8	18	45.3	6	44.9	12	46.1
Total	36	136.1	34	138.7	32	134.7	34	138.6

Nothing significant

Table 6

Mean Birth Weight, and Weight and Height at Five to Six Years of Various Fraternal Twin Groups

(Two-way Analysis of Variance—Sex of Sib and Social Class)

Social class	Male				Female			
	DZSS		DZOS		DZSS		DZOS	
	N	M	N	M	N	M	N	M
Birth Weight (Pounds)								
I	12	5.5	6	5.8	8	4.9	6	5.1
II	14	5.3	4	6.1	10	4.7	4	5.9
III	6	6.1	5	4.6	12	5.7	5	4.0
Total	32	16.9	15	16.5	30	15.3	15	15.0

Nothing significant

Weight at Five to Six Years (Pounds)								
I	12	42.0	6	47.4	12	48.3	6	48.2
II	14	44.1	4	54.9	10	46.7	4	44.1
III	6	45.2	5	46.5	12	45.3	5	44.4
Total	32	131.3	15	148.8	34	140.3	15	136.7

Sex of sib — $F = 4.12$; $p = .05$ Sex of sib x class — $F = 3.31$;
Sex of sib x class — $F = 3.0$; $p = .10 - .05$ $p = .05$

Height at Five to Six Years (Inches)								
I	12	44.1	6	47.6	12	46.6	6	47.1
II	14	45.7	4	47.1	10	46.0	4	46.1
III	6	44.9	5	47.0	12	46.1	5	46.5
Total	32	134.7	15	141.7	34	138.7	15	139.7

Nothing significant

Size and Maturity Characteristics of Newborn Twins and Some Features of Their Mothers Relevant to Childbearing

Variables	MZ				DZSS				DZOS			
	N	Male	N	Female	N	Male	N	Female	N	Male	N	Female
Mean birth weight (oz.)	36	86.6	34	79.5	32	87.6	30	83.2	15	87.1	15	74.7
Intraclass r for birth weight	18	82	17	65	16	49	15	84	15	73	15	
Mean pair member difference in birth weight (oz.)	36	7.6	34	10.4	32	12.1	30	11.5	15	12.4	15	12.4
Per cent with birth weight under 4 1/2 lbs.	36	28	34	44	32	16	30	33	15	27	15	33
Per cent with birth weight 4 1/2 to 5 1/2 lbs.	36	25	34	18	32	28	30	33	15	33	15	40
Per cent with birth weight over 5 1/2 lbs.	36	47	34	38	32	56	30	33	15	40	15	27
Incidence of prematurity	36	53	34	62	32	44	30	66	15	60	15	73
Mean birth weight of first-borns (oz.)	17[a]	85.2	17	80.2	16	91.6	15	84.8	11	87.5	3	71
Mean birth weight of second-borns (oz.)	17	86.3	17	78.7	16	84.1	15	81.6	3	71.7	11	75.7
Per cent of times first-born is heavier member of pair	17	59	17	65	16	63	15	71	14	73	14	33
No. of prematures among first-borns	17	9	17	10	16	7	15	10	14	6	14	2
No. of prematures among second-borns	17	10	17	11	16	7	15	10	14	2	14	9
Mean age of mother at marriage (yrs.)	16	22.6	17	23.6	16	24.6	15	24.5	15	23.1	15	23.1
Mean age of mother at birth of twins (yrs.)	16	26.1	17	26.8	16	28.9	15	30.6	15	28.8	15	28.8
Mean interval between mother's age at marriage and birth of twins (yrs.)	16	3.5	17	3.2	16	5.8	15	6	15	4.2	15	4.2

[a]In a few instances, since the twins were delivered by Cesarian section, birth order was not known.

Table 8

Size Characteristics of Twins and Matched Singletons at Ages Five to Six Years; Comparison of First- and Second-born[a]

Group	MZ[b]								DZSS[b]								DZOS								Total twin	
	N	Twin male	N	Matched singleton	N	Twin female	N	Matched singleton	N	Twin male	N	Matched singleton	N	Twin female	N	Matched singleton	N	Twin male	N	Matched singleton	N	Twin female	N	Matched singleton	N	
Mean weight (lbs.) of first-born	17	49.4	17	50.7	17	45.6	17	49.8	16	44.6	15	51.1	15	46.8	30	50.4	12	45.4	48	51.4	3	44.9	12	50.0		
Mean weight (lbs.) of second-born[c]	17	48.9	17	53.3	17	44.9	17	47.5	16	43.7	15	52.0	15	45.4	30	48.5	3	47.9	12	54.7	12	46.1	48	48.0		
Mean height (inches) of first-born	17	45.4	17	46.7	17	46.0	17	46.6	16	44.9	15	46.9	15	46.3	30	46.5	12	46.4	48	47.1	3	45.4	12	47.0		
Mean height (inches) of second-born	17	45.2	17	47.3	17	45.7	17	45.4	16	45.2	15	47.1	15	46.0	30	45.9	3	49.9	12	47.3	12	46.7	48	46.4		
% of first-borns who are heavier member of pair	17	68			17	59			16	65			15	69			12	58			3	33				
% of first-borns who are taller member of pair	17	53			17	53			16	35			15	63			12	58			3	0				
% of pair members maintaining same relative status in weight up to 5-6 years	34	67			34	94			32	67			30	80			15	53			15	53				
% of first-borns with higher IQ	17	35			17	38			16	36			17	57			12	33			3	67				
% of first-borns who are dominant co-twins	17	58			17	59			16	53			17	56			12	17			3	100				
Mean health rating	36	4.17	34	3.92	34	4.09	34	3.98	34	3.59		3.9	34	4.0		4.0	19	3.8	76	4.1	19	3.8	76	4.1		
Mean pair-member difference in weight	18	1.8			17	2.6			16	4.5			17	4.3											15	6.3
Mean pair-member difference in height	18	.6			17	.4			16	1.7			17	1.8											15	3.1
Intraclass r for weight	18	95			17	77			16	65			17	37											15	70
Intraclass r for height	18	97			17	95			16	63			17	45											15	58

[a]The N's for the different variables are not always in agreement because of incomplete information.

[b]Significant at the .05 levels or better are the following twin-singleton differences: MZm, mean heights; DZSSm, mean weights and heights.

[c]The second-born singletons are not strictly comparable to second-born twins, as the latter are essentially first-born children.

Two-way Analysis of Variance of Same-sex Twin-singleton Differences in Weight and Height at Five to Six Years

Group	Weight, mean difference						Height, mean difference					
	Male		Female		Total		Male		Female		Total	
	N	M	N	M	N	M	N	M	N	M	N	M
MZ	18	−2.07	17	−3.45	35	−2.77	18	−1.53	17	−.01	35	−.78
DZSS	16	−5.90	17	−3.19	33	−4.56	16	−1.43	17	−.01	33	−.73
Total	34	−4.01	34	−3.34			34	−1.48	34	−.01		
Interaction MZ		−1.03		−1.06				−.02		.02		
DZSS		−1.00		1.03				.02		−.02		

DZSSm < matched single – p = .05

MZM < matched singleton – p = .05
DZSSm < matched singleton – p = .05

Table 10

Relation of Birth Weight to Number of Individuals in Various Twin Groups Having at Least One Defect

Group	Birth weight									Prematures with defects			
	Under 4 1/2 lbs.			4 1/2 to 5 1/2 lbs.			Over 5 1/2 lbs.						
	Total N	N with some defect	% with defect	Total N	N with some defect	% with defect	Total N	N with some defect	% with defect	Total N	No. prematures	No. prematures with defect	% Prematures with defect
MZm	10	7	70	9	1	11	17	10	59	36	19	8	42
MZf	15	1	7	6	0	0	13	5	38	34	21	1	05
DZSSm	5	4	80	9	3	33	18	1	06	32	14	7	50
DZSSf	10	3	30	10	1	10	10	0	00	30	20	4	20
DZOSm	4	3	75	5	1	20	6	1	17	15	9	4	44
DZOSf	5	2	40	6	4	67	4	1	25	15	11	6	55
Total	49	20	41	45	10	22	68	18	26	162	94	30	32

Table 11

Number and Type of Defect in Various Twin Subgroups

	Twin subgroups									Grand total
	MZm	MZf	MZ (total)	DZSSm	DZSSf	DZSS (total)	DZOSm	DZOSf	DZOS (total)	
No. of subjects	36	34	70	34	34	68	17	17	34	172
No. of dental and oral defects	5	0	5	4	2	6	1	2	3	14
No. of ocular defects at school age	6	3	9	4	1	5	5	8	13	27
No. of other physical defects (clubfoot, heart, kidney, etc.)	3	1	4	1	1	2	1	1	2	8
I.Q. below 90	7	0	7	2	1	3	0	2	2	12
Defect per individual	.58	.12	.36	.32	.15	.24	.41	.76	.59	.35

Table 12

Incidence of Those Wearing Glasses at Five to Six Years of Age among Subjects with Different Birth Weights

Maturity level	Twin subgroup																	
	MZm		MZf		MZ (total)		DZSSm		DZSSf		DZSS (total)		DZOSm		DZOSf		DZOS (total)	
	N	%	N	%	N	%	N	%	N	%	N	%	N	%	N	%	N	%
Birth weight under 4 1/2 lbs.	1	10	1	07	2	08	1	20	1	10	2	13	2	50	2	40	4	44
Birth weight, 4 1/2 to 5 1/2 lbs.	2	22	0	00	2	13	3	33	0	0	3	15	1	20	3	50	4	36
Birth weight over 5 1/2 lbs.	3	18	2	15	5	17	0	0	0	0	0	0	0	0	1	25	1	10

Table 13

Age at Certain Critical Periods in the Life of Mothers of Twins in Various Sub-twin and Social-class Groups

(Three-way Analysis of Variance in Same-sex Pairs (Zygosity, Sex, and Social Class) and Two-way Analysis in Fraternal Pairs (Sex of Sib and Class)

Social class	MZ				DZSS				DZOS			
	Male		Female		Male		Female		Male		Female	
	N	M	N	M	N	M	N	M	N	M	N	M
Mean Age of Mothers at Marriage												
I	7	21.4	5	22.8	6	23.5	4	23.5	6	25.8	6	25.8
II	3	24.0	3	24.7	7	26.3	5	26.2	4	21.8	4	21.8
III	6	22.3	9	23.3	3	24.0	6	23.8	5	21.8	5	21.8
Total	16	67.7	17	70.8	16	73.8	15	73.5	15	69.4	15	69.4

Nothing significant

Social class	MZ				DZSS				DZOS			
Mean Age of Mothers at Birth of Twins												
I	7	26.6	5	26.4	6	30.5	4	26.3	6	29.3	6	29.3
II	3	26.7	3	26.3	7	29.4	5	33.6	4	27.5	4	27.5
III	6	25.0	9	27.7	3	26.7	6	31.8	5	29.6	5	29.6
Total	16	78.3	17	80.4	16	86.6	15	91.7	15	86.4	15	86.4

Zygosity - F = 4.58; p = .05 - .01

Table 14

Correlation between Birth Weight of Twins and Mother Variables

Group	N	Mother variables		
		Mother's age at marriage	Mother's age at birth of twins	Interval between mother's age at marriage and at birth of twins
Total group	158	12	−01	−01
MZm	32	28	52[a]	35[a]
MZf	34	−06	−19	−27
DZSSm	32	06	−32	−41[a]
DZSSf	30	30	−28	−08
DZOSm	15	−21	03	21
DZOSf	15	−23	23	05

[a]Significant at 5% level or better.

Table 15

Mean Health Rating for Various Twin Subgroups; MZ vs. DZSS
(Three-way Analysis of Variance; Zygosity, Sex, and Social Class)

Social class	MZ				DZSS			
	Male		Female		Male		Female	
	N	M	N	M	N	M	N	M
I	16	4.02	10	3.84	12	3.66	12	3.79
II	8	4.37	6	4.40	16	3.75	10	4.51
III	12	4.23	18	4.03	8	3.15	12	4.39
Total	36	12.62	34	12.27	36	10.56	34	12.69

Zygosity x sex — F = 5.18; p = .05 − .01

Table 16

Mean Health Ratings for Various Fraternal Twin Groups
(Two-way Analysis of Variance; Sex of Sib and Social Class)

Social class	Male				Female			
	DZSS		DZOS		DZSS		DZOS	
	N	M	N	M	N	M	N	M
I	12	3.66	7	4.33	12	3.79	7	4.15
II	16	3.75	5	2.98	10	4.51	5	3.43
III	8	3.15	7	3.95	12	4.39	7	3.73
Total	36	10.56	19	11.26	34	12.69	19	11.31

Sex of sib x class; F = 4.53; p = .05 − .01	Nothing significant

Table 17

Three-way Analysis of Variance (Zygosity, Sex, Social Class) of Various PMA Subtest Quotients, and the Quotient Scores for the Total Test

(Mean Quotient Score for Various Twins and Social-class Subgroups)

Social class	MZ				DZSS				DZOS			
	Males		Females		Males		Females		Males		Females	
	N	M	N	M	N	M	N	M	N	M	N	M
Total Test Quotient Scores												
I	16	109.3	8	104.6	8	107.0	10	115.1	6	113.3	6	118.0
II	8	108.1	6	109.7	16	109.0	10	110.9	5	115.2	5	109.4
III	10	93.2	18	102.8	6	105.8	10	103.0	6	100.5	6	97.0
Total	34	310.6	32	317.1	30	321.8	30	329.0	17	329.0	17	324.4

Zygosity - F^a = 4.65; p = .05 - .01
Class - F = 8.99; p = .01 - .001

Social class	MZ				DZSS				DZOS			
	Males		Females		Males		Females		Males		Females	
	N	M	N	M	N	M	N	M	N	M	N	M
Verbal Test Quotients												
I	16	104.4	8	110.3	8	107.9	10	111.8	6	115.0	6	113.3
II	8	106.9	6	98.3	16	110.4	10	106.2	5	117.2	5	113.0
III	10	87.1	18	104.4	6	102.0	10	103.3	6	99.8	6	97.8
Total	34	298.4	32	313.0	30	320.3	30	321.3	17	332.0	17	324.1

Zygosity - F = 6.15; p = .05 - .01
Class - F = 7.42; p = .01 - .001

[a] F's given are for the MZ - DZSS comparison.
There are no significant DZSS - DZOS differences.

Table 17 (continued)

Social class	MZ				DZSS				DZOS			
	Males		Females		Males		Females		Males		Females	
	N	M	N	M	N	M	N	M	N	M	N	M
Perceptual Test Quotients												
I	16	114.6	8	118.9	8	103.4	10	120.3	6	111.2	6	119.0
II	8	108.1	6	115.2	16	108.0	10	121.5	5	124.6	5	123.6
III	10	100.4	18	109.0	6	106.8	10	106.7	6	109.8	6	98.8
Total	34	323.1	32	343.1	30	318.2	30	348.5	17	345.6	17	341.4

Sex - F = 13.15; p = .001
Class - F = 5.44; p = .05 - .01

Social class	MZ				DZSS				DZOS			
	Males		Females		Males		Females		Males		Females	
	N	M	N	M	N	M	N	M	N	M	N	M
Quantitative Test Quotients												
I	16	113.5	8	96.9	8	102.7	10	117.9	6	114.2	6	121.0
II	8	110.1	6	118.3	16	110.6	10	114.3	5	106.2	5	110.8
III	10	94.0	18	100.4	6	108.0	10	105.0	6	105.0	6	99.3
Total	34	317.6	32	315.6	30	321.3	30	337.2	17	325.4	17	331.1

Class - F = 5.76; p = .05 - .01

Social class	MZ				DZSS				DZOS			
	Males		Females		Males		Females		Males		Females	
	N	M	N	M	N	M	N	M	N	M	N	M
Spatial Test Quotient												
I	16	105.2	8	98.5	8	107.0	10	110.2	6	108.3	6	122.2
II	8	102.6	6	104.2	16	98.9	10	106.7	5	121.2	5	104.6
III	10	99.2	18	97.9	6	110.5	10	101.1	6	101.7	6	97.8
Total	34	307.0	32	300.6	30	316.4	30	318.0	17	331.2	17	324.6

Nothing significant

214

Table 18

PMA Mean Quotient Scores of Twins and Matched Singletons

Group	N	Test				
		Total	V	P	Q	S
MZm	34	104.3	98.8	107.6	105.9	102.8
Matched singleton	68	109.3	116.9	100.8	113.7	107.3
Significance of difference		.05−.02	<.001	.10−.05	.05−.02	.05−.02
MZf	32	105.4	105.8	113.0	103.4	100.1
Matched singleton	64	107.8	111.7	104.4	111.7	107.3
Significance of difference			.05−.02	.05−.02		
DZSSm	30	107.8	107.9	106.2	107.8	103.4
Matched singleton	60	111.6	119.5	103.4	114.1	109.6
Significance of difference			.01−.001			
DZSSf	30	108.7	105.7	115.7	110.9	104.4
Matched singleton	60	107.5	111.5	103.3	110.9	106.3
Significance of difference			.05−.02	.01−.001		
DZOSm	17	109.0	110.4	114.7	105.7	109.5
Matched singleton	68	108.6	114.6	102.4	112.8	105.4
Significance of difference				.01−.001		
DZOSf	17	108.6	106.1	113.2	110.3	108.3
Matched singleton	68	110.4	113.4	106.6	115.1	107.4
Significance of difference						

215

Table 19

Reliability Coefficients of Various Measures of Language Performance Based on the Children's Apperception Test

Type of reliability	First vs. second scoring		Interscorer correlations		Test-retest correlations		Split-halves correlations		Corrected split-halves correlations	
Measure	N	r	N	r	N	r	N	r	N	r
Syntax error count	116	97					164	86	164	92
Word count	83	99	12	99	50	78	167	88	167	92
Thematic-descriptive score	113	99	36	99	50	70	167	99	167	99
Incoherence rating			12	84	50	59	167	70	167	82

216

Intercorrelations of Measures of Various Aspects of Language and Speech Performance in the Total Twin Population

	Teacher's rating of speech form	K's rating of speech form	Syntax error counts	Rating of talkativeness	CAT, word count	CAT, thematic-descriptive score	CAT, incoherence score	PMA, verbal test	PMA, total test	PMA, perceptual test	PMA, quantitative test	PMA, motor test	PMA, spatial test
Mother's rating of difficulty in speech learning	-55[b]	73	37	-12	07	-17	27	-31	-34	-15	-40	-14	-08
Teacher's rating of speech form		-49	-35	16	02	17	-22	38	32	25	28	13	11
K's rating of speech form			38	00	-01	-10	26	-24	-35	-22	-43	-18	-20
Syntax error counts				-20	-11	-17	39	-26	-31	-19	-32	-10	-09
Rating on talkativeness					06	08	-07	18	14	14	08	07	-03
CAT, Word count						49	-04	14	10	04	09	09	-11
CAT, Thematic-descriptive score							-34	19	11	20	07	-02	04
CAT, Incoherence score								-13	-23	-20	-26	-05	-21
PMA, Verbal test									74	40	39	37	34

[a] In items 1, 3, 4, and 8 a high score means poor performance, whereas in the other items a high score indicates merit. Correlations over 15 are significant.

[b] Decimal points omitted in all correlations.

Table 21

Intertwin Group Differences in Speech and Language Performance; MZ vs. DZSS Means
(Three-way Analysis of Variance Involving Zygosity, Sex, and Social Class)

Social class	MZ				DZSS			
	Male		Female		Male		Female	
	N	M	N	M	N	M	N	M
Teacher's Rating of Speech Form								
I	16	3.96	10	3.41	12	4.12	12	4.25
II	8	4.14	6	3.42	16	3.79	10	4.83
III	12	2.39	18	3.81	8	3.60	12	4.17
Total	36	10.49	34	10.64	36	11.51	34	13.25

Zygosity — F = 11.33; p = < .001. Class — F = 3.50; p = .05 — .01
Sex x class — F = 3.91; p = .05 — .01

	K's Rating of Speech Form[a]							
I	16	3.00	10	4.58	10	4.40	12	2.40
II	8	2.88	6	3.83	14	3.07	6	3.50
III	12	4.58	18	3.50	6	3.67	12	2.71
Total	36	10.46	34	11.91	30	11.14	30	8.61

Zygosity x sex — F = 6.51; p = .01 — .001

	CAT, Syntax Error Count							
I	16	15.8	10	20.2	9	23.4	10	14.6
II	8	18.1	6	20.8	14	16.4	6	13.5
III	12	36.8	18	19.3	4	21.2	12	16.3
Total	36	70.7	34	60.3	27	61.0	28	44.4

Zygosity — F = 7.25; p = .01 — .001. Sex — F = 11.5; p = .01 — .001

	Teacher's Rating of Talkativeness							
I	16	3.93	10	3.87	12	3.93	12	3.62
II	8	3.59	6	3.89	16	4.07	10	4.27
III	12	3.45	18	4.09	8	3.71	12	3.75
Total	36	10.97	34	11.85	36	11.71	34	11.64

Nothing significant

	CAT, Word Count							
I	16	870	10	1090	9	550	10	700
II	8	550	6	560	14	600	6	780
III	12	470	18	590	6	350	12	730
Total	36	1890	34	2240	29	1500	28	2210

Nothing significant

	CAT, Thematic-descriptive Score							
I	16	36.4	10	39.4	9	30.4	10	37.7
II	8	25.6	6	35.3	14	36.1	6	41.7
III	12	28.3	18	31.0	6	29.0	12	29.3
Total	36	90.3	34	105.7	29	95.5	28	108.7

Sex — F = 5.27; p = .05 — .01.   Class — F = 3.76; p = .05 — .01

	CAT, Incoherence Score[a]							
I	16	26.0	10	27.2	9	28.9	10	26.6
II	8	28.8	6	26.0	14	23.3	6	18.8
III	12	30.9	18	29.4	6	28.7	12	30.3
Total	36	85.7	34	82.6	29	80.9	28	75.7

Class — F = 5.56; p = .01 — .001

[a]Lower score here indicates better form.

Table 22

Fraternal Twin Group Differences in Speech and Language Performance; DZSS vs. DZOS Means

(Two-way Analysis of Variance; Sex of Sib and Social Class)

Social class	Males				Females			
	DZSS		DZOS		DZSS		DZOS	
	N	M	N	M	N	M	N	M
Teacher's Rating of Speech Form								
I	12	4.12	7	3.88	12	4.25	7	4.39
II	16	3.79	5	3.01	10	4.83	5	3.32
III	8	3.60	7	4.25	12	4.17	7	4.17
Total	36	11.51	19	11.14	34	13.25	19	11.88

Nothing significant

	K's Rating of Speech Form[a]							
I	10	4.40	7	3.57	12	2.40	7	2.86
II	14	3.07	5	3.60	6	3.50	5	2.80
III	6	3.67	7	4.86	12	2.71	7	3.43
Total	20	11.14	19	12.03	30	8.61	19	9.09

Nothing significant

	CAT, Syntax Error Count							
I	9	23.4	7	18.6	10	14.6	7	14.6
II	14	16.4	5	20.0	6	13.5	5	15.4
III	4	21.2	7	14.9	12	16.3	7	14.6
Total	27	61.0	19	53.5	28	44.4	19	44.6

Nothing significant

	Teacher's Rating of Talkativeness							
I	12	3.93	7	4.04	12	3.62	7	3.57
II	16	4.07	5	3.40	10	4.27	5	3.87
III	8	3.71	7	3.65	12	3.75	7	3.83
Total	36	11.71	19	11.09	34	11.64	19	11.27

Nothing significant

	CAT, Word Count							
I	9	550	7	1210	10	700	7	780
II	14	600	5	650	6	780	5	1070
III	6	350	7	560	12	730	7	850
Total	29	1500	19	2420	28	2210	19	2700

Nothing significant

	CAT, Thematic-descriptive Score							
I	9	30.4	7	42.0	10	37.7	7	36.2
II	14	36.1	5	32.8	6	41.7	5	41.6
III	6	29.0	7	33.4	12	29.3	7	43.0
Total	29	95.5	19	108.2	28	108.7	19	120.8

Nothing significant

	CAT, Incoherence Score[a]							
I	9	28.9	7	21.7	10	26.6	7	23.6
II	14	23.3	5	27.2	6	18.8	5	22.8
III	6	28.7	7	27.4	12	30.3	7	20.7
Total	29	80.9	19	76.3	28	75.7	19	67.1

Nothing significant

[a]Lower score here indicates better form.

Table 23

Mean of Twin and Singleton Scores on Various Aspects of Speech and Language Performance as well as in Social Involvement (t-test)

| Measure | MZ | | | | DZSS | | | | DZOS | | | |
| | Males | | Females | | Males | | Females | | Males | | Females | |
	N	M	N	M	N	M	N	M	N	M	N	M
Teachers' Rating of Speech Form												
Twin	36	3.48	34	3.62	36	3.86	34	4.36	19	3.79	19	4.03
Matched singleton	72	4.03	68	3.86	72	4.04	68	4.00	76	3.72	76	4.11
p diff.	.10-.05		N.S.		N.S.		.10-.05		N.S.		N.S.	
K's Rating of Speech Form[a]												
Twin	36	3.50	34	3.94	30	3.66	30	2.77	19	4.00	19	3.05
Matched singleton	72	3.82	68	3.81	60	3.81	60	3.67	76	3.90	76	3.59
p diff.	N.S.		N.S.		N.S.		.01		N.S.		N.S.	
Syntax Error Counts[a]												
Twin	36	23.6	32	20.1	27	20.0	28	14.8	19	17.8	19	14.8
Matched singleton	12	16.1	12	18.7	12	16.1	12	18.8	12	17.9	12	19.5
p diff.	.01		N.S.		.01		.01		N.S.		.05	
Teachers' Rating of Talkativeness												
Twin	36	3.69	34	4.06	36	3.94	34	3.85	19	3.73	19	3.75
Matched singleton	72	4.02	68	3.88	72	4.23	68	3.85	76	4.04	76	3.99
p diff.	N.S.		N.S.		.02		N.S.		N.S.		N.S.	

| | MZ | | | | DZSS | | | | DZOS | | | |
| | Males | | Females | | Males | | Females | | Males | | Females | |
Measure	N	M	N	M	N	M	N	M	N	M	N	M
CAT, Word Count												
Twin	36	655	34	675	29	532	28	823	19	1195	19	875
Matched singleton	36	699	34	775	29	666	28	783	19	665	19	1141
p diff.	N.S.		N.S.		N.S.		N.S.		N.S.		N.S.	
CAT, Thematic-descriptive Score												
Twin	36	31.3	34	34.5	29	32.1	28	34.9	19	36.4	19	40.2
Matched singleton	36	33.3	34	34.9	29	32.9	28	35.4	19	38.6	19	39.6
p diff.	N.S.		N.S.		N.S.		N.S.		N.S.		N.S.	
CAT, Incoherence Score[a]												
Twin	36	28.3	34	27.9	29	26.1	28	26.9	19	35.3	19	22.3
Matched singleton	36	29.9	34	29.4	29	31.3	28	28.1	19	30.9	19	30.1
p diff.	N.S.		N.S.		.01		N.S.		.05		.01	
PMA V-test Quotient												
Twin	34	98.8	32	105.8	30	107.9	30	105.7	17	110.4	17	106.1
Matched singleton	68	116.9	64	111.8	60	119.5	60	111.5	68	114.6	68	113.4
p diff.	.01-.001		05		.01-.001		.02		.20-.10		.10-.05	

[a]Lower score means greater merit.

221

Table 24

Correlations between Various Measures of Speech and Language Performance and Certain Measures of Social Experience or Involvement

	Mother's rating of speech progress	Teacher's rating of speech form	K's rating of articulation errors	Syntax error count	Rating of talkativeness	CAT word count	CAT thematic-descriptive score	CAT incoherence score	PMA V-subtest
Twin closeness	−05[a]	07	01	08	06	−12	−04	09	−08
No. of playmates	−22	16	−15	−10	08	02	12	−07	01
Rating of gregariousness	−16	28	−25	−21	30	09	29	−24	29
Involvement with adults	−12	13	01	−35	48	01	14	−07	08
Involvement with children	−27	36	−30	−34	45	14	33	−27	33
Rating of popularity	−34	42	−35	−27	14	13	33	−26	32
Social class	11	−12	06	11	−02	−19	−22	15	−32

[a]Decimal point is omitted in all correlations. Correlations of 15 or over are significant.

222

Mean of Twin Pair and Mean of Four Matched Singleton Scores for Various Measures of Social Involvement (t-test)

	MZ				DZSS				DZOS			
	Males		Females		Males		Females		Males		Females	
	N	M	N	M	N	M	N	M	N	M	N	M
Involvement with Adults												
Twin	18	3.89	17	4.28	18	3.97	17	4.13	19	3.87	19	3.94
Matched singleton	18	3.88	17	4.03	18	3.97	17	4.08	19	3.90	19	4.14
p diff.	N.S.		.10–.05		N.S.		N.S.		N.S.		.10–.05	
Involvement with Children												
Twin	18	3.62	17	4.30	18	3.87	17	4.27	19	4.00	19	4.01
Matched singleton	18	3.93	17	3.96	18	3.95	17	4.07	19	3.87	19	4.21
p diff.	.10		.05–.02		N.S.		.02–.01		N.S.		N.S.	
Number of Playmates												
Twin	18	4.6	17	4.4	15	4.6	16	4.3	19	3.6	19	4.1
Matched singleton	18	4.2	17	4.0	15	4.2	16	4.1	19	3.8	19	4.8
p diff.	N.S.		N.S.		N.S.		N.S.		N.S.		N.S.	
Rating of Gregariousness												
Twin	18	3.35	17	4.12	18	4.03	17	4.33	19	4.05	19	3.77
Matched singleton	18	3.90	17	3.98	18	3.94	17	4.12	19	3.80	19	4.29
p diff.	.05–.02		N.S.		N.S.		N.S.		N.S.		.05–.02	
Rating of Popularity												
Twin	18	3.71	17	4.75	18	3.92	17	4.75	19	4.12	19	4.41
Matched singleton	18	3.95	17	4.00	18	3.87	17	4.17	19	3.84	19	4.15
p diff.	N.S.		.01–.001		N.S.		.01–.001		N.S.		N.S.	

Table 26

Intertwin Group Differences in Social Involvements; MZ vs. DZSS Means
(Three-way Analysis of Variance; Zygosity, Sex, and Social Class)

	MZ				DZSS			
Social class	Male		Female		Male		Female	
	N	M	N	M	N	M	N	M
	Twin Closeness Score							
I	16	7.8	10	7.7	10	6.7	10	6.0
II	8	7.3	6	7.8	14	5.4	8	9.6
III	12	7.5	18	8.9	6	6.2	12	7.0
Total	36	22.6	34	24.4	30	18.3	30	22.6

Zygosity — F = 5.24; p = .05 — .01
Sex — F = 5.46; p .05 — .01

	Involvement with Adults							
I	16	4.10	10	4.13	12	3.98	12	4.07
II	8	4.02	6	4.35	16	3.92	10	4.21
III	12	3.55	18	4.33	8	3.93	12	4.13
Total	36	11.67	34	12.81	36	11.83	34	12.41

Sex — F = 8.96; p = .01 — .001

	Involvement with Children							
I	16	3.84	10	4.32	12	3.82	12	4.28
II	8	3.91	6	4.13	16	3.99	10	4.41
III	12	3.13	18	4.36	8	3.69	12	4.17
Total	36	10.88	34	12.81	36	11.50	34	12.86

Sex — F = 25.78; p = < .001

	Number of Playmates Listed							
I	16	4.3	10	4.8	10	3.1	12	4.2
II	8	5.3	6	3.0	14	6.0	8	4.0
III	12	4.6	18	4.6	6	3.7	12	4.6
Total	36	14.2	34	12.4	30	12.8	32	12.8

Sex x class — F = 6.54; p = .01

	Rating of Gregariousness							
I	16	3.59	10	4.29	12	3.92	12	4.04
II	8	3.71	6	4.21	16	4.05	10	4.66
III	12	2.80	18	3.96	8	4.15	12	4.26
Total	36	10.10	34	12.46	36	12.12	34	12.96

Zygosity — F = 7.55; p = .01 — .001
Sex — F = 12.11; p < .001

	Rating of Popularity							
I	16	4.14	10	4.90	12	4.00	12	4.91
II	8	4.28	6	4.34	16	4.11	10	5.17
III	12	2.78	18	4.68	8	3.41	12	4.48
Total	36	11.20	34	13.92	36	11.52	34	14.56

Sex — F = 33.17 ; p = < .001
Class — F = 6.65; p = .01

Table 27

Intertwin Group Differences in Social Involvements; DZSS vs. DZOS Means
(Two-way Analysis of Variance; Sex of Sibling and Social Class)

Social class	Male				Female			
	DZSS		DZOS		DZSS		DZOS	
	N	M	N	M	N	M	N	M
Twin Closeness Score								
I	10	6.7	7	4.7	10	6.0	7	4.6
II	14	5.4	5	4.8	8	9.6	5	5.4
III	6	6.2	7	4.6	12	7.0	7	5.7
Total	30	18.3	19	14.1	30	22.6	19	15.7
					Sex of sibling — F = 9.25; p = < .01			
Involvement with Adults								
I	12	3.98	7	3.88	12	4.07	7	3.99
II	16	3.92	5	3.67	10	4.21	5	3.64
III	8	3.93	7	4.00	12	4.13	7	4.10
Total	36	11.83	19	11.55	34	12.41	19	11.73
Nothing significant								
Involvement with Children								
I	12	3.82	7	4.10	12	4.28	7	4.05
II	16	3.99	5	3.91	10	4.41	5	4.15
III	8	3.69	7	3.98	12	4.17	7	3.85
Total	36	11.50	19	11.99	34	12.86	19	12.05
Nothing significant								
Number of Playmates Listed								
I	10	3.1	7	4.1	12	4.2	7	4.9
II	14	6.0	5	3.4	8	4.0	5	3.4
III	6	3.7	7	3.3	12	4.6	7	3.9
Total	30	12.8	19	10.8	32	12.8	19	12.2
Nothing significant								
Rating of Gregariousness								
I	12	3.92	7	4.13	12	4.04	7	3.54
II	16	4.05	5	3.98	10	4.66	5	3.95
III	8	4.15	7	4.03	12	4.26	7	3.63
Total	36	12.12	19	12.14	34	12.96	19	11.12
Nothing significant								
Rating of Popularity								
I	12	4.00	7	4.32	12	4.91	7	4.39
II	16	4.11	5	3.87	10	5.17	5	4.76
III	8	3.41	7	4.10	12	4.48	7	4.19
Total	36	11.52	19	12.29	34	14.56	19	13.34
Nothing significant								

Table 28

Intercorrelations of Various Measures of Social Experience and Involvement, Total Twin Group (N = 163–72)[a]

	No. of playmates	Rating of gregariousness	Involvement with adults	Involvement with children	Rating on popularity	Social class
Twin closeness	02	–02	16	09	07	08
No. of playmates		19	11	15	13	02
Rating on gregariousness			35	75	50	–06
Involvement with adults				47	24	–02
Involvement with children					61	–09
Rating on popularity						–16
Social class						

[a]Minimal significant r = .15.

Table 29

Per Cent of Subjects in Various Twin Subgroups Who Were Sinistral at Some Time before Seven Years or Who Were Sinistrals at Five to Six Years

	MZ			DZSS			DZOS			Total group
	Male	Female	Total	Male	Female	Total	Male	Female	Total	
Sinistral at some time before seven years	39	22	31	35	21	28	18	24	21	28
Sinistral at five to six years	24	6	15	12	15	13	12	18	15	14

x^2 – Left preference at five to six years and zygosity (MZ vs. DZSS) = .0014; N.S.
x^2 – Left preference some time before seven years and zygosity (MZ vs. DZSS) = .0508; N.S.
x^2 – Left preference some time before seven years and sex (MZ + DZSS) = 3.66; p = .05
x^2 – Left preference at five to six years and sex (MZ + DZSS) = .7459; N.S.

226

Table 30

Comparison of Members of Pairs Having One Member Righthanded and the Other Lefthanded

Trait	Lefthanded	Righthanded	Pair members equal	Total	p
	N	N	N	N^a	
Born first	16	13	-	29	N.S.
Heavier at birth	16	16	-	32	N.S.
Heavier at five to six years	19	12	-	31	.10-.20
Stutterer	6	5	-	11	N.S.
Possessed of some speech disorder	7	12	-	19	N.S.
Taller at five to six years	13	15	2	30	N.S.
Dominant member of pair	23	9	-	32	<.01-.001
More competitive	11	4	17	32	.10-.05
More active	9	12	11	32	N.S.
More involved with children	18	14	-	32	N.S.
Higher IQ	17	12	2	31	N.S.

[a]The N's differ here, in part, because of the incompleteness of the data for some variables.

Table 31

Number of Twins Lefthanded at Five to Six Years Who Had a Birth Weight under or over Four-and-a-half Pounds

Birth weight	Hand preference		Total
	Number lefthanded	Number righthanded	
Birth weight under 4 1/2 pounds	10	41	51
Birth weight over 4 1/2 pounds	19	96	115
Total	29	137	166

x^2 = .120; N.S.

Table 32

Number of Twins Who Showed a Left Preference at Any Time up to Seven Years and Who Had a Birth Weight under Five-and-a-half Pounds

Birth weight	Hand preference		Total
	Number lefthanded	Number righthanded	
Birth weight under 5 1/2 pounds	31	64	95
Birth weight over 5 1/2 pounds	48	53	71
Total	79	117	166

x^2 = .715; N.S.

Table 33

Number of Twins of Various Types Who Experienced a Period of Stuttering at Some Time before Seven Years of Age

Groups	Number stuttering	Number not stuttering	Total number	x^2	p
Male	13	76	89		
Female	6	81	87		
Total	19	157	176	1.974	.10-.20 (N.S.)
MZ	5	71	76		
DZSS	10	58	68		
Total	15	129	144	1.740	.10-.20 (N.S.)
Birth weight under 4 1/2 pounds	5	46	51		
Birth weight over 4 1/2 pounds	14	101	115		
Total	19	147	166	.032	N.S.
Birth weight under 5 1/2 pounds	10	85	95		
Birth weight over 5 1/2 pounds	9	62	71		
Total	19	147	166	.034	N.S.
Lefthanded at some period before 7 years	7	42	49		
Righthanded always	12	115	127		
Total	19	157	176	.430	N.S.
Left preference at 5 to 6 years	6	19	25		
Right preference at 5 to 6 years	13	138	151		
Total	19	157	176	3.798	.05

Table 34

Number of Twins of Various Types Stuttering at Ages Five to Six

Group	Number stuttering	Number not stuttering	Total Number	$\underline{x}^2$	$\underline{p}$
Lefthanded at 5 to 6 years	2	23	25		
Righthanded at 5 to 6 years	9	142	151		
Total	11	165	176	.003	N.S.
MZ	5	71	76		
DZSS	6	62	68		
Total	11	133	144	.036	N.S.

Table 35

Various Types of Reliability Estimates for Measures Based on the Children's Apperception Test

Measure	Reliability type							
	Scoring I and scoring II		Interjudge		Test-retest		Corrected split-halves	
	N	$\underline{r}$	N	$\underline{r}$	N	$\underline{r}$	N	$\underline{r}$
Hostility	83	97	36	89	50	75	167	85
Catastrophe	83	95	36	89	50	83	167	78
Negative themes	167	99	33	99	50	88	167	84
Negative outcomes	167	96	33	95	50	56	167	81
Mother mentions	87	96	20	97	50	45	167	65
Father mentions	87	97	20	96	50	54	167	56
Mother-child +	87	92	20	93	50	75	167	71
Mother-child −	87	82	20	88	50	24	167	62
Father-child +	87	91	20	93	50	13	167	50
Father-child −	87	86	20	96	50	44	167	70

Table 36

CAT-based Measure Intercorrelations with and without Word Count Partialled Out[a]

	Hostility	Catastrophe	Negative Outcome	Negative Theme	Mother-mentions	Father-mentions	Mother-child +	Mother-child −	Father-child +	Father-child −	Thematic-descriptive
Hostility	-	49[c]	30	67	36	39	36	41	50	49	64
Catastrophe	48[b]	-	51	63	17	10	15	31	15	26	49
Negative outcome	37	55	-	62	18	13	16	31	4	31	42
Negative theme	76	72	64	-	36	40	39	52	37	49	81
Mother mentions	44	28	23	44	-	64	73	57	42	30	45
Father mentions	45	20	18	37	66	-	33	41	64	52	33
Mother – child +	50	33	24	52	75	43	-	52	49	28	52
Mother – child –	53	44	37	61	61	46	61	-	46	54	42
Father – child +	60	31	13	49	48	67	58	54	-	47	42
Father – child –	54	26	35	54	35	53	36	58	52	-	39
Thematic descriptive	73	61	47	86	51	40	62	53	53	46	-
Word count	53	49	24	50	28	24	43	39	39	27	49

[a] All decimal points are omitted.

[b] All first-order correlations are significant and positive.

[c] First-order correlations are below the diagonal, partial correlations (word count partialled out) above the diagonal.

Table 37

Intercorrelations for All Twin Subjects between CAT-based Measures and Various Other Measures of Social Attitudes and Skills[a]

Ratings of social attitudes and other measures	CAT-based measures											
	Hostility	Catastrophe	Negative outcome	Negative theme	Mother mentions	Father mentions	Mother-child +	Mother-child −	Father-child +	Father-child −	Thematic-descriptive	Word count
Involvement with adults	7	10	16	15	12	8	0	0	10	6	14	1
Involvement with children	27	17	15	33	26	18	17	28	26	24	33	14
Gregariousness (rating)	24	08	12	26	18	22	16	24	19	8	29	9
Leadership (rating)	22	13	19	25	21	16	17	21	17	20	23	13
Popularity (rating)	23	18	15	29	29	18	25	21	18	20	33	13
Social apprehensiveness (rating)	-14	-5	-12	-22	-20	-20	-12	-17	-20	-14	-22	-4
Number of playmates	13	15	13	14	3	5	4	9	13	7	12	2
Twin closeness score	-3	-4	4	-7	-3	-4	-6	-6	-2	-4	-4	-12
Femininity complex	-18	13	6	22	29	16	12	26	12	20	24	3
Masculinity complex	-12	-7	4	-10	-20	-6	-11	-21	-9	-18	-14	-2
Social class	18	18	-9	22	25	26	19	17	15	13	22	19
PMA, IQ Total	5	10	1	16	22	29	10	15	18	16	11	10
PMA, V subtest	13	14	-1	21	25	30	16	16	23	15	19	14
Originality (rating)	8	-4	6	11	21	13	13	11	8	12	11	2
No. of interests (rating)	13	14	16	24	-5	7	7	-5	13	15	29	0
Hostility complex	4	-4	15	8	-4	12	-3	-11	8	1	5	6
Emotionality and tension complex	4	10	12	8	15	18	-12	9	13	8	4	6
Intensity (rating)	9	19	19	17	17	-1	-1	19	1	14	17	4
Cheerfulness (rating)	20	14	16	26	0	8	8	0	10	14	23	11
Activeness (rating)	5	4	12	12	21	-3	-3	22	8	12	10	-4
Competitiveness (rating)	10	11	14	16	21	7	7	22	8	13	13	3

[a]An r of about 15 is needed for significance.

232

Table 38

Responses Made to Questions Presented in the Interview by Various Twin Groups in which the Co-twins Were of Like Sex

Interview item	Group	Response percentages			x^2	p
Subject sees likeness between himself and twin		Yes	No			
	MZm	77	23		4.23	.05–.02
	DZSSm	48	52			
	MZ total	78	22		6.61	.01–.001
	DZSS total	54	46			
Twins dress alike		Rarely	Sometimes	Usually		
	MZm	6	19	75	22.47	.001
	DZSSm	67	13	20		
Amount of play with twin		Very little	Medium	Much		
	MZ total	0	43	57	7.11	.05–.025
	DZSS total	5	57	38		
Preference for play with sib over play alone		Sib	Indifferent	Alone		
	MZf	71	26	3	6.28	.05–.02
	DZSSf	60	17	23		
Subject feels accepted by sib's friends		Rarely	Sometimes	Usually		
	MZf	0	13	87	6.88	.05–.20
	DZSSf	15	23	62		
Amount of play with sib's friends		Little	Medium	Much		
	MZm	3	28	69	10.36	.01–.005
	DZSSm	10	60	30		
Sib uses subject's possessions without permission		Seldom	Medium	Usually		
	MZf	43	4	53	7.95	.025–.01
	DZSSf	50	25	25		
Subject objects if sib uses possessions without permission		Seldom	Medium	Usually		
	MZf	70	10	20	5.00	.10–.05
	DZSSf	59	0	41		
Age of best friend		Older	Same Age	Younger		
	MZf	35	56	9	4.17	.20–.10
	DZSSf	7	93	0		
Sex preference in playmates		Male	Indifferent	Female		
	MZ total	36	49	15	12.28	.003–.001
	DZSS total	27	30	43		

233

Table 39

DZSS and DZOS Twin-group Responses Made to Questions Presented in the Interview

Question	Group	Response percentages			$\underline{x}^2$	$\underline{p}$
		Yes	No			
Desire to be like sib	DZSSf	64	36		7.99	.005–.001
	DZOSf	8	92			
	DZSS total	57	43		9.30	.005–.001
	DZOS total	16	84			
S wants sib in class	DZSSf	93	7		12.04	.0005
	DZOSf	50	50			
	DZSS total	73	23		7.54	.01–.005
	DZOS total	56	44			
Desire to share bed-room with sib	DZSS total	70	30		6.41	.025–.01
	DZOS total	13	87			
Happier without sib	DZSS total	13	87		10.45	.005–.001
	DZOS total	34	66			
		Little	Moderate	Much		
Amount of play with sib	DZSS total	5	57	38	6.36	.05–.02
	DZOS total	18	61	21		
		Sib	Indifferent	Alone		
Preference for play with sib over alone	DZSS total	62	19	19	8.61	.02–.01
	DZOS total	47	11	42		
		Like	Indifferent	Dislike		
Reaction to play alone	DZSS total	14	20	66	6.29	.05–.025
	DZOS total	26	5	69		
		Sib	Indifferent	Others		
Preference for play with sib over others	DZSSf	27	43	30	7.14	.05–.025
	DZOSf	16	16	68		
	DZSSm	53	33	14	6.94	.05–.025
	DZOSm	21	37	42		
		Rarely	Moderate	Much		
Sib bossy	DZSS total	40	40	20	5.05	.10–.05
	DZOS total	18	53	29		
Amount of play with sib's friends	DZSS total	8	60	32	5.48	.10–.05
	DZOS total	24	57	19		
S feels accepted by sib's friends	DZSS total	9	14	77	4.22	.20–.10
	DZOS total	7	30	63		
		Male	Indifferent	Female		
Sex of sib preferred	DZSS total	56	6	39	14.52	.001–.0005
	DZOS total	39	29	32		

234

Table 39

Question	Group	Response percentages			x^2	p
		Male	Indifferent	Female		
Sex of baby preferred	DZSSm	57	3	40	5.40	.10–.05
	DZOSm	78	11	11		
	DZSSf	33	7	60	10.39	.01–.005
	DZOSf	0	5	95		
		Rarely	Sometimes	Much		
S minds if sib uses his possessions without permission	DZSSf	59	0	41	10.30	.01–.005
	DZOSf	13	13	74		
		Child	Both	Sib		
Initiator of quarrels	DZSSm	3	47	50	9.57	.01
	DZOSm	36	32	32		
	DZSS total	9	43	48	7.17	.05–.025
	DZOS total	24	29	47		
Victor in quarrel	DZSS total	53	35	12	8.40	.02–.01
	DZOS total	47	21	32		
		No	Indifferent	Yes		
Desire to dress alike	DZSS total	27	5	68	6.23	.05–.02
	DZOS total	50	10	40		
		Sib	Neither	Child		
Father favors	DZSSf	12	80	7	9.83	.01–.005
	DZOSf	6	50	44		
		Yes	No			
Sib is permitted to do what S is not	DZSS total	19	81		9.68	.01–.001
	DZOS total	44	56			
	DZSSf	14	86		6.23	.05–.01
	DZOSf	53	47			
Sib is made to do what S need not	DZSSf	21	79		6.14	.02–.01
	DZOSf	63	27			
	DZSS total	22	78		10.30	<.001
	DZOS total	48	52			
Child has friends who are not sib's	DZSSf	40	60		4.03	.05–.02
	DZOSf	74	26			
		Dislike	Indifferent	Like		
Child's reaction to school	DZSSm	7	17	76	6.25	.05–.02
	DZOSm	11	47	42		
	DZSS total	2	14	84	5.20	
	DZOS total	5	26	69		.10–.05

Table 40

Mean Ratings on Various Social Traits of MZ and DZSS Groups
(Three-way Analysis of Variance; Zygosity, Sex, Social Class)

Social class	Group							
	MZ				DZSS			
	Male		Female		Male		Female	
	N	M	N	M	N	M	N	M
Responsiveness to Adult Sympathy and Approval								
I	16	4.02	10	3.89	12	4.12	12	3.85
II	8	3.61	6	4.39	16	3.46	10	3.86
III	12	3.18	18	4.31	8	4.10	12	3.82
Total	36	10.81	34	12.59	36	11.68	34	11.53

Zygosity x sex — F = 5.07; p = .05 — .01

Social class	MZ Male N	M	Female N	M	DZSS Male N	M	Female N	M
Leadership								
I	16	3.97	10	4.54	12	3.94	12	4.48
II	8	3.79	6	3.86	16	3.99	10	4.77
III	12	2.84	18	4.37	8	3.77	12	4.34
Total	36	10.60	34	12.77	36	11.70	34	13.59

Zygosity — F = 4.73; p = .05 — .01
Sex — F = 21.07; p = < .001

Social class	MZ Male N	M	Female N	M	DZSS Male N	M	Female N	M
Finalty								
I	16	3.88	10	3.78	12	4.31	12	4.33
II	8	4.09	6	3.68	16	3.75	10	4.60
III	12	3.62	18	3.98	8	3.16	12	4.37
Total	36	11.59	34	11.44	36	11.22	34	13.30

Zygosity x sex — F = 5.09; p = .05 — .01

Social class	MZ Male N	M	Female N	M	DZSS Male N	M	Female N	M
Planfulness								
I	16	3.62	10	4.40	12	4.04	12	4.37
II	8	4.65	6	3.34	16	3.48	10	4.22
III	12	3.16	18	3.77	8	2.76	12	3.64
Total	36	11.43	34	11.51	36	10.28	34	12.23

Sex — F = 4.27; p = .05 — .01
Class — F = 8.05; p = .005 — .001
Zygosity x sex — F = 3.41; p = .10 — .05
Sex x class — F = 3.66; p = .05 — .01

Social class	MZ Male N	M	Female N	M	DZSS Male N	M	Female N	M
Originality								
I	16	4.11	10	4.48	12	4.25	12	4.52
II	8	4.21	6	3.74	16	3.73	10	4.65
III	12	2.88	18	3.62	8	3.22	12	4.22
Total	36	11.20	34	11.84	36	11.20	34	13.39

Sex — F = 10.69; p = .01 — .001
Zygosity x sex — F = 3.19; p = .10 — .05
Class — F = 12.20; p = .001 — .0001

Social class	MZ Male N	M	Female N	M	DZSS Male N	M	Female N	M
Number of Interests								
I	16	3.97	10	4.64	12	3.52	12	4.70
II	8	4.14	6	4.17	16	4.14	10	4.52
III	12	2.85	18	3.80	8	3.03	12	3.77
Total	36	10.96	34	12.61	36	10.69	34	12.99

Sex — F = 13.77; p = .001 — .0001
Class — F = 10.49; p = .01 — .001

Table 41

Mean Ratings on Various Social Traits of MZ and DZSS Groups

Social class	Group							
	MZ				DZSS			
	Male		Female		Male		Female	
	N	M	N	M	N	M	N	M
	Resistance							
I	16	4.08	10	3.34	12	4.07	12	3.87
II	8	4.29	6	4.90	16	4.61	10	3.36
III	12	4.30	18	3.68	8	3.71	12	3.62
Total	36	12.67	34	11.92	36	12.39	34	10.85

Sex — F = 7.01; p = .05 — .01
Class — F = 4.46; p = .05 — .01
Zygosity x Class — F = 3.11; p = .10 — .05

	Cruelty							
I	16	4.24	10	3.41	12	4.16	12	4.25
II	8	3.53	6	4.26	16	4.38	10	3.60
III	12	3.86	18	3.69	8	4.10	12	3.92
Total	36	11.63	34	11.36	36	12.64	34	11.77

Zygosity — F = 4.99; p = .05 — .01

	Faultfinding							
I	16	4.11	10	4.19	12	3.97	12	3.84
II	8	3.70	6	4.59	16	4.07	10	3.35
III	12	3.24	18	3.54	8	3.66	12	3.73
Total	36	11.05	34	12.32	36	11.70	34	10.92

Zygosity x Sex — F = 4.64; p = .05 — .01

	Selfishness							
I	16	3.75	10	3.77	12	4.17	12	4.04
II	8	3.84	6	4.26	16	4.14	10	2.96
III	12	3.56	18	3.37	8	4.12	12	3.94
Total	36	11.15	34	11.40	36	12.43	34	10.94

Zygosity x Class — F = 4.72; p = .01
Zygosity x Sex — F = 3.75; p = .10 — .05
Zygosity — F = 3.75; p = .10 — .05

	Exhibitionism							
I	16	3.83	10	4.11	12	4.19	12	4.22
II	8	3.64	6	3.86	16	4.29	10	3.86
III	12	3.60	18	3.62	8	3.82	12	3.99
Total	36	11.07	34	11.59	36	12.30	34	12.07

Zygosity — F = 3.25; p = .10 — .05

	Insistence on Rights							
I	16	3.83	10	4.47	12	4.03	12	4.37
II	8	3.59	6	3.67	16	4.20	10	3.95
III	12	3.21	18	3.81	8	3.20	12	4.08
Total	36	10.63	34	11.95	36	11.43	34	12.40

Zygosity — F = 3.15; p = .10 — .05
Sex — F = 10.65; p = .005 — .001
Class — F = 8.72; p = .01 — .001

	Indirectness of Response to Fear and Frustrations							
I	16	3.67	10	3.92	12	3.67	12	4.31
II	8	3.42	6	3.75	16	4.26	10	3.84
III	12	3.17	18	3.38	8	3.71	12	4.06
Total	36	10.26	34	11.05	36	11.64	34	12.21

Zygosity — F = 7.38; p = .01 — .005

Table **42**

Significant Twin-singleton Trait Mean Differences and Sigmas of the Mean Differences; MZ and DZSS Groups

	MZ				DZSS			
	Male		Female		Male		Female	
	Mean diff.	σ_{md}	Mean diff.	σ_{md}	Mean diff.	σ_{md}	Mean diff.	σ_{md}
PMA IQ total	−5.3	2.37						
PMA V-test	−18.0	2.77	−6.0	2.65	−11.5	3.46	−5.9	2.49
PMA P-test	6.8	3.40	8.5	3.63			+12.4	3.49
PMA Q-test	−8.7	3.72						
PMA S-test	−5.2	2.57						
Height at 5−6 years	−1.5	.65			−1.6	.47		
Weight at 5−6 years			−3.7	1.57	−6.6	1.61	−3.6	1.38
Involvement with children	−3.11	.19	.35	.13			.20	.07
Friendliness to children							.43	.19
Involvement with adults			.26	.13				
Friendliness to adults			.53	.25				
Gregariousness	−.55	.22						
Responsibleness			.41	.22				
Leadership	−.37	.22	.53	.24			.49	.15
Popularity			.75	.22			.58	.19
Masculinity			−.41	.13				
Sissiness	.33	.16						
Femininity			.34	.11				
Social apprehensiveness			−.52	.24			−.30	.15
Moodiness			−.54	.23				
Intensity	−.33	.17						
Cheerfulness			.61	.18	−.41	.21		
No. of interests			.45	.18				
Competitiveness	−.41	.18						
Insistence on rights	−.44	.20						
Tendency to alibi	−.47	.21	−.42	.24	−.42	.17		
CAT−negative theme			1.5	.52				
CAT−negative outcome			1.1	.51				
CAT−incoherence					−5.07	1.56		
CAT−mother-child −					−.5	.26		
CAT−father-child +								
Articulation							.36	.19
K Articulation score							−.98	.27
Talkative					.29	.11		

238

Table 43

Number and Character of the Playmates of the Identical and Same-sex Fraternal Twins[a]
(Three-way Analysis of Variance; Zygosity, Sex, and Social Class)

Social class	Group							
	MZ				DZSS			
	Male		Female		Male		Female	
	N	M	N	M	N	M	N	M
	Number of Male Playmates Listed by Child							
I	16	3.4	10	1.7	10	2.0	12	1.3
II	8	4.6	6	.7	14	3.8	8	.8
III	12	2.8	18	1.6	6	1.8	12	1.0
Total	36	10.8	34	4.0	30	7.6	32	3.1

Zygosity — F = 6.71; p = .05 — .01
Sex — F = 54.19; p = < .0001
Sex x class — F = 9.21; p = .01 — .001

	Number of Female Playmates Listed by Child							
I	16	.9	10	3.1	10	1.1	12	3.0
II	8	.6	6	2.3	14	2.2	8	3.3
III	12	1.8	18	3.1	6	1.8	12	3.6
Total	36	3.3	34	8.5	30	5.1	32	9.9

Zygosity — F = 3.74; p = .05
Sex — F = 33.94; p = < .0001

	Number of Same-age Playmates Listed by Child							
I	16	2.3	10	2.4	10	1.8	12	2.7
II	8	3.1	6	2.8	14	3.3	8	3.3
III	12	2.6	18	2.8	6	3.0	12	3.1
Total	36	8.0	34	8.0	30	8.1	32	9.1

Class — F = 3.24; p = .05

[a]See data in Tables 26 and 27 for description of total number of playmates listed by the various twin groups.

Table 44

Sex Role Behavior and Attitudes of Twins from Identical and Same-sex Fraternal Pairs
(Three-way Analysis of Variance; Zygosity, Sex, and Social Class)

Social class	Group							
	MZ				DZSS			
	Male		Female		Male		Female	
	N	M	N	M	N	M	N	M
Preference for Own Sex								
I	16	4.8	10	3.9	10	4.3	10	4.4
II	8	4.9	6	5.0	14	4.6	8	4.9
III	12	5.0	18	4.3	6	3.4	12	4.4
Total	36	14.7	34	13.2	30	12.3	30	13.7

Zygosity — F = 5.58; p = .05 — .01

Social class	Group							
	MZ				DZSS			
	Male		Female		Male		Female	
	N	M	N	M	N	M	N	M
Femininity-complex Score								
I	16	3.78	10	4.42	12	3.91	12	4.28
II	8	4.01	6	4.05	16	3.64	10	4.36
III	12	3.40	18	4.45	8	3.77	12	3.97
Total	36	11.19	34	12.92	36	11.32	34	12.61

Sex — F = 28.58; p = < .0001

Social class	Group							
	MZ				DZSS			
	Male		Female		Male		Female	
	N	M	N	M	N	M	N	M
Masculinity-complex Score								
I	16	4.08	10	3.58	12	4.05	12	3.94
II	8	4.13	6	4.17	16	4.34	10	3.53
III	12	4.11	18	3.48	8	3.93	12	3.69
Total	36	12.32	34	11.23	36	12.32	34	11.16

Sex — F = 19.81; p = .001 — .0001

Table 45

Twin-singleton Trait Mean Differences and Sigmas of the Mean Differences; MZ and DZSS Groups

Measure	Male				Female			
	N	Mean diff.	σ_{md}	p	N	Mean diff.	σ_{md}	p
MZ								
Masculinity complex	18	.07	.10		17	−.41	.13	< .01
Femininity complex	18	−.12	.15		17	.34	.11	< .01
Rating – tomboyishness					16	.23	.27	
Rating – sissyness	18	.33	.16	.05				
Involvement with adults	18	.02	.20		17	.26	.13	< .10
Involvement with children	18	−.31	.19		17	.35	.13	< .02
Emotionality and tension complex	18	−.13	.10		17	−.06	.11	
Hostility complex	18	−.15	.13		17	−.19	.14	
DZSS								
Masculinity complex	18	−.01	.14		17	−.13	.13	
Femininity complex	18	−.08	.12		17	−.15	.11	
Rating – tomboyishness					17	−.24	.24	
Rating – sissiness	17	−.03	.23					
Involvement with adults	18	.00	.11		17	.05	.12	
Involvement with children	18	−.08	.16		17	.20	.07	.01
Emotionality and tension complex	18	−.08	.11		17	.08	.09	
Hostility complex	18	−.15	.15		17	.03	.13	

Table 46

Comparison of MZ and DZSS Groups on CAT-based Measures
(Three-way Analysis of Variance; Zygosity, Sex, and Social Class)

Social class	MZ				DZSS			
	Male		Female		Male		Female	
	N	M	N	M	N	M	N	M
Mother-mentions								
I	16	4.8	10	6.3	9	4.1	12	4.8
II	8	2.6	6	3.3	14	3.4	6	6.2
III	12	2.5	18	3.8	6	1.7	12	4.2
Total	36	9.9	34	13.5	29	9.2	30	15.2

Sex — F = 16.66; p = < .001
Class — F = 8.46; p = .01 — .001
Zygosity x class — F = 4.91; p = .01

Social class	MZ				DZSS			
	Male		Female		Male		Female	
	N	M	N	M	N	M	N	M
Father-mentions								
I	16	3.2	10	3.8	9	4.1	12	4.2
II	8	2.6	6	2.8	14	3.3	6	3.2
III	12	1.8	18	2.7	6	1.8	12	2.9
Total	36	7.6	34	9.3	29	9.2	30	10.3

Class — F = 6.22; p = .01 — .001

Social class	MZ				DZSS			
	Male		Female		Male		Female	
	N	M	N	M	N	M	N	M
Mother-child Pleasant								
I	16	2.6	10	3.2	9	1.7	10	1.6
II	8	.6	6	1.2	14	1.5	6	3.3
III	12	.9	18	1.1	6	.5	12	1.8
Total	36	4.1	34	5.5	29	3.7	28	6.7

Sex — F = 4.84; p = .05 — .01
Class — F = 4.26; p = .05 — .01
Sex x class — F = 5.79; p = .01 — .001

Social class	MZ				DZSS			
	Male		Female		Male		Female	
	N	M	N	M	N	M	N	M
Mother-child Unpleasant								
I	16	.8	10	1.7	9	.2	10	1.1
II	8	.3	6	.5	14	.6	6	1.5
III	12	.4	18	.8	6	.0	12	1.1
Total	36	1.5	34	3.0	29	.8	28	3.7

Sex — F = 11.81; p = .01 — .001

Social class	MZ				DZSS			
	Male		Female		Male		Female	
	N	M	N	M	N	M	N	M
Father-child Pleasant								
I	16	1.1	10	1.0	9	1.3	10	1.6
II	8	.5	6	.7	14	1.5	6	1.5
III	12	.8	18	.9	6	.0	12	.8
Total	36	2.4	34	2.6	29	2.8	28	3.9

Sex x class — F = 3.04; p = .05

Table 46 (continued)

Social class	MZ				DZSS			
	Male		Female		Male		Female	
	N	M	N	M	N	M	N	M
	Father-child Unpleasant							
I	16	1.0	10	.6	9	.2	10	1.0
II	8	.3	6	1.0	14	.6	6	.7
III	12	.2	18	.8	6	.2	12	.5
Total	36	1.5	34	2.4	29	1.0	28	2.2

Sex — F 5.14; $\underline{p}$ = .05 — .01

Social class	MZ				DZSS			
	Male		Female		Male		Female	
	N	M	N	M	N	M	N	M
	CAT-hostility Score							
I	16	8.4	10	9.2	9	4.1	10	7.6
II	8	3.1	6	6.8	14	8.1	6	7.2
III	12	4.4	18	4.7	6	2.3	12	6.6
Total	36	15.9	34	20.7	29	14.5	28	21.4

Sex — F = 3.81; $\underline{p}$ = .05

Social class	MZ				DZSS			
	Male		Female		Male		Female	
	N	M	N	M	N	M	N	M
	CAT-catastrophe Score							
I	16	3.4	10	4.5	9	.9	10	3.4
II	8	1.1	6	3.7	14	2.6	6	2.8
III	12	2.8	18	2.6	6	2.0	12	1.8
Total	36	7.4	34	10.8	29	5.5	28	8.0

Nothing significant

Social class	MZ				DZSS			
	Male		Female		Male		Female	
	N	M	N	M	N	M	N	M
	CAT-negative Outcome							
I	16	3.8	10	3.1	9	1.0	10	1.7
II	8	1.1	6	3.5	14	2.4	6	2.7
III	12	1.8	18	2.4	6	1.7	12	1.5
Total	36	5.7	34	9.0	29	5.1	28	5.9

Zygosity — F = 3.19; $\underline{p}$ = .10 — .05
Sex — F = 3.53; $\underline{p}$ = .10 — .05

Social class	MZ				DZSS			
	Male		Female		Male		Female	
	N	M	N	M	N	M	N	M
	CAT-negative Theme							
I	16	5.6	10	6.3	9	3.0	10	6.4
II	8	2.5	6	6.0	14	5.6	6	6.2
III	12	3.2	18	4.6	6	3.2	12	4.2
Total	36	11.3	34	16.9	29	11.8	28	16.8

Sex — F = 9.28; $\underline{p}$ = .01 — .001

Table 47

Twin-matched Singleton Comparison of a Number of Responses of Various Types Given in the Interview by All Child Subjects from Same-sex Pairs (X^2 is Based on McNemar's Formula for Matched Groups)

Question		Response	Twin group Yes	Twin group No	Twin group Total	X^2	p
Plays with sib often or moderately often	Singleton	Yes No Total	33 40 73	18 33 51	51 73 124	7.60	.01–.001
Prefers play with sib to play with others or is indifferent	Singleton	Yes No Total	45 26 71	27 26 53	72 52 124	.00	N.S.
Likes to play alone or is indifferent	Singleton	Yes No Total	15 13 28	14 80 94	29 93 122	.00	N.S.
Has friends sib does not have	Singleton	Yes No Total	49 15 64	36 21 57	85 36 121	7.84	.01–.001
Sib often uses child's possessions without permission or moderately	Singleton	Yes No Total	18 25 43	21 59 80	39 84 123	.20	N.S.
Much quarreling with sib	Singleton	Yes No Total	15 24 39	28 56 84	43 80 123	.20	N.S.
Child initiates quarrels or both sibs do equally	Singleton	Yes No Total	16 17 33	19 71 90	35 88 123	.03	N.S.
Child usually victor in quarrels or sibs about equal	Singleton	Yes No Total	27 47 74	21 28 49	48 75 123	9.19	.01–.001

Question		Response	Twin group Yes	Twin group No	Twin group Total	X^2	p
Plays with sib rarely or moderately often	Singleton	Yes No Total	15 2 17	16 91 107	31 93 124	9.39	.01–.001
Prefers play alone to play with sib or is indifferent	Singleton	Yes No Total	17 17 34	23 67 90	40 84 124	.63	N.S.
Dislikes to play alone or is indifferent	Singleton	Yes No Total	53 25 78	25 19 44	78 44 122	.02	N.S.
Happier without sib	Singleton	Yes No Total	14 17 31	38 55 93	52 72 124	7.27	.01–.001
Sib rarely or moderately uses child's possessions	Singleton	Yes No Total	27 24 51	24 48 72	51 72 123	.02	N.S.
Child wishes to change places with sib	Singleton	Yes No Total	25 20 45	32 46 78	57 66 123	2.33	N.S.
Sib initiates quarrels or both do equally	Singleton	Yes No Total	29 24 53	39 31 70	68 55 123	3.11	.10–.05
Sib usually victor in quarrel or both sibs equal	Singleton	Yes No Total	7 15 22	51 50 101	58 65 123	18.50	< .001

244

Table 47 (continued)

Left section

Question		Response	Twin group			X^2	p
			Yes	No	Total		
Child plays with sib's friends often or moderately	Singleton	Yes No Total	25 37 62	12 46 58	37 83 120	11.76	.001
Sib very bossy	Singleton	Yes No Total	18 18 36	21 65 86	39 83 129	.10	N.S.
Wish to share bedroom with sib	Singleton	Yes No Total	38 29 67	22 25 47	60 54 114	.71	N.S.
Child favored by mother, or mother is neutral	Singleton	Yes No Total	18 18 36	28 59 87	46 77 123	1.76	.20–.10
Child favored by father, or father is neutral	Singleton	Yes No Total	13 20 33	35 50 85	48 70 118	3.56	.10–.05
Preferred playmate is older or of same age	Singleton	Yes No Total	19 15 34	32 55 87	51 70 121	5.45	.02
Best friend is older or of same age	Singleton	Yes No Total	19 23 42	23 48 81	52 71 123	1.45	.30–.20
Rather go to school than stay home	Singleton	Yes No Total	18 13 31	23 48 71	41 61 102	2.25	.20–.10

Right section

Question		Response	Twin group			X^2	p
			Yes	No	Total		
Child plays rarely or moderately with sib's friends	Singleton	Yes No Total	9 10 19	51 50 101	60 60 120	26.23	< .001
Child well treated by sib's friends	Singleton	Yes No Total	37 31 68	24 27 51	61 58 119	.65	N.S.
Child desires infant sib	Singleton	Yes No Total	59 29 88	20 16 36	79 45 124	1.31	N.S.
Sib favored by mother, or mother is neutral	Singleton	Yes No Total	17 8 25	32 66 98	49 74 123	13.22	< .001
Sib favored by father, or father is neutral	Singleton	Yes No Total	14 10 24	22 72 94	36 82 118	3.78	.05
Preferred playmate is younger or of same age	Singleton	Yes No Total	13 17 30	15 76 91	28 93 121	.03	N.S.
Best friend is younger or of same age	Singleton	Yes No Total	14 11 25	13 85 98	27 96 123	.04	N.S.
Likes teacher	Singleton	Yes No Total	66 10 76	9 18 27	75 28 103	.00	N.S.

245

Table 48

Number and Characteristics of Playmates Listed by Twins and Matched Singletons
(Means and Sigma Means for MZ and DZSS Groups)

	Male							Female						
	Twin			Singleton				Twin			Singleton			
	N	Mean	σ_m	Mean	σ_m	$\underline{t}$	p	N	Mean	σ_m	Mean	σ_m	$\underline{t}$	p
MZ														
No. playmates	36	4.6	.38	4.2	.29	.85	N.S.	34	4.4	.27	4.0	.29	1.23	N.S.
No. male play-mates	36	3.5	.28	3.3	.24	.36	N.S.	34	1.4	.18	1.4	.26	.20	N.S.
No. female play-mates	36	1.1	.31	.8	.16	.74	N.S.	34	2.9	.22	2.6	.24	1.10	N.S.
No. older play-mates	36	1.3	.24	1.1	.21	.18	N.S.	34	1.1	.24	1.2	.22	.33	N.S.
No. same-age playmates	36	2.6	.19	1.8	.21	2.39	<.05	34	2.7	.27	1.6	.23	3.43	<.01
No. younger playmates	36	.7	.29	1.1	.19	1.11	N.S.	34	.7	.29	1.2	.20	2.05	<.05
DZSS														
No. playmates	30	4.6	.47	4.2	.30	.75	N.S.	32	4.3	.26	4.1	.22	.68	N.S.
No. male play-mates	30	2.8	.33	3.1	.24	.75	N.S.	32	1.0	.23	1.2	.18	.80	N.S.
No. female play-mates	30	1.8	.31	1.1	.18	1.99	<.10	32	3.3	.21	2.9	.23	1.26	N.S.
No. older play-mates	30	1.2	.18	1.5	.23	.73	N.S.	32	1.0	.20	1.1	.22	.28	N.S.
No. same-age playmates	30	2.4	.33	1.6	.25	2.09	<.05	32	3.0	.23	1.9	.22	3.93	<.01
No. younger playmates	30	.6	.18	1.1	.25	1.93	N.S.	32	.4	.13	1.1	.20	2.69	<.05

Table 49

Mean and Sigma of Means for Various Twin Groups of Twin-singleton Differences in Scores
Derived from the Children's Apperception Test

Measure	Male				Female			
	N	Mean	σ_m	p	N	Mean	σ_m	p
MZ								
Thematic-descriptive score	18	−2.0	3.18		17	−.4	1.95	
Incoherence score	18	−1.6	2.38		17	−1.6	1.87	
Word count	18	−43.9	142.71		17	−99.7	111.41	
Hostility score	18	−1.1	1.48		17	+.8	1.01	
Catastrophe score	18	+.0	.83		17	.1	.96	
Mother mentions	18	.7	.45		17	−.9	.49	
Father mentions	18	−.1	.35		17	−.1	.48	
Mother-child +	18	+.1	.40		17	−.5	.41	
Mother-child −	18	.3	.25		17	−.1	.25	
Father-child +	18	.2	.29		17	−.0	.23	
Father-child −	18	.1	.23		17	+.2	.15	
Negative outcome	18	.4	.32		17	1.1	.51	.05
Negative theme	18	.2	.82		17	1.5	.52	.01
DZSS								
Thematic-descriptive score	15	−.5	3.16		14	−.5	2.54	
Incoherence score	15	−5.0	1.56	.01	14	−1.1	1.65	
Word count	15	−130.7	97.37		14	+39.7	202.87	
Hostility score	15	−.9	1.39		14	1.7	1.64	
Catastrophe score	15	−.7	.65		14	−1.3	.98	
Mother mentions	15	−.7	.67		15	.5	.48	
Father mentions	15	+.8	.56		15	+.2	.65	
Mother-child +	15	.2	.24		14	.4	.58	
Mother-child −	15	−.5	.26	.05	14	.0	.35	
Father-child +	15	+.6	.30	.05	14	.4	.46	
Father-child −	15	.0	.17		14	.2	.24	
Negative outcome	15	.1	.40		14	.3	.54	
Negative theme	15	.5	.62		14	1.1	.74	

Table 50

Two-way Analysis of Variance of Twin-singleton Differences (Same-sex Twin Pairs)

	Mean differences			Mean differences		
	Male	Female	Total	Male	Female	Total
	Height at 5–6 Years			Femininity Complex		
MZ	−1.5	−0.	−.8	−.12	.32	.10
DZSS	−1.4	−0.	−.7	−.08	.15	.04
Total	−1.5	−0.		−.10	.23	
	Sex−F = 8.51; p = .01−.001			Sex−F = 7.36; p = .01−.001		
	Involvement with Children			Masculinity Complex		
MZ	−.31	.33	.00	.07	−.39	−.16
DZSS	−.08	.20	.06	−.01	−.13	−.07
Total	−.19	.26		.03	−2.57	
	Sex−F = 10.26; p = < .001			Sex−F = 5.65; p = .01−.001		
	Leadership			Popularity		
MZ	−.37	.50	.06	−.23	.70	.23
DZSS	−.03	.49	.23	.04	.58	.31
Total	−.20	.49		−.09	.64	
	Sex−F = 10.91; p = < .001			Sex−F = 9.17; p = < .001		
	Friendliness to Adults			Gregariousness		
MZ	.08	.50	.29	−.55	.13	−.21
DZSS	.01	.47	.24	.09	.21	.15
Total	.05	.48		−.23	.17	
	Sex−F = 3.57; p = .10−.05			Sex−F = 3.56; p = .10−.05		
	Confidence			Social Apprehensiveness		
MZ	−.24	.18	−.03	.28	−.49	−.10
DZSS	−.19	−.10	−.05	.08	−.30	−.11
Total	−.22	.14		.18	−.39	
	Sex−F = 3.57; p = .10−.05			Sex−F = 6.80; p = .01−.001		
	Friendliness to Children			Insistence on Rights		
MZ	−.36	.30	−.03	−.44	.11	−.17
DZSS	.05	.43	.24	−.19	.23	.02
Total	−.15	.37		−.32	.17	
	Sex−F = 5.80; p = .05−.01			Sex−F = 7.17; p = .01−.001		
	Intensity			Finality		
MZ	−.33	.25	−.04	−.23	.14	−.05
DZSS	−.18	.08	−.05	−.18	.34	.08
Total	−.25	.16		−.20	.24	
	Sex−F = 3.93; p = .05−.01			Sex−F = 4.16; p = .05−.01		
	Cheerfulness			Originality		
MZ	−.19	.57	.19	−.34	.11	−.12
DZSS	−.41	.11	−.15	−.10	.33	.11
Total	−.30	.34		−.22	.22	
	Sex−F = 11.13; p = < .001			Sex−F = 4.24; p = .05−.01		
	Number of Interests			PMA V-test		
MZ	−.35	.42	+.03	−18.0	−5.3	−11.8
DZSS	−.44	.19	−.13	−10.2	−5.5	−7.9
Total	−.39	.30		−14.1	−5.4	
	Sex−F = 6.82; p = .01−.001			Sex−F = 10.28; p = < .001		

Table 51

Intercorrelations of Measures of Attitude toward Own Sex and Sex Role

	Females from Same-sex Pairs[a] (N = 64–70)				
Measures	Female preference for own sex	Female complex score	Male complex score	Mother mentions (CAT)	Father mentions (CAT)
Rating on					
Tomboyishness	−3	−20	66	−11	−23
Female identification score	-	− 3	5	− 3	4
Femininity-complex score	-	-	−60	29	16
Masculinity-complex score	-	-	-	−20	− 6
Mother-mentions (CAT)	-	-	-	-	66

	Males from Same-sex Pairs[a] (N = 67–72)				
Measures	Male preference for own sex	Male complex score	Female complex score	Mother mentions (CAT)	Father mentions (CAT)
Rating on					
Sissiness	7	−00	−11	− 8	2
Male identification score	-	27	10	− 7	−12
Masculinity-complex score	-	-	−59	−18	− 8
Femininity-complex score	-	-	-	20	5
Mother-mentions (CAT)	-	-	-	-	67

[a]The minimal significant r is .23–.25.

249

Table 52

Own-sex Preference, Sex-typical Behavior, and Sex of Playmates in DZSS and DZOS Twin Groups

(Two-way Analysis of Variance; Sex of Sib, Social Class)

Social class	Male				Female			
	DZSS		DZOS		DZSS		DZOS	
	N	M	N	M	N	M	N	M
Preference for Own Sex								
I	10	4.3	7	3.7	10	4.3	7	5.1
II	14	4.6	5	4.5	8	4.9	5	4.3
III	6	3.4	7	5.2	12	4.4	7	3.9
Total	30	12.3	19	13.4	30	13.7	19	13.4

Nothing significant

Femininity-complex Score								
I	12	3.91	7	3.95	12	4.28	7	4.24
II	16	3.64	5	3.11	10	4.36	5	4.27
III	8	3.77	7	4.08	12	3.97	7	4.07
Total	36	11.32	19	12.14	34	12.61	19	12.58

Nothing significant

Masculinity-complex Score								
I	12	4.05	7	4.05	12	3.94	7	4.05
II	16	4.34	5	3.55	10	3.53	5	3.57
III	8	3.93	7	4.02	12	3.69	7	3.89
Total	36	12.32	19	11.62	34	11.16	19	11.51

Nothing significant

	Sissiness				Tomboyishness			
I	12	4.14	7	4.31	12	3.67	7	3.84
II	10	3.89	5	4.27	10	4.57	5	3.98
III	12	3.76	7	4.31	12	4.12	7	4.13
Total	34	11.79	19	12.89	34	12.36	19	11.95

Nothing significant

	Number of Male Playmates Listed by Child							
I	10	2.0	7	2.6	12	1.3	7	1.4
II	14	3.8	5	2.2	8	.8	5	.8
III	6	1.8	7	2.7	12	1.0	7	1.7
Total	30	7.6	19	7.5	32	3.1	19	3.9

Nothing significant

	Number of Female Playmates Listed by Child							
I	10	1.1	7	1.6	12	3.0	7	3.4
II	14	2.2	5	1.2	8	3.3	5	2.6
III	6	1.8	7	.6	12	3.6	7	2.1
Total	30	5.1	19	3.4	32	9.9	19	8.1

Nothing significant

	Number of Same-age Playmates Listed by Child							
I	10	1.8	7	2.9	12	2.7	7	3.4
II	14	3.3	5	2.4	8	3.3	5	3.0
III	6	3.0	7	1.9	12	3.1	7	2.1
Total	30	8.1	19	7.2	32	9.1	19	8.5

Nothing significant

250

Table 53

Characteristics of Fraternal Twins from Same- and Opposite-sex Pairs
(Two-way Analysis of Variance; Sex of Sib and Social Class)

Social class	Male				Female			
	DZSS		DZOS		DZSS		DZOS	
	N	M	N	M	N	M	N	M
Health								
I	12	3.66	7	4.33	12	3.79	7	4.15
II	16	3.75	5	2.98	10	4.51	5	3.43
III	8	3.15	7	3.95	12	4.39	7	3.73
Total	36	10.56	19	11.26	34	12.69	19	11.31

Sex of sib x class — F = 4.53; p = .05 — .01

Social class	Male				Female			
Activeness								
I	12	4.15	7	4.00	12	4.10	7	3.50
II	16	4.20	5	3.42	10	3.92	5	3.73
III	8	3.80	7	3.59	12	4.33	7	3.67
Total	36	12.15	19	11.01	34	12.35	19	10.90

Sex of sib — F = 3.93; p = .05

Social class	Male				Female			
Sensitiveness								
I	12	3.55	7	3.82	12	4.24	7	3.58
II	16	3.93	5	3.02	10	4.13	5	2.72
III	8	4.25	7	4.01	12	3.66	7	3.94
Total	36	11.73	19	10.85	34	12.03	19	10.24

Sex of sib — F = 5.66; p = 05 — .01
Sex of sib x class — F = 3.79;
p = .05 — .01

Social class	Male				Female			
Tendency to Project Blame								
I	12	3.75	7	3.92	12	3.78	7	4.24
II	16	4.33	5	3.28	10	3.30	5	3.54
III	8	4.22	7	3.98	12	3.90	7	4.21
Total	36	12.30	19	11.18	34	10.98	19	11.99

Nothing significant

Social class	Male				Female			
Exhibitionism								
I	12	4.19	7	4.16	12	4.23	7	3.61
II	16	4.29	5	3.32	10	3.86	5	3.62
III	8	3.82	7	3.69	12	3.99	7	3.55
Total	36	12.30	19	11.17	34	12.07	19	10.78

Nothing significant

Social class	Male				Female			
Selfishness								
I	12	4.17	7	3.34	12	4.04	7	3.99
II	16	4.14	5	3.66	10	2.96	5	3.66
III	8	4.12	7	3.83	12	3.94	7	3.87
Total	36	12.43	19	10.83	34	10.94	19	11.52

Nothing significant

Social class	Male				Female			
Aggressiveness								
I	12	3.87	7	4.02	12	4.11	7	4.04
II	16	3.81	5	3.43	10	4.02	5	3.90
III	8	3.86	7	4.18	12	4.11	7	4.04
Total	36	11.54	19	11.63	34	12.24	19	11.98

Nothing significant

Social class	Male				Female			
Uncooperativeness with Group								
I	12	4.61	7	4.09	12	3.76	7	3.69
II	16	3.91	5	3.62	10	3.21	5	3.37
III	8	4.56	7	4.02	12	3.74	7	4.34
Total	36	13.07	19	11.73	34	10.71	19	11.40

Class — F = 3.96; p = .05 — .01

Table 54

Characteristics of Fraternal Twins from Same- and Opposite-sex Pairs
(Two-way Analysis of Variance; Sex of Sib and Social Class)

| Social class | Male | | | | Female | | | |
| | DZSS | | DZOS | | DZSS | | DZOS | |
	N	M	N	M	N	M	N	M
				Obedience				
I	12	3.60	7	3.75	12	4.47	7	4.37
II	16	3.69	5	4.49	10	4.23	5	3.91
III	8	4.34	7	4.34	12	3.87	7	3.93
Total	36	11.63	19	12.58	34	12.57	19	12.21

Class — F = 5.23; p = .05 — .01

				Tendency to Tattle				
I	12	4.00	7	4.05	12	4.18	7	3.82
II	16	4.21	5	3.00	10	4.07	5	3.00
III	8	3.92	7	4.17	12	4.26	7	4.18
Total	36	12.13	19	11.22	34	12.51	19	11.00

Nothing significant

				Emotionality and Tension Complex				
I	12	4.06	7	4.06	12	3.93	7	3.81
II	16	3.98	5	3.47	10	4.02	5	3.50
III	8	4.00	7	3.85	12	3.98	7	3.78
Total	36	12.04	19	11.38	34	11.93	19	11.09

Sex of sib — F = 4.74;
p = .05 — .01

				Intensity				
I	12	4.07	7	3.89	12	4.07	7	3.50
II	16	3.88	5	2.87	10	4.33	5	3.61
III	8	3.72	7	3.43	12	3.95	7	3.76
Total	36	11.67	19	10.19	34	12.35	19	10.87

Nothing significant

				Cheerfulness				
I	12	3.82	7	4.44	12	3.94	7	4.08
II	16	3.43	5	4.09	10	4.16	5	4.70
III	8	3.19	7	4.30	12	4.12	7	3.85
Total	36	10.44	19	12.83	34	12.22	19	12.63

Sex of sib — F = 8.02; p = .01 — .001

				Moodiness				
I	12	4.09	7	4.01	12	4.60	7	3.97
II	16	4.46	5	3.07	10	3.58	5	3.33
III	8	3.81	7	3.93	12	3.65	7	3.39
Total	36	12.36	19	11.01	34	11.83	19	10.69

Class — F = 3.83; p = .05 — .01

Table 55

Characteristics of Fraternal Twins from Same- and Opposite-sex Pairs
(Two-way Analysis of Variance; Sex of Sib and Social Class)

Social class	Male				Female			
	DZSS		DZOS		DZSS		DZOS	
	N	M	N	M	N	M	N	M
				Ambition				
I	12	4.18	7	3.60	12	4.65	7	4.50
II	16	3.37	5	4.09	10	4.20	5	4.09
III	8	3.51	7	3.59	12	4.20	7	3.73
Total	36	11.06	19	11.28	34	13.05	19	12.32

Nothing significant

Social class	Male				Female			
				Planfulness				
I	12	4.04	7	4.22	12	4.37	7	4.62
II	16	3.48	5	3.84	10	4.22	5	4.01
III	8	2.76	7	3.94	12	3.64	7	4.34
Total	36	10.28	19	12.00	34	12.23	19	12.97

Sex of sib — $F = 3.56$; $p = .10 - .05$
Class — $F = 3.76$; $p = .05 - .01$

Social class	Male				Female			
				Number of Interests				
I	12	3.52	7	3.91	12	4.70	7	3.78
II	16	4.14	5	3.44	10	4.52	5	3.68
III	8	3.03	7	4.09	12	3.77	7	4.28
Total	36	10.69	19	11.44	34	12.99	19	11.74

Sex of sib x class — $F = 3.01$; $p = .10 - .05$ Sex of sib x class — $F = 3.14$; $p = .05$

Social class	Male				Female			
				Originality				
I	12	4.25	7	4.09	12	4.52	7	4.89
II	16	3.73	5	3.96	10	4.65	5	4.20
III	8	3.22	7	3.79	12	4.22	7	3.76
Total	36	11.20	19	11.84	34	13.39	19	12.85

Class — $F = 5.27$; $p = .01 - .001$

Social class	Male				Female			
				Tenacity				
I	12	3.96	7	3.54	12	4.42	7	4.62
II	16	3.51	5	3.89	10	4.09	5	4.32
III	8	3.63	7	4.01	12	4.04	7	4.34
Total	36	11.10	19	11.44	34	12.55	19	13.28

Nothing significant

Table 56

CAT-based Measures of Fraternal Twins from Same- and Opposite-sex Pairs
(Two-way Analysis of Variance; Sex of Sib and Social Class)

Social class	Group							
	Male				Female			
	DZSS		DZOS		DZSS		DZOS	
	N	M	N	M	N	M	N	M
Catastrophe Score								
I	9	.9	7	9.1	10	3.4	7	4.4
II	14	2.6	5	2.4	6	2.8	5	2.8
III	6	2.0	7	1.9	12	1.8	7	3.3
Total	29	5.5	19	13.4	28	8.0	19	10.5

Sex of sib — F = 4.85; p = .05 — .01
Sex of sib x class — F = 5.00; p = .05 — .01

Hostility Score								
I	9	4.1	7	11.7	10	7.6	7	7.3
II	14	8.1	5	6.2	6	7.2	5	10.4
III	6	2.3	7	6.3	12	6.6	7	8.9
Total	29	14.5	19	24.2	28	21.4	19	26.6

Nothing significant

Negative Outcome								
I	9	1.0	7	3.1	10	1.7	7	2.9
II	14	2.4	5	2.2	6	2.7	5	3.2
III	6	1.7	7	1.6	12	1.5	7	1.6
Total	29	5.1	19	6.9	28	5.9	19	7.7

Nothing significant

Negative Theme								
I	9	3.0	7	8.4	10	6.4	7	6.0
II	14	5.6	5	5.0	6	6.2	5	7.8
III	6	3.2	7	4.3	12	4.2	7	6.1
Total	29	11.8	19	17.7	28	16.8	19	19.9

Sex of sib — F = 3.97; p = .10 — .05
Sex of sib x class — F = 3.18; p = .10 — .05

Mother-child Pleasant								
I	9	1.7	7	2.1	10	1.6	7	2.6
II	14	1.5	5	1.9	6	3.3	5	3.6
III	6	.5	7	1.1	12	1.8	7	4.1
Total	29	3.7	19	5.1	28	6.7	19	10.3

Nothing significant

Mother-child Unpleasant								
I	9	.2	7	1.9	10	1.1	7	1.7
II	14	.6	5	1.2	6	1.5	5	1.6
III	6	.0	7	.6	12	1.1	7	1.0
Total	29	.8	19	3.7	28	3.7	19	4.3

Sex of sib — F = 10.12; p = .01 — .001

Table 57

Attitudes toward Sibling and Others Expressed in Interview by Fraternal Twins from Opposite-sex Pairs and by Matched Singletons (Sign Test or McNemar's X^2)

DZOS Male

	Group	Little	Moderate	Much	Significance level
Amt. S plays with sib	Twin	5	58	37	N.S.
	Singleton	26	53	21	
Sib is bossy	Twin	21	37	42	.05
	Singleton	37	47	16	
Amt. of quarreling with sib	Twin	00	58	42	N.S.
	Singleton	26	37	37	
		Sib	**Both**	**Child**	
Usual initiator of sibling quarrels	Twin	21	32	47	N.S.
	Singleton	53	26	21	
Usual victor in sibling quarrels	Twin	16	16	68	.02
	Singleton	53	16	31	
		Yes	**No**		
Child has some friends sib does not have	Twin	56	44		.20–.30 (N.S.)
	Singleton	78	22		
		Bad	**Indifferent**	**Good**	
Treatment received from sib's friends	Twin	12	47	41	N.S.
	Singleton	18	35	47	
		Sib	**Neither**	**Child**	
Mother favors	Twin	11	68	21	N.S.
	Singleton	21	37	42	
Father favors	Twin	16	58	26	N.S.
	Singleton	32	32	37	
		Male	**Indifferent**	**Female**	
Sex preference in play-mates	Twin	47	48	5	N.S.
	Singleton	37	47	16	

DZOS Female

	Group	Little	Moderate	Much	
Amt. S plays with sib	Twin	16	63	21	N.S.
	Singleton	5	58	37	
Sib is bossy	Twin	16	68	16	N.S.
	Singleton	31	53	16	
Amt. of quarreling with sib	Twin	5	53	42	N.S.
	Singleton	11	47	42	
		Sib	**Both**	**Child**	
Usual initiator of sibling quarrels	Twin	58	26	16	N.S.
	Singleton	58	16	26	
Usual victor in sibling quarrels	Twin	48	26	26	N.S.
	Singleton	47	11	42	
		Yes	**No**		
Child has some friends sib does not have	Twin	74	26		N.S.
	Singleton	84	16		
		Bad	**Indifferent**	**Good**	
Treatment received from sib's friends	Twin	5	58	37	N.S.
	Singleton	11	37	52	
		Sib	**Neither**	**Child**	
Mother favors	Twin	11	53	36	N.S.
	Singleton	16	47	37	
Father favors	Twin	6	50	44	N.S.
	Singleton	33	33	33	
		Male	**Indifferent**	**Female**	
Sex preference in play-mates	Twin	5	37	58	N.S.
	Singleton	11	47	42	

255

Table 58

Number and Characteristics of Playmates Listed by Twins from Same- and Opposite-sex Fraternal Pairs and by Matched Singletons

Playmates	Male							Female						
	Twin			Singleton		t	p	Twin			Singleton		t	p
	N	M	σ_m	M	σ_m			N	M	σ_m	M	σ_m		
DZSS														
No. playmates	30	4.6	.47	4.2	.30	.75	N.S.	32	4.3	.26	4.1	.22	.68	N.S.
No. male playmates	30	2.8	.33	3.1	.24	.75	N.S.	32	1.0	.23	1.2	.18	.80	N.S.
No. female playmates	30	1.8	.31	1.1	.18	1.99	<.10	32	3.3	.21	2.9	.23	1.26	N.S.
No. older playmates	30	1.2	.18	1.5	.23	.73	N.S.	32	1.0	.20	1.1	.22	.28	N.S.
No. same-age playmates	30	2.4	.33	1.6	.25	2.09	<.05	32	3.0	.23	1.9	.22	3.93	<.01
No. younger playmates	30	.6	.18	1.1	.25	1.92	N.S.	32	.4	.13	1.1	.20	2.69	<.05
DZOS														
No. playmates	19	3.6	.26	3.8	.35	.36	N.S.	19	4.1	.50	4.8	.51	.97	N.S.
No. male playmates	19	2.5	.23	2.5	.34	.00	N.S.	19	1.4	.36	1.7	.31	.66	N.S.
No. female playmates	19	1.1	.18	1.3	.22	.49	N.S.	19	2.7	.31	3.1	.43	.61	N.S.
No. older playmates	19	.8	.16	1.0	.28	.63	N.S.	19	.7	.20	1.7	.38	2.10	<.05
No. same-age playmates	19	2.5	.62	1.4	.33	2.28	<.05	19	2.8	.26	1.9	.27	2.12	<.05
No. younger playmates	19	.3	.11	1.4	.24	4.37	<.01	19	.6	.16	1.2	.29	1.90	N.S.

Table 59

Significant Twin-matched Singleton Differences in a Variety of Traits, Including Some of Special Interest; Fraternal Twins from Opposite-sex Pairs

Trait	DZOS males				DZOS females			
	N	md	σmd	p	N	md	σmd	p
Rating								
Emotion-tension complex	19	−.24	.115	.05	19	−.23	.107	.05
Confidence	19	−.37	.180	.10−.05				
Intensity	19	−.46	.246	.10−.05	19	−.38	.198	.10−.05
Moodiness	19				19	−.44	.229	.10−.05
Exhibitionism	19	−.43	.224	.10−.05	19	−.51	.142	.01−.001
Activeness	19	−.42	.229	.10−.05				
Voice volume	19	−.34	.147	.05−.01				
Selfishness	19	−.47	.248	.10−.05				
Sensitiveness	19				19	−.63	.292	.05
Tendency to alibi	19	−.41	.206	.05	19	−.47	.163	.01
Jealousy					19	−.58	.192	.01
Gregariousness					19	−.53	.239	.05
CAT−incoherence	19	−5.58	2.494	.05	19	−7.79	2.142	.01
CAT−negative theme					19	2.2	.66	.01
CAT−catastrophe					19	1.5	.69	.05
Masculinity complex	19	−.21	.156	N.S.	19	−.13	.151	N.S.
Femininity complex	19	−.23	.141	N.S.	19	.10	.099	N.S.
Rating−tomboyishness					19	−.13	.204	N.S.
Rating−sissiness	19	.12	.126	N.S.				
Involvement with adults complex	19	−.03	.154	N.S.	19	−.20	.122	N.S.
Involvement with children complex	19	.13	.170	N.S.	19	−.20	.160	N.S.

Table 60

MZ and DZSS Group Differences with Birth Maturity (Weight) Level Controlled
(Three-way Analysis of Variance; Zygosity, Sex, Birth Weight)

Birth maturity (weight) level[a]	Group							
	MZ				DZSS			
	Male		Female		Male		Female	
	N	M	N	M	N	M	N	M
Involvement with Adults								
I	17	3.83	13	4.15	18	3.86	11	4.11
II	9	4.19	6	4.25	9	4.27	11	4.19
III	10	3.75	13	4.28	5	3.75	10	4.09
Total	36	11.77	32	12.68	32	11.88	32	12.39

Sex — $F = 5.82$; $p = .05 - .01$
Maturity — $F = 2.91$; $p = .10 - .05$

Involvement with Children								
I	17	3.70	13	4.22	18	3.83	11	4.19
II	9	3.69	6	4.21	9	4.28	11	4.25
III	10	4.40	13	3.84	5	3.60	10	4.43
Total	36	10.79	32	12.27	32	11.71	32	12.87

Sex — $F = 8.40$; $p = .01 - .001$

Gregariousness								
I	17	3.41	13	4.30	18	4.00	11	4.21
II	9	3.54	6	3.96	9	4.42	11	4.80
III	10	3.03	13	4.02	5	3.35	10	4.09
Total	36	9.98	32	12.28	32	11.77	32	13.10

Sex — $F = 13.22$; $p = .01 - .001$
Zygosity — $F = 6.85$; $p = .01$
Maturity — $F = 3.85$; $p = .05 - .01$

Aggressiveness								
I	17	3.47	13	3.84	18	3.87	11	3.99
II	9	4.08	6	4.09	9	4.52	11	4.24
III	10	3.86	13	4.24	5	3.19	10	3.97
Total	36	11.41	32	12.17	32	11.58	32	12.20

Maturity — $F = 3.45$; $p = .05 - .01$

[a]Maturity level: I = birth weight under 4 1/2 pounds; II = 4 1/2 - 5 1/2 pounds; and III = over 5 1/2 pounds.

Table 60 (continued)

Birth maturity (weight) level[a]	Group							
	MZ				DZSS			
	Male		Female		Male		Female	
	N	M	N	M	N	M	N	M
Exhibitionism								
I	17	3.68	13	3.82	18	3.84	11	4.02
II	9	3.97	6	4.28	9	4.79	11	4.20
III	10	3.67	13	3.61	5	3.62	10	3.32
Total	36	11.32	32	11.71	32	12.25	32	11.54

Maturity — F = 5.16; p = .01 — .001

Talkativeness								
I	17	3.79	13	3.81	18	3.86	11	3.61
II	9	3.82	6	4.18	9	4.49	11	3.62
III	10	3.65	13	4.24	5	3.53	10	3.60
Total	36	11.26	32	12.23	32	11.88	32	10.83

Zygosity x sex — F = 3.62; p .10 — .05

Finality								
I	17	3.87	13	3.75	18	3.59	11	3.92
II	9	3.27	6	3.94	9	4.26	11	4.33
III	10	3.75	13	4.18	5	4.39	10	4.64
Total	36	10.89	32	11.87	32	12.24	32	12.89

Zygosity — F = 5.41; p = .05 — .01
Maturity — F = 2.98; p = .10 — .05

Femininity-complex Score								
I	17	3.71	13	4.21	18	3.81	11	4.01
II	9	3.20	6	4.36	9	3.91	11	4.28
III	10	3.43	13	4.52	5	3.63	10	4.49
Total	36	10.54	32	13.09	32	11.35	32	12.78

Sex — F = 43.91; p = < .0001
Zygosity x sex — F = 3.5; p = .10 — .05
Sex x maturity — F = 4.61; p = .05 — .01
Zygosity x sex x maturity — F = 8.73; p = .10 — .001

Masculinity-complex Score								
I	17	4.16	13	3.83	18	4.16	11	3.76
II	9	4.20	6	3.70	9	4.07	11	3.77
III	10	3.96	13	3.41	5	4.08	10	3.36
Total	36	12.32	32	10.94	32	12.31	32	10.89

Sex — F = 29.03; p = < .001

Table 61

Fraternal Same- and Opposite-sex Group Differences with Birth Maturity (Weight) Controlled

(Two-way Analysis of Variance; Sex of Sib and Birth Weight)

Birth maturity (weight) level	Group							
	Male				Female			
	DZSS		DZOS		DZSS		DZOS	
	N	M	N	M	N	M	N	M
Emotion-tension Complex								
I	18	4.04	6	3.71	11	3.87	4	3.49
II	9	3.89	5	4.07	11	4.03	6	3.99
III	5	4.00	4	3.89	10	4.03	5	3.86
Total	32	11.93	15	11.67	32	11.93	15	11.34

Nothing significant

	Aggressiveness							
I	18	3.87	6	3.54	11	3.99	4	3.83
II	9	4.52	5	4.26	11	4.24	6	4.45
III	5	3.19	4	3.98	10	3.97	5	3.87
Total	32	11.58	15	11.78	32	12.20	15	12.15

Maturity — F = 4.28; p = .01 — .001

	Gregariousness							
I	18	4.00	6	3.54	11	4.21	4	3.77
II	9	4.42	5	4.61	11	4.80	6	4.04
III	5	3.35	3	3.82	10	4.09	4	3.23
Total	32	11.77	14	11.97	32	13.10	14	11.04

Maturity — F = 5.41; p = .01 — .001

	Exhibitionism							
I	18	3.84	6	3.36	11	4.02	4	3.68
II	9	4.79	5	4.31	11	4.20	6	3.82
III	5	3.62	4	4.06	10	3.32	5	3.52
Total	32	12.25	15	11.73	32	11.54	15	11.02

Maturity — F = 2.71; p = .10 — .05

	Talkativeness							
I	18	3.86	6	3.62	11	3.61	4	3.14
II	9	4.49	5	3.95	11	3.62	6	4.25
III	5	3.53	4	3.68	10	3.60	5	4.13
Total	32	11.88	15	11.25	32	10.83	15	11.52

Maturity — F = 2.81; p = .10 — .05

	Finality							
I	18	3.59	6	3.33	11	3.92	4	3.73
II	9	4.26	5	3.88	11	4.33	6	4.04
III	5	4.39	4	3.67	10	4.64	5	4.13
Total	32	12.24	15	10.88	32	12.89	15	11.90

Maturity — F = 2.98; p = .10 — .05
Sex of sib — F = 3.65; p = .10 — .05

Table 62

Intraclass Correlations for Co-twins' Closeness Scores

MZ						DZSS						DZOS	
Male		Female		Total		Male		Female		Total		Total	
N	$\underline{r}$	N	$\underline{r}$	N	$\underline{r}$	N	$\underline{r}$	N	$\underline{r}$	N	$\underline{r}$	N	$\underline{r}$
18	41	17	33	35	34	15	41	15	15	30	34	19	−04

Table 63

Correlations between Closeness Score and Various Measures of Sex Attitude and Behavior

Variables correlated	Group															
	MZ				DZSS				DZOS							
	Male		Female		Male		Female		Male		Female					
	N	$\underline{r}$	N	$\underline{r}$	N	$\underline{r}$	N	$\underline{r}$	N	$\underline{r}$	N	$\underline{r}$				
Closeness and sex preference	36	12	34	3	30	20	30	14	19	−20	19	− 7				
Closeness and masculinity–complex score	36	5	34	−4	30	−15	30	01	19	−29	19	21				
Closeness and feminity–complex score	36	11	34	−2	30	17	30	−04	19	57[a]	19	27				

[a]Significant at 5% level; no other $\underline{r}$'s are significant.

Table 64

Correlation (ρ) between Co-twin Differences in Closeness Score and Differences in Degree of Preference for Own Sex

MZ				DZSS				DZOS	
Male		Female		Male		Female			
N	$\underline{\text{p}}$	N	$\underline{\text{p}}$	N	$\underline{\text{p}}$	N	$\underline{\text{p}}$	N	$\underline{\text{p}}$
18	52[a]	17	28	15	46[a]	15	-28	19	9

[a]Significant at between .05 and .02 level.

Table 65

Statistically Significant Correlations Between the Measure of Closeness of Co-twins and Other Traits and Social Circumstances

Variables correlated	Group													
	Total		MZ				DZSS				DZOS			
			Male		Female		Male		Female		Male		Female	
	N	r	N	r	N	r	N	r	N	r	N	r	N	r
	152–180		34–36		30–34		26–36		28–34		15–19		15–19	
Rating on articulation						−42								
Syntax error count (CAT)								37		−37				
Story length (CAT)														−43
Rating on talkativeness				−31										50
Rating—freedom from stuttering		19						47		33				
Right-hand preference												50		
PMA—Total—IQ														
PMA V-subtest								33						
PMA P-subtest								39						
PMA S-subtest								34						
PMA M-subtest						−42								
Rating—no. of interests		17												49
Rating—responsibleness		17		41										
Rating—affectionateness		15										55		
Rating—jealousy														
Involvement with children														
Rating—popularity												45		
Rating—gregariousness		−14		−35								45		
Rating—social apprehensiveness		18												
Rating—confidence		16										−51		
Involvement with adults														
Dominance in pair												−53		
Stability of dominance in pair				36										
Rating—cheerfulness												44		
Mother—child + (CAT)														
Mother—mentions (CAT)								36		30				−52
Father—mentions (CAT)												57		
Femininity—complex score		17				38								
Age of mother at birth of twins		22		−37										
Co-twins in same class at school														

264

Table 66

School Placement of Twins of Various Types

Placement	Group												
	MZ						DZSS						DZOS
	Male		Female		Total		Male		Female		Total		
	N	%	N	%	N	%	N	%	N	%	N	%	N	%
Same class	7	39	15	88	22	63	11	61	13	76	24	69	10	53
Different class	11	61	2	12	13	37	7	39	4	24	11	31	9	47

Table 67

Frequency of Expressed Desire to Have Sib as Classmate

Desire	MZ				DZSS				DZOS			
	Male		Female		Male		Female		Male		Female	
	N	%	N	%	N	%	N	%	N	%	N	%
To be class-mates	24	67	26	76	20	67	30	94	11	58	9	47
Not to be class-mates	12	33	8	24	10	33	2	6	8	42	10	53

Table 68

Frequency of Agreement of Twins' Desire as to Placement and Actual Placement in School

	Group											
	MZ				DZSS				DZOS			
	Male		Female		Male		Female		Male		Female	
	N	%	N	%	N	%	N	%	N	%	N	%
Agreement	20	56	25	74	21	70	26	81	12	63	16	84
Disagreement	16	44	9	26	9	30	6	19	7	37	3	16

Table 69

Significant Biserial Correlations Between Separation at School and Various Personality Traits (Same Class = 1; Different Class = 2)

Variables Correlated	MZ		DZSS		DZOS		
	Male	Female	Male	Female	Male	Female	Total
Age					−74	−74	20
Social class	40						−13
Weight at 5−6 years			33	44			26
Height at 5−6 years			36	33	47		
Health (rating)			30				18
Mother's age at birth of twins	−35			44	46	46	−18
PMA quotient total		46		−31			
PMA quotient V							
PMA quotient P	−32			−35			−19
PMA quotient Q	−30	43					
PMA quotient S	−30						
PMA quotient M		−39					
Ambition (rating)							−18
No. of interests (rating)			41				
Tenacity (rating)							−14
Originality (rating)				−34			
Baby talk persistence		−35	−33				−14
Articulation (rating)		34	−33				−14
Syntax errors (CAT)			−44				
Talkativeness (rating)	38						
Word count (CAT)	−46						
Stutter (rating)				36			
Thematic-descriptive (CAT)			32				
Incoherence (CAT)			−36		−45		
Closeness to twin	−37		46				−22
Involvement with children			31				
No. of playmates listed			50				22
Popularity (rating)							−18
Social apprehensiveness (rating)			−39				
Involvement with adults complex		−36					
Obedience (rating)	−39	−32					−22
Responsibleness (rating)	−34						−26
Jealousy (rating)	33						16
Mother mentions (CAT)							−17
Father mentions (CAT)							−13
Mother-child − (CAT)			32				
Father-child − (CAT)			40				
Mother-child + (CAT)	−32						
Father-child + (CAT)							
Hostility score (CAT)			30				
Hostility complex (rating)			38				23
Moodiness (rating)			−56			50	25
Stability of dominance	43	44					23
Negative outcomes (CAT)			40				
Negative themes (CAT)			38				
Catastrophe (CAT)			46		46		
Masculinity complex			35	28			28
Femininity complex							−24

Table 70

Two-way Analysis of Variance (Zygosity and Sex) of Dominant-matched Nondominant Twin Differences (Seventy Same-sex Pairs of Twins)[a]

Item		Difference Means		
	Group	Male	Female	Total
Weight at 5-6 years	MZ	1.0	−1.6	−.3
	DZSS	.5	2.2	1.3
	Total	.7	.3	
Interaction — F = 4.34; p = .05 − .025				
Health (rating)	MZ	−.45	−.09	−.27
	DZSS	−.03	.26	.11
	Total	−.24	.09	
Zygosity — F = 5.02; p = .025 − .01 Sex — F = 3.69; p = .10 − .05				
Indirectness of response (rating)	MZ	.27	−.28	.00
	DZSS	−.15	.15	.00
	Total	.06	−.06	
Interaction — F = 3.72; p = .10 − .05				
Stuttering (rating)	MZ	−.13	.07	−.03
	DZSS	.57	−.05	.26
	Total	.22	.01	
Interaction — F = 4.14; p = .05 − .01				
Friendliness to adults (rating)	MZ	−.00	.07	.03
	DZSS	.29	−.38	−.04
	Total	.15	−.16	
Interaction — F = 4.03; p = .05 − .01				
Father-child + (CAT)	MZ	.6	−.2	.2
	DZSS	−.2	.7	.2
	Total	.2	.2	
Interaction — F = 5.87; p = .025 − .01				
Affectionateness (rating)	MZ	−.05	.01	−.02
	DZSS	.19	−.51	−.16
	Total	.07	−.25	
Interaction — F = 4.54; p = .05 − .025				
Obedience (rating)	MZ	−.18	−.22	−.20
	DZSS	−.52	.19	−.17
	Total	−.36	−.01	
Sex — F = 4.27; p = .05 − .025 Interaction — F = 5.0; p = .05 − .025				
Tendency to dawdle (rating)	MZ	.16	−.15	.01
	DZSS	.52	−.49	.02
	Total	.34	−.32	
Sex — F = 8.89; p = < .005				

[a]Only data for items showing some significant or near-significant difference are presented.

267

Table 70 (continued)

Item	Group	Difference Means		
		Male	Female	Total
Friendliness to children (rating)	MZ	.03	−.04	−.00
	DZSS	.55	.00	.28
	Total	.30	−.02	

Zygosity − F = 2.37; $\underline{p}$ = .10 − .05
Sex − F = 2.96; N.S.

Item	Group	Male	Female	Total
Non-cooperation with peers (rating)	MZ	−.21	.20	.01
	DZSS	.25	−.11	.07
	Total	.02	.04	

Interaction − F = 3.56; $\underline{p}$ = .10 − .05

Item	Group	Male	Female	Total
Tendency to tease	MZ	−.08	−.16	−.12
	DZSS	.47	.21	.34
	Total	.19	.03	

Zygosity − F = 5.50; $\underline{p}$ = .025 − .01

Item	Group	Male	Female	Total
Number of same-age playmates	MZ	.4	.5	.5
	DZSS	1.1	.1	.6
	Total	.8	.3	

Sex − F = 2.16; N.S.
Interaction − F = 2.33; N.S.

Item	Group	Male	Female	Total
Number of playmates who are younger	MZ	.3	4.6	2.4
	DZSS	−11.3	−5.7	−8.6
	Total	−5.6	−.6	

Zygosity − F = 5.90; $\underline{p}$ = .025 − .01

Item	Group	Male	Female	Total
Tendency to projection of blame	MZ	−.25	.43	.08
	DZSS	.00	.24	.12
	Total	−.12	.33	

Sex − F = 4.34; $\underline{p}$ = .05 − .025

Item	Group	Male	Female	Total
Tendency to alibi (rating)	MZ	−.03	.04	.00
	DZSS	.72	.22	.47
	Total	.35	.13	

Zygosity − F = 4.32; $\underline{p}$ = .05 − .025

Item	Group	Male	Female	Total
Syntax error count (CAT)	MZ	3.3	2.1	2.7
	DZSS	−.9	−2.4	−1.6
	Total	1.2	−.2	

Zygosity − F = 6.18; $\underline{p}$ = .025 − .01

Item	Group	Male	Female	Total
Curiosity (rating)	MZ	−.10	−.14	−.12
	DZSS	.26	.31	.28
	Total	.09	.09	

Zygosity − F = 5.17; $\underline{p}$ = .025 − .01

Table 11

Number of Responses Given to Questions in the Interview by Matched Groups of Dominant and Nondominant Co-twins (McNemar's X^2 for Matched Groups or Cochran's Q)

Nondominant co-twin

Item	Group	Response	Dominant co-twin		
			Yes	No	Total
Sib is thought to be bossy	Total	Yes	4	15	19
		No	7	57	64
		Total	11	72	83
		$X^2 = 2.23$; $p = .10 - .20$			
Wish to change places with sib	Total	Yes	4	18	22
		No	11	51	62
		Total	15	69	84
		$X^2 = 1.24$; $p = .20 - .30$			
Prefers to go on visit without sib	Total	Yes	8	9	17
		No	17	43	60
		Total	25	52	77
		$X^2 = 1.88$; $p = .10 - .20$			
Prefers play with sib to play alone	DZSSm	Yes	6	0	6
		No	4	5	9
		Total	10	5	15
		$X^2 = 2.25$; $p = .10 - .20$			
Likes to play alone	DZSSm	Yes	1	4	5
		No	0	10	10
		Total	1	14	15
		$X^2 = 2.25$; $p = .10 - .20$			
Plays much with sib	DZOS	Yes	3	4	7
		No	0	11	11
		Total	3	15	18
		$X^2 = 2.25$; $p = .10 - .20$			
Playmate choice—favors others over sib	MZf	Yes	2	1	3
		No	7	7	14
		Total	9	8	17
		$X^2 = 3.13$; $p = .10 - .05$			
Much quarreling with sib	DZSSm	Yes	1	6	7
		No	0	8	8
		Total	1	14	15
		$X^2 = 4.17$; $p = .02 - .05$			

Dominant co-twin

Group	Response	Dominant co-twin		
		Yes	No	Total
DZOS	Yes	1	8	9
	No	0	9	9
	Total	1	17	18
	$X^2 = 6.13$; $p = .02 - .01$			
DZOS	Yes	0	6	6
	No	0	12	12
	Total	0	18	18
	$X^2 = 4.17$; $p = .02 - .05$			
DZOS	Yes	5	5	10
	No	1	4	5
	Total	6	9	15
	$X^2 = 1.50$; $p = .20 - .30$			

269

Table 71 (continued)

Left section (Nondominant co-twin)

Item	Group	Response	Dominant co-twin		
			Yes	No	Total
Sib usually initiates quarrels	DZSSf	Yes	5	6	11
		No	1	4	5
		Total	6	10	16
		$X^2 = 2.29$; $p = .10 - .20$			
Sib usually victor in quarrels	Total	Yes	3	16	19
		No	5	59	64
		Total	8	75	83
		$X^2 = 4.76$; $p = .02 - .05$			
Is able to do what sib cannot	MZf	Yes	5	1	6
		No	6	2	8
		Total	11	3	14
		$X^2 = 2.29$; $p = .10 - .20$			
Desire baby sib	DZOSf	Yes	2	4	6
		No	11	1	12
		Total	13	5	18
		$X^2 = 2.40$; $p = .10 - .20$			
Preferred playmate is younger	Total	Yes	3	6	9
		No	0	74	74
		Total	3	80	83
		$X^2 = 4.17$; $p = .01 - .05$			
Likes school	Total	Yes	54	9	63
		No	15	4	19
		Total	69	13	82
		$X^2 = 1.04$; $p = .30$			
Right hand always preferred	Total	Yes	46	21	67
		No	13	6	19
		Total	59	27	86
		$X^2 = 1.44$; $p = .20 - .30$			
S had considerable difficulty in learning to speak	Total	Yes	12	7	19
		No	2	66	68
		Total	14	73	87
		$X^2 = 1.78$; $p = .10 - .20$			

Right section

Group	Response	Dominant co-twin		
		Yes	No	Total
DZOS	Yes	3	2	5
	No	7	6	13
	Total	10	8	18
	$X^2 = 1.76$; $p = .10 - .20$			
MZm	Yes	9	5	14
	No	1	3	4
	Total	10	8	18
	$X^2 = 1.50$; $p = .20 - .30$			
MZf	Yes	9	6	15
	No	1	1	2
	Total	10	7	17
	$X^2 = 2.29$; $p = .10 - .20$			

270

Table 72

Mean Scores for Twin Subgroups with Social Class Controlled

Variable	MZ Male N	MZ Male M	MZ Female N	MZ Female M	DZSS Male N	DZSS Male M	DZSS Female N	DZSS Female M	DZOS Male N	DZOS Male M	DZOS Female N	DZOS Female M	MZ vs DZSS — Nothing significant	Zygosity	Sex	Class	Zygosity x sex	Zygosity x class	Sex x class	DZSS vs DZOS Male — Nothing significant	Male Sex of sib	Male Class	Male Sex of sib x class	Female — Nothing significant	Female Sex of sib	Female Class	Female Sex of sib x class
Age	36	74.2	34	69.5	36	70.7	34	72.7	19	74.5	19	74.5	0[b]							0				0			
Birth weight (lbs.)	36	5.5	34	5.2	32	5.6	30	5.1	15	5.5	15	5.0	0								x						x
Weight at 5-6 years (lbs.)	36	49.0	34	46.1	32	43.7	34	46.8	15	49.6	15	45.6	0							0				0			
Height at 5-6 years (in.)	36	45.3	34	46.3	32	44.9	34	46.2	15	47.3	15	46.6	0							0				0			
C[a] Rating, health	36	4.21	34	4.09	36	3.52	34	4.23	19	3.75	19	3.77			n		x						n	0			
PMA - total (quotient)	34	103.5	32	105.7	30	107.3	30	109.7	17	109.7	17	108.1	0							0				0			
PMA - V (quotient)	34	99.5	32	104.3	30	106.7	30	107.1	17	110.8	17	108.0	0							0				0			
PMA - P (quotient)	34	107.7	32	114.3	30	106.1	30	116.2	17	115.2	17	113.8	0							0				0			
PMA - Q (quotient)	34	105.9	32	105.2	30	107.1	30	112.4	17	108.5	17	110.4	0							0				0			
PMA - M (quotient)	36	106.4	32	116.3	30	110.1	30	111.5	17	112.4	17	106.9	0							0				0			
PMA - S (quotient)	34	102.3	32	100.2	30	105.5	30	106.0	17	110.4	17	108.2	0							0				0			
Rating																											
F originality	36	3.73	34	3.95	36	3.73	34	4.46	19	3.95	19	4.28			xx	xxx				0				0			
C no. of interests	36	3.65	34	4.20	36	3.56	34	4.33	19	3.81	19	3.91			xxx	xxx				0				0			
F curiosity	36	3.68	34	3.91	36	3.93	34	3.93	19	3.99	19	3.89			xxxx	xxx				0				0			
C responsibleness	36	3.67	34	4.39	36	3.74	34	4.18	19	4.13	19	4.12			xx	xx	n			0				0			
F planfulness	36	3.81	34	3.84	36	3.43	34	4.08	19	4.00	19	4.32			x						n			0			
F tenacity	36	3.75	34	4.00	36	3.70	34	4.18	19	3.81	19	4.43			xx	x				0				0			
C ambition	36	3.66	34	4.18	36	3.69	34	4.35	19	3.76	19	4.10			xx	n				0				0			
C speech form	36	3.50	34	3.55	36	3.84	34	4.42	19	3.71	19	3.96		xxx	xx		xx		x	0				0			
speech form K	36	3.49	34	3.97	30	3.71	30	2.87	19	4.01	19	3.03					xx			0				0			
CAT																											
syntax error count	36	23.6	32	20.1	27	20.3	28	14.8	19	17.8	19	14.9								0				0			
story word count	36	630.0	34	747.0	29	500.0	28	737.0	19	707.0	19	900.0	0							0				0			
incoherence score	36	28.6	34	27.5	29	27.0	28	25.2	15	25.4	14	22.3			xx	xx				0				0			
thematic-descriptive	36	30.1	34	35.2	29	31.8	28	36.2	19	36.1	19	40.3			x	x				0				0			

[a]C, item from California Rating Scales; F, item from Fels Behavior Rating Scales.
[b]0, no significant relations observed.
n, near significance at .05 level.
x, < .05 level of significance.
xx, < .01 level of significance.
xxx, < .001 level of significance.
xxxx, < .0001 level of significance.

Table 72 (continued)

	Variable	MZ Male N	MZ Male M	MZ Female N	MZ Female M	DZSS Male N	DZSS Male M	DZSS Female N	DZSS Female M	DZOS Male N	DZOS Male M	DZOS Female N	DZOS Female M	MZ vs. DZSS Nothing signif.	Zygosity	Sex	Class	Zygosity x sex	Zygosity x class	Sex x class	DZSS vs DZOS Male Nothing signif.	Male Sex of sib	Male Class	Male Sex of sib x class	Female Nothing signif.	Female Sex of sib	Female Class	Female Sex of sib x class
	Rating																											
C	stammering	36	3.72	34	3.70	36	4.00	34	3.61	19	4.15	19	3.98	0							0				0			
C	voice volume	36	3.71	34	3.98	36	3.23	34	3.95	19	3.70	19	3.69	0							0				0			
C	talkativeness	36	3.66	34	3.95	36	3.90	34	3.88	19	3.69	19	3.76	0							0				0			
	Closeness score	36	7.5	34	8.1	30	6.1	30	7.5	19	4.7	19	5.2		x	x				n	0					xx		
	Rating																											
F	jealousy	36	3.81	34	3.86	36	4.13	34	3.96	19	3.96	19	3.67	0							0				0			
C	selfishness	36	3.72	34	3.80	36	4.14	34	3.65	19	3.61	19	3.84			xx		n				n			0			
C	insistence on rights	36	3.54	34	3.98	36	3.81	34	4.13	19	3.78	19	3.96				xx		x		0				0			
F	friendliness to adults	36	3.86	34	4.21	36	3.98	34	4.42	19	4.20	19	4.38			x				n	0				0			
F	Involvement with adults (complex)	36	3.89	34	4.27	36	3.94	34	4.14	19	3.85	19	3.91			xx					0				0			
F	Rating - social apprehensiveness	36	4.35	34	3.61	36	4.21	34	3.73	19	4.03	19	3.91			xxx					0				0			
	Rating																											
F	resistance	36	4.21	34	3.97	36	4.13	34	3.62	19	4.08	19	3.91			xx	x				0				0			
F	obedience	36	3.87	34	4.22	36	3.88	34	4.19	19	4.19	19	4.07			x							x				x	
F	affectionateness	34	3.79	34	4.38	34	3.84	34	4.36	19	3.94	19	4.08			xx					0				0			
C	tendency to tattle	36	3.96	34	4.11	36	4.04	34	4.17	19	3.74	19	3.67	0							0				0			
F	friendliness to children	36	3.48	34	4.40	36	3.92	34	4.45	18	4.05	18	4.16			xxx					0				0			
	Involvement with children	36	3.62	34	4.27	36	3.83	34	4.28	19	4.00	19	4.02			xxxx					0				0			
	No. of playmates listed	36	4.7	34	4.1	30	4.3	32	4.3	19	3.6	19	4.0			xxxx					0				0			
	No. of male playmates listed	36	3.6	34	1.3	30	2.5	32	1.0	19	2.5	19	1.3		x	xxxx				xx	0				0			
	No. of female playmates listed	36	1.1	34	2.8	30	1.7	32	3.3	19	1.1	19	2.7		x	xxxx				xx	0				0			
	No. of same-age playmates listed	36	2.7	34	2.7	30	2.7	32	3.0	19	2.4	19	2.9				x							x	0			
	No. of older playmates listed (variance not computed)	36	1.2	34	1.0	30	1.0	32	.9	19	.8	19	.7								0				0			
	No. of younger playmates listed (variance not computed)	36	.8	34	.5	30	.5	32	.3	19	.5	19	.5															

Table 72 (continued)

	MZ Male N	MZ Male M	MZ Female N	MZ Female M	DZSS Male N	DZSS Male M	DZSS Female N	DZSS Female M	DZOS Male N	DZOS Male M	DZOS Female N	DZOS Female M	MZ vs DZSS: Nothing sig.	Zygosity	Sex	Class	Zyg×sex	Zyg×class	Sex×class	DZSS vs DZOS Male: Nothing sig.	Sex of sib	Class	Sex of sib×class	DZSS vs DZOS Female: Nothing sig.	Sex of sib	Class	Sex of sib×class
Rating																											
F gregariousness	36	3.37	34	4.15	34	4.04	34	4.32	19	4.05	19	3.71		xx	xxxx					0				0			
F aggressiveness	36	3.66	34	3.95	34	3.85	34	4.08	19	3.88	19	3.99	0							0				0			
C popularity	36	3.75	34	4.64	34	3.84	34	4.85	19	4.10	19	4.45			xx	xx				0				0			
F leadership	36	3.53	34	4.26	34	3.90	34	4.53	19	3.76	19	4.12		x	xxx					0				0			
F competitiveness	36	3.54	34	4.07	34	3.98	34	4.14	19	3.95	19	3.83			x					0				0			
C tendency to tease	36	3.89	34	3.71	34	4.00	34	3.66	19	3.83	19	3.66	0							0				0			
C tendency to project blame	36	4.01	34	3.81	34	4.10	34	3.66	19	3.73	19	3.97			x						n				n		
C tendency to alibi	36	3.61	34	3.79	34	3.68	34	3.74	19	3.79	19	3.47	0							0				0			
C exhibitionism	36	3.69	34	3.86	34	4.10	34	4.02	19	3.72	19	3.59	0							0				0			
C uncooperative with group	36	4.01	34	3.64	34	4.36	34	3.57	19	3.91	19	3.80			xxx						x			0			
Hostility complex	36	3.91	34	3.84	34	4.00	34	3.91	19	3.81	19	3.83	0							0				0			
F Quarrelsomeness	36	3.71	34	3.73	34	3.88	34	3.83	19	3.72	19	3.85	0							0				0			
CAT																											
hostility score	36	5.31	34	6.89	28	4.83	28	7.11	19	8.06	19	8.85			xx						x	x			x		
catastrophe	36	2.5	34	3.6	28	1.8	28	2.7	19	4.5	19	3.5	0								x	x	x		x		
negative outcome	36	1.9	34	3.0	28	1.7	28	2.0	19	2.3	19	2.5	0	n	n							n			n		
negative theme	36	3.8	34	5.6	28	3.9	28	5.6	19	5.9	19	6.7			xx			xx			x		x				
mother mentions	36	3.3	34	4.5	28	3.1	28	5.1	19	4.1	19	5.6			xx	xx								0			
father mentions	36	2.5	34	3.1	30	3.1	30	3.4	19	3.0	19	3.8			xxx	xx				0				0			
mother-child +	36	1.4	34	1.8	28	1.2	28	2.2	19	1.7	19	3.4			x	x					x				x		
mother-child −	36	.5	34	1.0	28	.3	28	1.2	19	1.2	19	1.4			xx						xx			0			
father-child +	36	.8	34	.9	28	.9	28	1.3	19	1.2	19	1.2							xx	0				0			
father-child −	36	.5	34	.8	28	.3	28	.7	19	.6	19	.8							x	0				0			
Emotion-tension complex	36	3.91	34	3.92	34	4.04	34	4.00	19	3.76	19	3.69	0								x				x		
Rating																											
F intensity	36	3.65	34	4.21	34	3.89	34	4.12	19	3.39	19	3.62			x						x				x		
C criticalness	36	3.83	34	4.11	34	3.90	34	3.64	19	3.71	19	3.67	0			n	x			0				0			
F sensitiveness	36	3.84	34	4.10	34	3.91	34	4.01	19	3.62	19	3.41	0							0					x		
C moodiness	36	4.07	34	3.78	34	4.13	34	3.94	19	3.67	19	3.56			x		x				x				x		
C confidence	36	3.60	34	4.27	34	3.80	34	4.18	19	3.58	19	3.86	0							0				0		n	x

Table 72 (continued)

	Variable	MZ Male		MZ Female		DZSS Male		DZSS Female		DZOS Male		DZOS Female		Significance, MZ vs. DZSS							Significance, DZSS vs. DZOS Male				Female			
		N	M	N	M	N	M	N	M	N	M	N	M	Nothing significant	Zygosity	Sex	Class	Zygosity x sex	Zygosity x class	Sex x class	Nothing significant	Sex of sib	Class	Sex of sib x class	Nothing significant	Sex of sib	Class	Sex of sib x class
	Rating (continued)																											
F	cheerfulness	36	3.67	34	4.35	36	3.48	34	4.07	19	4.28	19	4.21			xxx						xx			0			
F	activeness	36	4.08	34	3.97	36	4.05	34	4.12	19	3.67	19	3.63	0								x					x	
C	indirectness	36	3.42	34	3.68	36	3.88	34	4.07	19	3.93	19	3.86		xx						0				0			
C	finality	36	3.86	34	3.81	36	3.74	34	4.43	19	3.72	19	4.23			xxx		x			0				0			
	Masculinity complex	36	4.11	34	3.74	36	4.11	34	3.72	19	3.87	19	3.83			xxxx					0				0			
	Femininity complex	36	3.73	34	4.20	36	3.77	34	4.23	19	4.05	19	4.19								0				0			
	Sissiness	36	4.30			34	3.93			19	4.30			0							0				0			
	Tomboyishness			32	4.12			34	4.12			19	4.00	0							0				0			
	Male preference score	36	4.9			30	4.1			19	4.5				x						0				0			
	Female preference score			34	4.32			30	4.6			19	4.5	0							0				0			
	Nervous habits	36	3.94	34	3.59	36	3.81	34	3.83	19	4.04	19	3.73	0							0				0			
	Mother's age at marriage	16	22.6	17	23.6	16	24.6	15	24.5	15	23.1	15	23.1	0							0				0			
	Mother's age at birth of twins	16	26.1	17	26.8	16	28.9	15	30.5	15	28.8	15	28.8		x						0				0			

Twin-singleton Differences—Pair Means of Twins Compared with Mean of Singleton Matches

Variable	MZm N[a]	MZm Mean[a]	MZm σmd[a]		MZf N	MZf Mean	MZf σmd		DZSSm N	DZSSm Mean	DZSSm σmd		DZSSf N	DZSSf Mean	DZSSf σmd		DZOSm N	DZOSm Mean	DZOSm σmd		DZOSf N	DZOSf Mean	DZOSf σmd	
Age	18	1.3	1.00		17	-.1	.59		18	.4	.59		17	.2	.55		19	1.2	.91		19	1.6	.90	
Weight at 5-6 years (lbs.)	18	-2.1	1.53		17	-3.7	1.57		16	-6.6	1.61		17	-3.6	1.38		15	-3.8	2.98		15	-2.9	1.60	n
Height at 5-6 years (inches)	18	-1.5	.65	x[b]	17	-.0	.52	x	16	-1.6	.47		17	-.0	.45	x	15	.4	.70		15	.1	.46	
Health rating	18	.25	.246		17	.11	.208		18	-.33	.240		14	-.01	.246		19	-.37	.245		19	-.24	.162	
PMA - total	17	-5.3	2.37	x	16	-2.4	3.13		15	-3.5	4.0		15	1.2	2.11		17	.0	3.40		17	-2.6	4.23	
PMA - V	17	-18.0	2.77	xxx	16	-6.0	2.65	x	15	-11.5	3.46	xx	15	-5.9	2.49	xx	17	-4.7	3.77		17	-8.0	4.91	
PMA - P	17	6.8	3.40	n	16	8.5	3.63	x	15	2.7	4.22		15	12.4	3.49	xx	17	11.4	4.07	x	17	6.6	4.57	
PMA - Q	17	-8.7	3.72	x	16	-8.2	5.75	x	15	-4.9	5.83		15	.0	2.97		17	-8.0	5.04		17	-5.2	4.56	
PMA - S	17	-5.2	2.57	x	16	-7.2	4.59		15	-5.7	3.91		15	-1.8	2.85		17	5.0	4.48		17	1.3	5.14	
Rating																									
originality	18	-.34	.272		17	.12	.207		18	-.10	.169		17	.33	.208		19	-.01	.231		19	.26	.233	
number of interests	18	-.35	.347		17	.45	.176	x	18	-.44	.255		17	.19	.254		19	.03	.250		19	-.09	.216	
responsibleness	18	-.18	.194		16	.41	.220	n	18	.01	.147		17	-.01	.226		19	.36	.264		19	-.19	.210	
tenacity	18	-.22	.271		17	.34	.233		18	-.21	.201		17	.04	.233		19	.03	.295		19	.22	.254	
speech form	18	-.55	.319		17	-.24	.316		18	-.18	.237		17	.36	.194	n	19	.07	.384		19	.08	.278	
speech form (K)	18	-.32	.355		17	.13	.386		15	-.27	.422		15	-.98	.266	xx	19	.11	.320	xx	19	-.54	.289	n
CAT																									
word count	18	-43.	142.		17	-99.	111.		15	-130.	97.		14	39.	202.		19	529.	395.		19	-265.	169.	
incoherence	18	-1.58	2.381	x	17	-1.56	1.871	x	15	-4.97	1.556	xx	14	-1.13	1.654		19	-5.58	2.490	x	19	-7.79	2.142	xx
thematic-descriptive score	18	-1.97	3.178		17	-.38	1.946		15	-.50	3.161		14	-.47	2.542		19	-2.16	3.176		19	.58	2.794	
Rating																									
tendency to stammer	18	-.27	.268		17	-.09	.193	x	18	-.11	.223		17	-.19	.188		19	-.11	.247		19	-.02	.161	
voice volume	18	-.28	.267		17	.13	.237		18	-.09	.208		17	.06	.184		19	-.34	.147	x	19	-.35	.228	
talkativeness	18	-.33	.289		17	.17	.225		18	-.29	.109	x	17	-.01	.204		19	-.31	.229		19	-.24	.196	
jealousy	18	-.00	.135		17	-.37	.201		18	.15	.163		17	-.02	.218		19	.08	.188		19	-.58	.192	
selfishness	18	-.25	.209		17	-.42	.249		18	.14	.216		17	-.22	.197		19	-.47	.248	n	19	-.17	.284	
insistence on rights	18	-.44	.198	x	17	.12	.193		18	-.19	.151		17	.23	.195		19	-.16	.177		19	.01	.191	
friendliness to adults	18	.08	.329		17	.53	.255	x	18	.01	.169		17	.47	.130	xx	19	.33	.223		19	.14	.202	
Involvement with adults	18	.02	.197		17	.26	.130		18	.00	.109		17	.05	.123		19	-.03	.154		19	-.20	.122	
Rating																									
social apprehensiveness	18	.28	.294		17	-.52	.236	x	18	.08	.181		17	-.30	.147	x	19	-.22	.262		19	.08	.199	
obedience	18	.12	.209		17	.32	.230		18	.05	.193		17	.02	.199		19	.19	.237		19	-.04	.228	
affectionateness	18	.11	.269		17	.23	.245		17	.07	.216		17	.05	.150		19	.23	.199		19	-.18	.260	
friendliness to children	18	-.36	.250		17	.32	.236		18	.05	.202		17	.43	.185	x	19	.141	.316		19	-.02	.223	

[a] N, number of comparisons; mean, mean algebraic difference between group means compared; σmd = sigma of mean differences.

[b] See Table 72, footnote b.

Table 73 (continued)

Variable	MZm N	MZm Mean	MZm σ_{md}	S	MZf N	MZf Mean	MZf σ_{md}	S	DZSSm N	DZSSm Mean	DZSSm σ_{md}	S	DZSSf N	DZSSf Mean	DZSSf σ_{md}	S	DZOSm N	DZOSm Mean	DZOSm σ_{md}	S	DZOSf N	DZOSf Mean	DZOSf σ_{md}	S
Involvement with children	18	-.31	.185		17	.35	.130	x	18	-.08	.160		17	.20	.075	x	19	.13	.170	x	19	-.20	.160	
No. of playmates	18	.4	.49		17	.4	.31		15	.4	.75		16	.2	.31		19	-.1	.45		19	-.7	.75	
No. male playmates	18	.1	.38		17	.1	.29		15	-.3	.75		16	-.2	.27		19	-.0	.43		19	-.4	.56	
No. female playmates	18	.3	.37	x	17	.3	.29		15	.7	.36	n	16	.4	.34		19	-.2	.31		19	-.4	.62	x
No. same-age playmates	18	.7	.31		17	1.1	.32	xx	15	.8	.37	x	16	1.1	.28	xx	19	1.2	.51	x	19	.9	.45	x
No. older playmates	18	.1	.31		17	-1.2	.35	xx	15	-.3	.36		16	-.1	.24		19	-.2	.33		19	-.9	.46	x
No. younger playmates	18	-.3	.30		17	-.6	.29	x	15	-.5	.24	n	16	-.7	.24	xx	19	-1.1	.25	xxx	19	-.6	.33	
Rating																								
gregariousness	18	-.55	.224	x	17	.14	.217		18	.09	.242		17	.21	.160		19	.25	.247		19	-.53	.239	
popularity	18	-.234	.272		17	.75	.220	xx	18	.04	.278		17	.583	.195	xx	19	.29	.280		19	.26	.226	
leadership	18	-.37	.216		17	.53	.243	x	18	-.03	.225		17	.49	.152	xx	19	-.15	.212		19	-.16	.191	
competitiveness	18	-.47	.179	x	17	.24	.250		18	.01	.191		17	.05	.201		19	-.04	.215		19	-.37	.244	
tendency to project blame	18	.47	.210	x	17	-.42	.237	n	18	-.42	.174	x	17	-.25	.177		19	-.42	.206	x	19	-.47	.163	
exhibitionism	18	-.32	.253		17	.14	.196		18	-.02	.180		17	.25	.253		19	-.43	.224	n	19	-.51	.142	xx
Hostility complex	18	-.15	.129		16	-.19	.138		18	-.15	.148		18	.03	.129		19	-.17	.149		19	-.16	.122	
CAT																								
hostility score	18	-1.14	1.480		17	.77	1.006		15	-.90	1.388		14	1.73	1.636		19	-.79	1.794		19	2.37	1.392	
catastrophe	18	.0	.83		17	.16	.96		15	-.77	.65		14	-1.37	.98		19	1.26	1.32		19	1.5	.70	x
negative theme	18	.2	.82		17	1.5	.52	xx	15	.5	.62		14	1.1	.74		19	.7	.93		19	2.2	.64	xx
negative outcome	18	.4	.32		17	1.1	.51	x	15	.1	.40		14	.3	.54		19	.0	.74		19	.5	.65	
mother mentions	18	-.7	.45		17	-.9	.49	n	15	-.7	.67		15	-.5	.48		19	1.2	1.14		19	-.7	.39	n
father mentions	18	-.1	.35		17	-.1	.48		15	.8	.56		15	.2	.65		19	.3	.65		19	-.4	.61	
mother-child +	18	.1	.40		17	-.5	.41		15	.2	.24		14	.4	.58		19	.0	.54		19	.5	.57	
mother-child -	18	-.3	.25		17	-.1	.25		15	-.5	.26		14	.0	.35		19	.2	.40		19	.1	.48	
father-child +	18	.2	.29		17	-.0	.23		15	.6	.30	x	14	.4	.46		19	.5	.49		19	.1	.41	
father-child -	18	.1	.23		17	.2	.15		15	.0	.17	x	14	.2	.24		19	-.3	.32		19	.4	.25	
Emotion-tension complex	18	-.13	.104		17	-.06	.106		18	-.08	.105		17	.08	.090		19	-.24	.115	x	19	-.23	.107	x
Rating																								
intensity	18	-.33	.170	n	17	.27	.211		18	-.18	.276		17	.08	.176		19	-.46	.246	n	19	-.38	.198	n
criticalness	18	-.32	.240		17	-.07	.222		18	-.15	.226		17	-.27	.238		19	-.33	.205		19	-.34	.200	
sensitiveness	18	-.20	.207		17	.18	.146	x	18	-.20	.247		17	-.02	.183		19	.30	.275		19	-.63	.292	
moodiness	18	.04	.172		17	-.54	.228	xx	18	.13	.208		17	.11	.240		19	-.33	.264		19	-.44	.229	
confidence	18	-.24	.215		17	.19	.132		18	-.19	.208		17	.10	.189		19	-.37	.180	x	19	-.26	.236	
cheerfulness	18	-.19	.231		17	.61	.178	xx	18	-.41	.215	n	17	.11	.133		19	.22	.218		19	.06	.155	
activeness	18	-.06	.244		17	.10	.207		18	-.10	.141		17	.26	.263		19	-.41	.229		19	-.3	.206	
finality	18	-.23	.246		17	.15	.151		18	-.18	.251		17	.34	.203		19	-.25	.225	n	19	.25	.188	
Masculinity complex	18	.07	.096		17	-.41	.125	xx	18	-.0	.137		17	-.13	.125		19	-.21	.156		19	-.13	.151	
Feminity complex	18	-.12	.149		17	-.12	.125	xx	18	-.08	.119		17	.15	.106		19	.23	.141		19	.25	.188	
Sissiness	18	.33	.160	x	17	.34	.115		16	-.03	.229		17				19	.12	.126		19	.10	.099	

Dominant-nondominant Twin Differences—Difference Means and Sigma of the Difference Means

	MZm			MZf			DZSSm			DZSSf		
	N	Dif. Mean	σ_{md}	N	Dif. Mean	σ_{md}	N	Dif. Mean	σ_{md}	N	Dif. Mean	σ_{md}
Birth weight (oz.)	18	2.8	2.76	17	-5.3	3.00	16	9.7	4.35	15	-3.1	3.20
Weight at 5-6 years (lbs.)	18	1.0	.55	17	-1.7	1.12	16	.5	1.45	17	2.4	1.17
Height at 5-6 years (ins.)	18	.2	.15	17	-.3	.16	16	.6	.58	17	.5	.42
Health rating	18	-.55	.16 x^a	17	-.09	.18	18	-.03	.17	17	.26	.19
PMA - total	17	.2	1.62	16	2.2	1.74	15	1.6	1.90	15	3.9	2.72
PMA - V	17	.1	2.37	16	1.1	3.06	15	1.0	2.42	15	1.3	3.52
PMA - P	17	.1	3.01	16	1.7	3.42	15	2.1	3.69	15	4.2	3.67
PMA - Q	17	1.2	1.84	16	3.6	3.37	15	-.7	3.13	15	4.6	2.96
PMA - M	18	4.4	3.45	16	-.6	3.48	15	-.5	3.29	15	4.7	3.19
PMA - S	17	-.1	3.11	16	.5	3.01	15	5.5	3.62	15	5.1	4.51
Rating												
originality	18	-.10	.19	17	.23	.17	18	.13	.24	17	.23	.18
no. of interests	18	-.23	.19	17	.20	.14	18	.07	.24	17	.17	.17
curiosity	18	-.10	.20	17	-.15	.13	18	.26	.20	17	.31	.18
responsibleness	18	-.17	.14	17	-.10	.19	18	-.22	.14	17	-.12	.22
tendency to dawdle	18	.16	.18	17	-.16	.20	18	.52	.27 n	17	-.49	.23
planfulness	18	.03	.21	17	.21	.13	18	-.15	.25	17	.03	.21
ambition	18	-.13	.16	17	.06	.17	18	.12	.20	17	.10	.22
speech form	18	-.02	.21	17	-.02	.12	18	.10	.21	17	.22	.20
speech form K	18	-.22	.15	17	.00	.21	15	.07	.32	15	-.47	.35
CAT												
syntax error	18	3.3	2.23	16	2.1	1.68	14	-1.2	1.99	14	-2.9	1.81
incoherence	18	-2.1	1.35	17	2.29	1.98	15	-1.79	2.21	14	-1.3	1.99
thematic-descriptive score	18	2.31	2.22	17	.88	3.79	15	-.57	4.66	14	-.93	4.32

^{a}See Table 72, footnote b.

Table 74 (continued)

Rating	MZm			MZf			DZSSm			DZSSf		
	N	Dif. Mean	σ_{md}	N	Dif. Mean	σ_{md}	N	Dif. Mean	σ_{md}	N	Dif. Mean	σ_{md}
intensity	18	−.04	.29	17	−.10	.30	18	.27	.23	17	−.29	.29
criticalness	18	.05	.25	17	−.19	.11	18	.15	.33	17	.28	.24
sensitiveness	18	−.15	.23	17	−.11	.26	18	−.36	.22	17	−.19	.27
moodiness	18	.09	.21	17	−.18	.19	18	.54	.25	x 17	.21	.28
confidence	18	.03	.16	17	.04	.19	18	.20	.29	17	.36	.30
aggressiveness	18	.24	.22	17	.24	.16	18	.68	.24	x 17	−.05	.36
cheerfulness	18	−.16	.20	17	.18	.16	18	−.11	.31	17	.02	.30
activeness	18	−.25	.25	17	.04	.20	18	.46	.42	17	.24	.28
finality	18	−.20	.12	17	.08	.20	18	.32	.24	17	−.09	.24
Masculinity complex	18	−.10	.09	17	.11	.10	18	.11	.14	17	.11	.14
Femininity complex	18	−.10	.07	17	−.03	.07	18	.01	.12	17	−.04	.10
Male preference	18	.1	.31	x 17			15	.3	.43			
Feminine preference				17	.2	.38				15	−.51	.27
Physical apprehensiveness	18	−.20	.16	17	−.02	.15	x 18	−.54	.24	x 17	−.25	.31
Indirectness of response	18	.27	.29	17	−.30	.14	18	−.15	.22	17	.16	.21
Tendency to alibi	18	−.03	.17	17	.04	.21	18	.72	.28	x 17	.22	.25
Tendency to tattle	18	.06	.25	17	−.23	.17	18	.20	.31	17	−.16	.23
Nervous habits	18	−.18	.29	17	.23	.18	18	.37	.26	17	−.13	.21

Table 74 (continued)

	MZm			MZf				DZSSm				DZSSf			
	N	Dif. Mean	σ_{md}	N	Dif. Mean	σ_{md}		N	Dif. Mean	σ_{md}		N	Dif. Mean	σ_{md}	
Rating															
Tendency to stammer	18	−.13	.20	17	.08	.19		18	−.57	.24	x	17	−.05	.18	
voice volume	18	.10	.20	17	−.15	.09		18	.30	.25		17	−.05	.33	
talkativeness	18	−.18	.19	17	−.02	.17		18	.34	.24		17	−.03	.39	
CAT															
word count	18	45.2	101.73	17	79.1	113.64		15	−167.5	142.93	x	17	166.7	199.41	
Closeness	18	.2	.63	17	.2	.57		15	.3	.81		15	.9	.83	
Rating															
tendency to tease	18	−.08	.14	17	−.17	.18		18	.47	.23		17	.21	.22	
jealousy	18	−.16	.17	17	−.32	.20		18	.07	.24		17	−.23	.18	
selfishness	18	.09	.22	17	−.09	.18		18	−.16	.19		17	−.14	.20	
insistence on rights	18	−.05	.18	17	.11	.20		18	.27	.18		17	−.19	.22	
friendliness to adults	18	−.00	.08	17	.08	.12		18	.29	.19		17	−.38	.28	
Involvement with adults	18	−.05	.06	17	−.05	.07		18	.12	.20		17	−.29	.21	
Rating															
social apprehensiveness	18	−.22	.14	17	.01	.17		18	.40	.28		17	−.13	.34	
obedience	17	−.19	.13	17	−.24	.09		18	−.52	.23	x	17	.19	.18	
resistance	18	.01	.21	17	.23	.15		18	.28	.34		17	.17	.23	
affectionateness	17	−.05	.14	17	.01	.12	x	17	.19	.18		17	−.50	.24	x
friendliness to children	18	.03	.17	17	−.04	.08		18	.55	.26	x	17	.00	.17	
Involvement with children	18	.05	.09	17	.05	.10		18	.23	.16		17	.06	.18	
No. of playmates, listed by child	18	.8	.53	17	.4	.49		15	.9	.77		16	−.1	.59	
% male playmates, listed by child	18	−7.3	4.38	17	−2.3	5.25		15	−1.5	7.66		16	3.0	4.22	
% female playmates, listed by child	18	7.3	4.38	17	2.3	5.25		15	1.5	7.66		16	−3.0	4.22	
% same-age playmates, listed by child	18	−3.9	6.26	17	−3.7	8.10		15	15.3	7.70	n	16	3.7	8.76	
% older playmates, listed by child	18	1.8	5.83	17	−.9	10.10		15	1.6	6.60		16	2.7	8.13	

Table 74 (continued)

	MZm			MZf			DZSSm			DZSSf		
	N	Dif. Mean	σ_{md}	N	Dif. Mean	σ_{md}	N	Dif. Mean	σ_{md}	N	Dif. Mean	σ_{md}
% younger playmates, listed by child	18	.3	3.90	17	4.6	5.65	15	−13.6	5.71	16	−6.4	3.91
Rating												
noncooperative with peers	18	−.21	.14	17	.21	.15	18	.25	.22	17	−.11	.28
gregariousness	18	.04	.14	17	−.02	.18	18	.36	.27	17	−.03	.20
popularity	18	.19	.17	17	−.04	.15	18	−.21	.24	17	−.22	.20
leadership	18	−.13	.17	17	.11	.10	18	−.17	.20	17	.23	.22
competitiveness	18	−.03	.10	17	.24	.21	18	.27	.22	17	.12	.26
tenacity	18	−.23	.25	17	.11	.11	18	.19	.31'	17	.00	.26
tendency to project blame	18	−.25	.17	17	.46	.24	18 x	.00	.23	17 x	.24	.24
responsibilities	18	−.17	.14	17	−.10	.19	18	−.22	.19	17	−.02	.22
exhibitionism	18	.02	.12	17	−.08	.18	18	.47	.25	17	−.06	.28
quarrelsomeness	18	.02	.18	17	−.12	.19	18	.36	.18	17	.09	.31
Hostility complex	18	.02	.11	17	−.09	.10	18	.20	.13	17	−.09	.16
CAT												
hostility score	18	1.00	1.27	17	−1.88	1.31	15	−2.64	2.22	14	−.47	2.58
catastrophe score	18	−.2	1.05	17	−.8	1.24	15	.2	1.27	14	.6	.68
negative theme	18	.3	.70	17	−.5	.85	15	.2	1.49	14	.3	1.18
negative outcome	18	.2	.65	17	−.2	.67	15	1.0	.74	14	.5	.76
mother mentions	18	.3	.75	17	.1	.67	15	.5	.77	14	.5	.79
father mentions	18	.8	.52	17	.1	.65	15	.0	.57	14	.6	.71
mother-child +	18	.5	.56	17	.4	.55	15	.0	.59	14	.8	.77
mother-child −	18	.4	.36	17	.0	.39	15	−.4	.34	14	.7	.47
father-child +	18	.6	.40	17	−.0	.32	15	−.3	.46	14	.8	.42
father-child −	18	.2	.73	17	.1	.30	15	.0	.26	14	.4	.41
Emotion-tension complex	18	−.05	.10	17	−.03	.10	18	.03	.12	17	−.11	.11

References

ALLEE, W. C. 1936. Analytical studies of group behaviour in birds. *Wilson Bull.* **48**:143–51.

ALLEN, G. 1955. Comments on the analysis of twin samples. *Acta Genet. Med. Gemellologioe* **4**:143–59.

ALLEN G. and KALLMAN, F. J. 1955. Frequency and types of mental retardation in twins. *Amer. J. Hum. Genet.* **7**:15–20.

ALM, I. 1953. The long-term prognosis of prematurely-born children. *Acta Paediat.* **42**:Suppl. 94.

ANDERSON, H. H. 1939. Domination and social integration in the behavior of kindergarten children and teachers. *Genet. Psychol. Monogr.* **21**:287–385.

ANDERSON, W. J. R. 1956. Still births and neonatal mortality in twin births. *J. Obstet. and Gynaecol.* **63**:205–16.

ANON. 1965. The fantastic drug that creates quintuplets. *Life* **59**:24–31.

ARCHER, J. 1810. Observations showing that a white woman by intercourse with a white man and a Negro may conceive twins one of which shall be white and the other mulatto. *Medical Repository*, 3d Hexade, **1**:319.

AREY, L. B. 1934. *Developmental anatomy*. Philadelphia: W. B. Saunders Co.

ASHER, C. and ROBERTS, J. A. F. 1949. A study of birth weight and intelligence. *Brit. J. Soc. Med.* **3**:56–68.

BALLARD, P. B. 1911–1912. Sinistrality and speech. *J. Exper. Ped.* **1**:298–310.

BARKER, R. G. and WRIGHT, H. F. 1954. *Midwest and its children*. Evanston, Ill.: Row Peterson and Co.

BECK, A. C. 1947. *Obstetrical practice*. Baltimore, Md.: Williams and Wilkins Co.

BELLAK, L. and BELLAK, S. 1950. *Children's apperception test*. 2d ed. Larchmont, N.Y.: C. P. S. Inc.

BENDER, S. 1952. Twin pregnancy; a review of 472 cases. *J. Obst. Gynaec. Brit. Empire* **59**:510–18.

BENNET, C. A. and FRANKLIN, N. L. 1954. *Statistical analysis in chemistry and the chemical industry*. New York: John Wiley and Sons. (P. 117; see formula developed by B. Welch and Alice A. Aspin.)

BENTON, A. L. 1940. Mental development of prematurely-born children. A critical review of the literature. *Amer. J. Orthopsychiat.* **10**:719–47.

BERKO, J. 1958. The child's learning of English morphology. *Word* **14**: 150–77.

BERNSTEIN, M. E. 1948. Recent changes in the secondary sex ratio of the upper social strata. *Hum. Biol.* **20**:182–94.

BOOKSTAVER, P. I. 1951. An analysis of premature delivery of live-born infants. *Amer. J. Obstet. Gynecol.* **61**:399–406.

BOOTH, P. B., PLANT, G., IKIN, E. W., MOORES, P., SANGER, R., and RACE, R. R. 1957. Blood chimerism in a pair of twins. *Brit. Med. J.* I, 1456– 58.

BRACKEN, H. VON. 1934. Mutual intimacy in twins. Types of social structure in pairs of identical and fraternal twins. *Character Pers.* **2**:293–309.

BRAIN, W. R. 1945. Speech and handedness. *Lancet* **249**:837–41.

BRODHAGE, G. and WENDT, G. G. 1951. Die Verwendung qualitativer Fingerleistenmerkmale in Vaterschaftgutachen. *Z. menschl. Vererb. Konstitutionslehre* **30**:221–41.

BROWNLEE, K. A. 1960. *Statistical theory and methodology in science and engineering*. New York: John Wiley and Sons.

BURLINGHAM, D. 1952. *Twins, a study of three pairs of identical twins*. New York: International Universities Press.

BURT, C. 1937. *The backward child*. New York: The Macmillan Co.

CARPENTER, J. and EISENBERG, P. 1938. Some relations between family background and personality. *J. Psychol.* **6**:115–36.

CARROTHERS, G. E. 1947. Left-handedness among school pupils. *Amer. Sch. Board J.* **114**:17–19.

CATTELL, R. B. 1946. *Description and measurement of personality*. Yonkers-on-Hudson, N.Y.: World Book Co.

CATTELL, R. B. and MALTENO, E. V. 1940. Contributions concerning mental inheritance. V. Temperament. *J. Genet. Psychol.* **37**:31–47.

CATTELL, R. B., BLEWETT, D. B., and BELOFF, J. R. 1955. The inheritance of personality: a multiple variance analysis determination of approximate nature-nurture ratios for primary personality factors: Q data. *Amer. J. Hum. Genet.* **7**:122–46.

CHOWN, B., LEWIS, M., and BOWMAN, J. M. 1963. A pair of newborn human blood chimeric twins. *Transfusion* **3**:494–95.

COCHRAN, W. G. 1950. The comparison of percentages in matched samples. *Biometrika* 37:256–66.

CONRAD, H. S. 1933. *The California behavior inventory for nursery school children.* Berkeley and Los Angeles: University of California Press.

CORNER, G. W. 1955. The observed embryology of human single-ovum twins and other multiple births. *Amer. J. Obstet. Gynecol.* 70:933–51.

CRITCHLEY, M. 1954. Parietal syndromes in ambidextrous and lefthanded subjects. *Zbl. Neurochir.* 14:4–16.

DAHLBERG, G. 1926. *Twin births and twins from a hereditary point of view.* Stockholm: Tidens.

DART, C. 1938. Studies in eye, hand, and foot preferences. Pt. 3. Eye, hand, and foot preferences of mentally subnormal subjects compared with individuals of normal or superior intelligence. *J. Juv. Res.* 22: 119–22.

DAVIS, E. A. 1937. Linguistic skill in twins, singletons with siblings and only children from age five to ten years. *Univ. Minn. Instit. Child Welfare Monogr. Series* No. 14.

DAY, E. 1932. The development of language in twins. Comparison of twins and single children. *Child Developm.* 3:179–99.

DENCKER, S. J. 1958. A follow-up study of 128 closed-head injuries in twins. *Acta Psychiat. Neurol. (Kbh.)* 33: Suppl. 123.

DENCKER, S. J., HAUGE, M., KAIJ, L., and NIELSEN, A. 1961. The use of anthropological traits and blood groups in the determination of the zygosity of twins. *Acta Genet. (Basel)* 11:265–85.

DENENBERG, V. H. 1960. Critical periods for the effects of infantile experience and adult learning. *Science* 31:227–29.

DENNIS, W. 1935. Laterality of function in early infancy under controlled developmental conditions. *Child Developm.* 6:242–52.

DONINI, P., PUZZUOLI, D., and MONTEZEMOLO, R. 1964. Purification of gonadotrophins from human menopausal urine. *Acta Endocrinol.* 45: 321–28.

DOUGLAS, J. W. B. 1956. Mental ability and school achievement of premature children at 8 years of age. *Brit. Med. J.* 4977:1210–14.

DOUGLAS, J. W. B. and MOGFORD, C. 1953. The results of a national inquiry into the growth of premature children from birth to four years. *Arch. Dis. Childhood* 28:436–45.

DRILLIEN, C. M. 1961. A longitudinal study of the growth and development of prematurely- and maturely-born children. Pt. VI. Physical development. *Arch. Dis. Childhood* 36:1–10.

———. 1961. Mental development in age period 2 to 5 years. *Arch. Dis. Childhood* 36:233–40.

DRILLIEN, C. M. 1964. *The growth and development of the prematurely born infant.* Baltimore, Md.: Williams and Wilkins Co.

DUNCAN, J. M. 1866. *Fecundity, fertility, sterility and allied topics.* Edinburgh: A & C Block.

DUNSFORD, I., BOWLEY, C. C., HUTCHISON, A. M., THOMPSON, J. S., SANGER, R. and RACE, R. R. 1953. A human blood group chimera. *Brit. Med. J.* 2:81.

DUROST, W. N. 1934. The development of a battery of objective group tests of manual laterality with the results of their applications to thirteen hundred children. *Genet. Psychol. Monogr.* 16:225–335.

ERNHART, C. B., GRAHAM, F. K., EICHMAN, P. L., MARSHALL, J. M., and THURSTON, D. 1963. Brain injury in the preschool child: Some developmental considerations. II. Comparison of brain injured and normal children. *Psychol. Monogr.* 77: Serial No. 574.

ETTLINGER, G., JACKSON, C. V., and ZANGWILL, O. L. 1956. Cerebral dominance in sinistrals. *Brain* 79:569–88.

EYSENCK, H. J. 1951. The organization of personality. *J. Pers.* 20:101–17.

———. 1951. Neuroticism in twins. *Eugen. Rev.* 43:79–82.

———. 1952. *The scientific study of personality.* New York: The Macmillan Co.

———. 1956. The inheritance and nature of extraversion. *Eugen. Rev.* 48:23–30.

FISHER, R. A. 1918. The correlation between relatives on the supposition of Mendelian inheritance. *Trans. Roy. Soc. Edinburgh* 52:399–433.

———. 1925. The resemblance between twins; a statistical examination of Lauterbach's measurements. *Genetics* 10:569–79.

FISHER, R. A. and YATES, F. 1957. *Statistical tables for biological and agricultural research.* New York: Hafner Publishing Co. Pp. 4–5, 60, Table VIII.

FOLSOME, C. E., STONE, M. L., HIRSCH, L., and KRUMHOLZ, B. 1956. Maternal factors in prematurity. *Amer. J. Obstet. Gynecol.* 72:60–65.

FREUD, A., and DANN, S. 1951. An experiment in group upbringing. *Psychoanal. Stud. Child,* 6:127–68.

GELLERT, E. 1961. Stability and fluctuation in the power relationships of young children. *J. Abnorm. Soc. Psychol.,* 62:8–15.

GEMZELL, C. A. 1965. Induction of ovulation with human gonadotrophins. *Recent Progr. Hormone Res.* 21:179–204.

GEMZELL, C. A. and KJESSLER, B. 1964. Treatment of infertility after partial hypophysectomy with human pituitary gonadotrophins. *Lancet* 21:644.

GESELL, A. 1925. *Mental growth of the preschool child.* New York: The Macmillan Co.

———. 1931. The developmental psychology of twins. In *A handbook of child psychology*, ed. C. MURCHUSON. Worcester, Mass.: Clark University Press.

GESELL, A and AMES, L. B. 1947. The development of handedness. *J. Genet. Psychol.*, 70:155–75.

GETZELS, J. W. and JACKSON, P. W. 1962. *Creativity and intelligence: explorations with gifted students.* New York: John Wiley and Sons.

GIESECKE, M. 1936. The genesis of hand preference. *Monogr. Soc. Res. Child Developm.* I: No. 5.

GINSBURG, B. E. 1949. Genetics and social behavior—a theoretical synthesis. *R. B. Jackson Mem. Lab. 20th Comm. Lect.* 101–24.

GINSBURG, B. and ALLEE, W. C. 1943. Some effects of conditioning on social dominance and subordination in inbred strains of mice. *Physiol. Zool.* 15:485–506.

GLICK, P. C. 1957. *American families.* New York: John Wiley and Sons.

GOODENOUGH, F. L. and ANDERSON, J. E. 1931. *Experimental child study.* New York: Century Co.

GOODGLASS, H. and QUADFASEL, F. A. 1954. Language laterality in left-handed patients. *Brain* 77:521–48.

GORDON, H. 1920. Left-handedness and mirror writing, especially among defective children. *Brain* 43:313–68.

GOTTESMAN, I. I. 1963. Heritability of personality: a demonstration. *Psychol. Monogr.* 77: Serial No. 572.

GRAHAM, F. K., ERNHART, C. B., CRAFT, M., and BERMAN, P. W. 1963. Brain injury in the preschool child: Some developmental considerations. 1. Performance of normal children. *Psychol. Monogr.* 77: Serial No. 573.

GREGORY, I. D. T. 1957. Retinopathy of prematurity (retrolental fibroplasia in children in whom the disease did not progress to complete blindness and the subsequent investigation of cases of myopia). *Brit. J. Ophth.* 41:321–37.

GREULICH, W. W. 1934. Heredity in human twinning. *Amer. J. Phys. Anthropol.* 19:391–431.

GRIEVE, J. and MORANT, G. M. 1946. Records of eye colours for British populations and a description of a new eye-colour scale. *Ann. Hum. Genet.* 13:161–71.

GUILFORD, J. P. and ZIMMERMAN, W. S. 1956. Fourteen dimensions of temperament. *Psychol. Monogr.* 70: No. 417.

GUTTMACHER, A. F. 1939. An analysis of 573 cases of twin pregnancy. *Amer. J. Obstet. Gynecol.* 38:277–88.

GUTTMACHER, A. F. and KOLL, S. G. 1958. The fetus of multiple gestations. *Obstet. Gynecol.* 12:528–61.

HAHN, E. F. and HAWK, S. S. 1943. *Stuttering: Significant theories and therapies.* Stanford: Stanford University Press.

HARTMAN, C. G. and LEATHEM, J. H. 1963. "Oögenesis and ovulation." In *Mechanisms concerned with conception,* ed. C. G. HARTMAN. New York: Pergamon Press.

HEINLEIN, J. H. 1930. Preferential manipulation in children. *Comp. Psychol. Monogr.* **7:** No. 33.

HESS, E. H. 1959. Imprinting. *Science* **130:**133–41.

HESS, H., MOHR, G. J., and BARTELME, P. F. 1934. *The physical and mental growth of prematurely born children.* Chicago: University of Chicago Press.

HILDRETH, G. 1948. Manual dominance in nursery school children. *J. Genet. Psychol.* **72:**29–45.

———. 1949a. The development and training of hand dominance. I. Characteristics of handedness. *J. Genet. Psychol.* **75:**197–220.

———. 1949b. The development and training of hand dominance. II. Developmental tendencies in handedness. *J. Genet. Psychol* **75:**221–54.

———. 1949c. The development and training of hand dominance. III. Origin of handedness and lateral dominance. *J. Genet. Psychol.* **75:** 255–75.

———. 1950. The development and training of hand dominance: IV. Developmental problems associated with handedness. *J. Genet. Psychol.* **76:**39–100.

JACK, L. M. 1934. An experimental study of ascendant behavior in preschool children. *Univ. Iowa Stud. Child Welfare* **9:**7–65.

JASPER, H. H. 1932. A laboratory study of diagnostic indices of bilateral organization in stutterers and normal speakers. *Psychol. Monogr.* **43:** 72–174.

JONES, H. E. 1931. Dextrality as a function of age. *J. Exper. Psychol.* **14:**125–44.

KAGAN, J. 1964. Acquisition and significance of sex typing and sex role identity. In *Review of child development research,* eds. M. L. HOFFMAN and L. W. HOFFMAN. New York: Russell Sage Foundation.

KAGAN, J. and MOSS, H. A. 1960. The stability of passive and dependent behavior from childhood through adulthood. *Child Developm.* **31:** 577–91.

———. 1962. *Birth to maturity.* New York: John Wiley and Sons.

KALLMANN, F. J. 1959. Psychogenetic studies of twins. In *Psychology: a study of a science.* Vol. 3. *Formulations of the person and the social context,* ed. S. KOCH, pp. 338–62. New York: McGraw-Hill Book Co.

KALLMANN, F. J. and BONDY, E. 1952. Applicability of the twin study method in the analysis of variations in male selection and marital adjustment. *Amer. J. Hum. Genet.* **4:**209–22.

KARN, M. N. 1953. Twin data: a further study of birth weight, gestation time, maternal age, order of birth, and survival. *Ann. Eugen.* **17:**233–48.

KARN, M. N. and PENROSE, L. S. 1952. Birth weight and length of gestation of twins together with maternal age, parity, and survival rate. *Ann. Eugen.* **16**:365–77.

KNOBLOCH, H., RIDER, R., HARPER, P., and PASAMANICK, B. 1956. Neuropsychiatric sequelae of prematurity: a longitudinal study. *J. A. M. A.* **161**:581–85.

Koch, Helen L. 1933. Popularity in preschool children: Some related factors and a technique for its measurement. *Child Developm.* **4**:164–75.

———. 1954. The relation of "Primary Mental Abilities" in five- and six-year-olds to sex of child and characteristics of his sibling. *Child Developm.* **25**:209–23.

———. 1955. Some personality correlates of sex, sibling position, and sex of sibling among five- and six-year-old children. *Genet. Psychol. Monogr.* **52**:3–50.

———. 1956a. Attitudes of children toward their peers as related to certain characteristics of their sibling. *Psychol. Monogr.* **70**: Serial No. 426.

———. 1956b. Sibling influences on children's speech. *J. Speech Hearing Disorders* **21**:322–28.

———. 1957. The relation in young children between characteristics of their playmates and certain attributes of their siblings. *Child Developm.* **28**:175–202.

———. 1960. The relation of certain formal attributes of siblings to attitudes held toward each other and toward their parents. *Monogr. Soc. Res. Child Developm.* **25**: Serial No. 78.

———. 1964. A study of twins born at different levels of maturity. *Child Developm.* **35**:1265–82.

KOMAI, T. and FUKUOKA, G. 1936. Frequency of multiple births among Japanese and related peoples. *Amer. J. Phys. Anthropol.* **21**:443–47.

LAUTERBACH, C. E. 1933. The measurement of handedness. *J. Genet. Psychol.* **43**:207–12.

LEDERER, R. K. and REDFIELD, J. 1939. An exploratory investigation of hand status in the first two years of life. *Univ. Iowa Stud. Infant Behavior* **16**:146–57.

LILLIE, F. R. 1916. The theory of the free-martin. *Science* **43**:611–13.

LILIENFELD, A. M. and PASAMANICK, B. 1955. A study of variations in the frequency of twin births by race and socio-economic status. *Amer. J. Hum. Genet.* **7**:204–17.

———. 1956. The association of maternal and fetal factors with the development of mental deficiency. Relationships to maternal age, birth order, previous reproductive loss, and degree of mental deficiency. *Amer. J. Ment. Defic.* **60**:557–69.

LIPPMAN, A. S. 1927. Certain behavior responses in early infancy. *J. Genet. Psychol.* **34**:424–40.

LITTLE, C. C. 1954. Discussion of conference on problems and methods in human genetics. *Amer. J. Hum. Genet.* **6**:95–107.

McARTHUR, J. W. 1938. Reliability of dermatoglyphics in twin diagnosis. *Hum. Biol.* **10**:12–35.

McCARTHY, D. 1930. The language development of the preschool child. *Univ. Minn. Inst. Child Welfare Monogr. Series* No. 4.

McNEMAR, Q. 1947. Note on the sampling error of the difference between correlated proportions or percentages. *Psychometrika* **12**:153–57.

MEIER, G. W. 1964. Behavior of infant monkeys: Differences attributable to mode of birth. *Science* **143**:968–70.

MERRELL, D. J. 1957. Dominance of eye and hand. *Hum. Biol.* **29**:314–28.

MEYER, A. W. 1919. The occurrence of superfetation. *J.A.M.A.* **72**:769–74.

MEYERS, C. E., ORPET, R. E., ATTWELL, A. A., and DINGMAN, H. F. 1962. Primary abilities at mental age six. *Monogr. Soc. Res. Child Developm.* **27**: Serial No. 82.

MINTZ, B. (ed.) 1958. *Environmental influences on prenatal development.* Chicago: University of Chicago Press.

MUELLER, B. 1930. Untersuchungen über die Erblichkeit von Fingerbeerenmustern unter besonderer Berücksichtigung rechtlicher Fragestellungen. *Z. indukt. Abst. Vererbungslehre* **56**:302–82.

MURRAY, A. A. 1938. *Explorations in personality.* New York: Oxford University Press.

NEEL, J. V. and SCHULL, W. J. 1958. *Human heredity.* Chicago: University of Chicago Press.

NEWMAN, H. H. 1917. *The biology of twins.* Chicago: University of Chicago Press.

———. 1923. *The physiology of twinning.* Chicago: University of Chicago Press.

———. 1930. The fingerprints of twins. *J. Genet.* **23**:415–46.

———. 1934. Dermatoglyphics and the problems of handedness. *Amer. J. Anat.* **55**:277–322.

NEWMAN, H. H., FREEMAN, F. N., and HOLZINGER, K. J. 1937. *Twins: A study of heredity and environment.* Chicago: University of Chicago Press.

NICHOLAS, J. W., JENKINS, W. J., and MARSH, W. L. 1957. Human blood chimeras. *Brit. Med. J.* **1**:1458–60.

NIXON, W. L. B. 1956. On the diagnosis of twin-pair ovularity and the use of dermatoelyphic data. *Novant Anni delle Leggi Mendeliane,* ed. L. GEDDA. Rome: Instituto Gregorio Mendel.

OATES, D. W. 1929. Left-handedness in relation to speech defects, intelligence, and achievement. *For. Educ.* **7**:91–105.

OETTLE, A. G. 1953. Paternal influence in polyzygotic births. *J. Obstet. Gynaecol., Brit. Empire* **60**:775–84.

OHIRA K. 1958. A study of the twin method of heredity as a factor determining differences in environment. *Jap. J. Psychol.* **28**:269–72.

OHNO, S., KLINGER, H. P., and ATKIN, N. B. 1962. Human oögenesis. *Cytogenet.* **1**:42–51.

ORTON, S. T. 1937. *Reading, writing and speech problems of children.* New York: W. W. Norton and Co.

OSBORNE, R. H. and DEGEORGE, F. V. 1957. Selective survival in dizygotic twins in relation to the ABO blood groups. *Amer. J. Hum. Genet.* **9**:321–30.

———. 1959. *Genetic basis of morphological variation: an evaluation and application.* Cambridge, Mass.: Harvard University Press.

OSBORNE, R. H., HOROWITZ, S. L., and DEGEORGE, F. V. 1958. Hereditary factors in tooth dimensions: A study of the anterior teeth of twins. *Angle Orthodontist* **28**:87–93.

PENFIELD, W. and ROBERTS, L. 1959. *Speech and brain mechanisms.* Princeton, N.J.: Princeton University Press.

PITZ, G. F. and ROSS, R. B. 1961. Imprinting as a function of arousal. *J. Comp. Physiol. Psychol.* **54**:602–4.

PLOTKIN, S. A. 1958. The A B O blood groups in relation to prematurity and stillbirth. *J. Pediat.* **52**:42–47.

POTTER, E. L. 1963. Twin zygosity and placental form in relation to the outcome of pregnancy. *Amer. J. Obstet. Gynecol.,* **87**:566–77.

PRICE, B. Primary biases in twin studies. 1950. *Amer. J. Hum. Genet.* **2**:293–352.

RECORD, R. G., GIBSON, J. R., and McKEOWN, T. 1952. The foetal and infant mortality in multiple pregnancy. *J. Obstet. Gynaecol., Brit. Empire* **59**:471–82.

RICHARDS, T. W. and POWELL, M. 1941. The Fels child behavior scales. *Genet. Psychol. Monogr.* **24**:259–311.

RIFE, D. C. 1933. Genetic studies of monozygotic twins. *J. Hered.* **24**: 339–45.

———. 1940. Handedness with special reference to twins. *Genetics* **25**: 178–86.

ROSANOFF, A. J. and INMAN-KANE, C. V. 1934. Relation of premature birth and underweight condition at birth to mental deficiency. *Amer. J. Psychiat.* **13**:829–52.

ROSANOFF, A. J., HANDY, L. M., and PLESSET, I. R. 1937. The etiology of mental deficiency with special reference to its occurrence in twins. *Psychol. Monogr.* **48**: Serial No. 216.

ROSENBERG, B. G. and SUTTON-SMITH, 1964. Ordinal position and sex role identification. *Genet. Psychol. Monogr.* **70**:297–328.

Rosenthal, D. (ed.) 1963. *The Genain quadruplets, a case study and analysis of heredity and environment in schizophrenia.* New York: Basic Books, Inc.

Ross, R. C. and Philpott, N. 1953. Five-year survey of multiple pregnancies. *Canadian Med. Assn. J.* **69**:247–53.

Russel, J. K. 1952. Maternal and foetal hazards associated with twin pregnancies. *J. Obstet. Gynaecol.* **59**:208–16.

Schachter, S. 1959. *The psychology of affiliation.* Stanford: Stanford University Press.

Schatz, F. 1882–1910. Die Gefässverbindungen der Placentakreislaufe eineiiger Zwillinge, ihre Entwicklung und ihre Folgen. *Arch. Gynaekol.* Vols. 19, 24, 27, 29, 30, 53, 55, 58, 60, 92.

Scheffé, H. 1956. A "mixed model" for the analysis of variance. *Ann. Math. Stat.* **27**:23–36.

———. 1959. *The analysis of variance.* New York: John Wiley and Sons.

Schjelderup-Ebbe, T. 1922. Beiträge zur Socialpsychologie des Haushuhnes. *Z. Psychol.* **88**:225–52.

Sears, R. R., Maccoby, E. E., and Levin, H. 1957. *Patterns of child rearing.* Evanston, Ill.: Row, Peterson and Co.

Shettles, L. B. 1960, *Ovum humanum.* New York: Hafner Publishing Co.

Shields, J. 1954. Personality differences and neurotic traits in normal twin school children. *Eugen. Rev.,* **45**:213–45.

———. 1962. *Monozygotic twins.* Oxford: Oxford University Press.

Siegel, S. 1956. *Non-parametric statistics.* New York: McGraw-Hill Book Co.

Siemens, H. W. 1927. The diagnosis of identity in twins. *J. Hered.* **18**:201–9.

Slater, E. 1953. Psychotic and neurotic illnesses in twins. *Spec. Rep. Ser. Med. Res. Coun. (London)* No. 278.

———. 1961. The thirty-fifth Maudsley lecture: Hysteria. *J. Ment. Sci.* **107**:359–81.

Smith, S. M. and Penrose, L. S. 1955. Monozygotic and dizygotic twin diagnosis. *Ann. Hum. Genet.* **19**:273–89.

Sorsby, A. 1953. *Clinical genetics.* St. Louis: C. V. Mosby.

Spiers, A. L. 1956. An anthropometric study of prematurely born children at the age of 5 years. *Arch. Dis. Childhood* **31**:395–99.

Stehle, F. L. 1939. Über Grössenverhältnisse und Schwangerschaftsdauer der Zwillingen. *Zeitsch. Geburtsh. Gynäk.* **119**:159–74.

Stevenson, S. S., Worcester, J., and Rice, R. G. 1950. 677 congenitally malformed infants and associated gestational characteristics; general considerations. *Pediatrics* **6**:37–50.

STINCHFIELD, S. M. 1921. Standardization of speech testing material. *Quart. J. Speech Educ.* **17**:360–69.

———. 1923. The formulation and standardization of a series of graded speech tests. *Psychol. Monogr.* **33**: Serial No. 179.

STOCKARD, C. R. 1921. Developmental rate and structural expression: An experimental study of twins, double monsters, and single deformities, and the interaction among embryonic organs during their origin and development. *Amer. J. Anat.* **28**:115–277.

STOCKS, P. 1930. A biometric investigation of twins and their brothers and sisters. *Ann. Eugen.* **4**:49–108.

STOCKS, P. and KARN, M. N. 1933. A biometric investigation of twins and their brothers and sisters. Pt. II. *Ann. Eugen.* **5**:1–55.

STRANDSKOV, H. H. 1954. A twin study pertaining to the genetics of intelligence. *Atte del IX Congresso Internazionale de Genetica. Caryologia*, vol. Suppl, 811–13.

STRANDSKOV, H. H. and EDELEN, E. W. 1946. Monozygotic and dizygotic twin birth frequencies in the total, the "white," and the "colored" U.S. populations. *Genet.* **31**:438–46.

STUDDIFORD, W. E. 1936. Is superfetation possible in the human being? *Amer. J. Obstet. Gynecol.* **31**:845–55.

SUTTON, H. E., CLARK, P. J., and SCHULL, W. J. 1955. The use of multiallele genetic characters in the diagnosis of twin zygosity. *Amer. J. Hum. Genet.* **7**:180–88.

TEMPLIN, M. C. 1957. *Certain language skills in children.* Minneapolis: University of Minnesota Press.

THOMPSON, W. P. and DUBANOSKI, R. A. 1964. Early arousal and imprinting in chicks. *Science* **143**:1187–88.

THURSTONE, L. L. 1951. The dimensions of temperament. *Psychometrika* **16**:11–20.

———. 1951. Experimental tests of temperament. In Ekman G. *et al.*, *Essays in psychology.* Upsala: Almqvist and Wiksells.

THURSTONE, L. L., THURSTONE, T. G., and STRANDSKOV, H. H. 1953. A psychological study of twins. I. Distribution of absolute twin differences for identical and fraternal twins. The Psychometric Laboratory, *Report No. 4.* Chapel Hill: University of North Carolina.

THURSTONE, T. G., THURSTONE, L. L. 1946. *SRA Primary Mental Abilities—Test—Primary: for age 5 to 7. Examiner's Manual.* Chicago: Science Research Associates.

TRAVIS, L. E. *Speech pathology.* New York: Appleton Century 1931.

TRAVIS, L. E. and Johnson, W. 1934. Stuttering and the concept of handedness. *Psychol. Rev.* **41**:531–62.

UPDEGRAFF, RUTH. 1932. Preferential handedness in young children. *J. Exper. Educ.* **1**:134–39.

VERSCHUER, O. VON. 1927. Die vererbungsbiologische Zwillingsforschung. *Ergebnisse der inneren Medizin und Kinderheilkunde* **31**:35–120.

————. 1939. Twin research from the time of Francis Galton to the present day. *Proc. Royal Soc. London (Series B)* **128**:62–81.

————. 1928. Die Ähnlichkeitsdiagnose der Eineiigkeit von Zwillingen. *Anthr. Anz.* **5**:244–48.

WALKER, N. F. 1957. Determination of zygosity of twins. *Acta Genet. Statistica (Basel)* **7**:33–38.

WALLIN, J. E. W. 1924. Studies of mental defects and handicaps. *Miami Univ. Bull.* Series 22, No. 5.

WATERHOUSE, J. A. H. 1950. Twinning in twin pedigrees. *Brit. J. Soc. Med.* **4**:197–216.

————. 1953. Twin studies. In *Clinical genetics*, ed. A. SORSBY. St. Louis: C. V. Mosby.

WATERHOUSE, J. A H. and HOGBEN, L. 1947. Incompatibility of mother and foetus with respect to the iso-agglutinogen A and its antibody. *Brit. J. Soc. Med.* **I**:1–17.

WEINBERG, W. 1901. Beiträge zur Physiologie und Pathologie der Mehrlingsgeburten beim Menschen. *Arch. ges. Physiol.* **88**:346–430.

————. 1902. Probleme der Mehrlingsgeburtenstatistik. *Z. Geburtsch. Gynäk.* **47**:12–22.

WELCH, B. L. 1947. The generalization of "students" problem when several different population variances are involved. *Biometrika* **34**:28–35.

WELLMAN, B. L., CASE, I. M., MENGERT I. G., and BRADBURY, D. E. 1931. Speech sounds of young children. *Univ. Iowa Stud. Child Welfare,* **5**: No. 2.

WIENER, G. 1962. Psychologic correlates of premature birth: A review. *J. Nerv. Ment. Dis.* **134**:129–44.

WIENER, A. S. and LUFF, I. L. 1940. Chances of establishing the non-identity of biovular twins with special reference to individuality tests of the blood. *Genet.* **25**:187–96.

WILE, I. S. 1934. *Handedness: Right and left.* Boston: Lothrop, Lee, and Shepard.

WILSON, P. T., and JONES, H. E. 1931. A study of like-sexed twins: I. The vital statistics and family data of the sample. *Hum. Biol.* **3**:107–32.

————. 1932. Lefthandedness in twins. *Genet.* **17**:560–71.

YERUSHALMY, J. and SHEERAR, S. E. 1940. Studies in twins: I. The reaction of order of birth and age of parent to the frequency of like-sexed and unlike-sexed twin deliveries. *Hum. Biol.,* **12**:95–113.

Index